THE RIGHTS REVOLUTION

The
RIGHTS
REVOLUTION

Rights and Community
in Modern America

SAMUEL WALKER

New York   Oxford
OXFORD UNIVERSITY PRESS
1998

Oxford University Press

Oxford   New York
Athens   Auckland   Bangkok   Bogotá   Buenos Aires
Calcutta   Cape Town   Chennai   Dar es Salaam
Delhi   Florence   Hong Kong   Istanbul   Karachi
Kuala Lumpur   Madrid   Melbourne   Mexico City
Mumbai   Nairobi   Paris   São Paulo   Singapore
Taipei   Tokyo   Toronto   Warsaw

and associated companies in
Berlin   Ibadan

Published by Oxford University Press, Inc.
198 Madison Avenue, New York, New York 10016

Oxford is a registered trademark of Oxford University Press

Library of Congress Cataloging-in-Publication Data
Walker, Samuel, 1942–
    The rights revolution : rights and community in
modern America / Samuel Walker.
        p.   cm.
    Includes index.
    ISBN 0–19–509025–X
    1. Civil rights movements—United States—History—
20th century.   2. Civil rights—United States—History—
20th century.   3. Communitarianism—United States.
4. Social values—United States.   I. Title.
E185.615.W28   1998
323'.0973—dc21   97–53203

9 8 7 6 5 4 3 2 1

Printed in the United States of America
on acid-free paper

Contents

INTRODUCTION

HOW QUICKLY WE FORGET. Patterns of daily life that were once familiar are swept aside, and old ways of life are forgotten. And for each new generation, past ways of life are "history," something remote and not personally experienced. Americans in particular are a people without a sense of history, forever inventing a new society and casting off the past. We take the present for granted and implicitly assume that life was always this way. But of course it wasn't. Change continues to alter the way we live and how we think about the way we live.

This book is about one of the great transformations of American society. I believe it involves the most important change of the past half century, which I call the *rights revolution*, the growth of a comprehensive set of individual rights. This revolution includes a broad array of formal rights codified in laws and court decisions; but even more important, it involves a new rights consciousness, a way of thinking about ourselves and our society. As some observers point out, this new "rights culture" is marked by an almost reflexive habit of defining all problems in terms of rights. The words, expressed as demands, fall quickly from our lips: "I have a right to . . ." These rights include an expectation of personal liberty, freedom from unwarranted government regulation of both public and private matters, a right to speak freely on public affairs, and a freedom to conduct our private—including especially our sexual—lives as we choose.

It was not always so. In fact, we need go back scarcely forty years, and in some cases less, to a time when these notions of rights did not even exist as concepts, much less as formal legal rights. The now highly prized right to privacy, for example, is a little more than thirty years old. The challenge for the historian, writing for an audience that is so very ahistorical, is to make the dimensions of this transformation of American society come alive. So, as an imaginative exercise, I offer the following fable, adapted from a well-known part of our literary heritage.

THE ADVENTURES OF REITZ VAN WINKLE

The story is told about Reitz van Winkle, the ne'er-do-well son of an old Atlanta family. With a family inheritance, Reitz could afford to indulge his preference for drink and spend his days wandering around the city, conversing with whomever he met.[1]

One day in the summer of 1956, Reitz drank a bit more than even he was accustomed to, and in a drunken stupor he slid down a ravine on the outskirts of town and fell into a deep sleep. He slept so well, in fact, that he did not awaken for forty years. Then, on a morning in the spring of 1996, he awoke, an old man with a long gray beard and tattered clothes.

After reviving, Reitz looked around to find himself at the bottom of a ravine that was now crossed by a series of massive highways. Later, he would learn that they were called "interstates," but he had not yet heard of such a thing, much less seen one. The steady stream of rush hour traffic over all four lanes immediately suggested that the pace of life in his hometown had quickened substantially. Slowly, and with much effort, he climbed up through the underbrush and out of the ravine. He marveled at the many skyscrapers that marked the center of the city. These, too, were new. After catching his breath, he set off in the direction of downtown.

As he wandered into the city, one of the first things to catch his eye was an adult movie theater advertising "Hard-Core Double Penetration." Nearby bars advertised "Live! Nude! Women!" These sights were truly shocking to poor Reitz. Such blatant displays of explicit sex were just not allowed—or at least they weren't when he fell asleep in 1956. Why, he wondered, weren't these establishments closed immediately, and their proprietors arrested?

Continuing on to Peachtree Street, Reitz looked up at the gleaming office buildings that were the symbols of Atlanta's booming economy and the city's role as the economic hub of the New South. The pace of life on the streets was much faster than he remembered, with everyone in a hurry. He also noticed that many of the people streaming in and out of these buildings were "Nigras." Only later would someone explain to him that this word was not used in polite company. Over the years it had been replaced first by "Negro," then by "black," and more recently by "African American." Just watching the fast parade of multiracial, professional Atlantans made Rip's head spin.

Whatever the correct name, Reitz noticed that these African American people were well dressed. He didn't remember ever seeing so many who were evidently in business or some profession. Equally startling, they were often in the company of equally well-dressed white men and women. A few of these interracial couples exchanged kisses. Noticing their wedding rings, Reitz concluded that they were actually married. His head spun even faster. He had never seen such casual intermingling of the races, and certainly not between black men and white women. Any fool knew that interracial marriage was illegal, he said to himself. In 1956 such behavior would have resulted in arrest, at the very least. The reprisals by vigilantes—a very real possibility— would be much worse.

The bewildered Reitz wandered down a side street, where he saw something even more bizarre. There, in broad daylight, were two men holding hands and engaged in what was obviously a very intimate conversation. He had always heard about such things, of course, but had never actually seen two people of the same sex acting like this, and certainly not in public. Behavior like this was deeply hidden in the shadows of society—whispered about, but not tolerated in public. In the world of 1956 Atlanta that he knew, such behavior quickly drew the attention of the police. Why were these men not promptly arrested and jailed for their gross and immoral conduct?

Actually, arrest was very much on Rip's mind. He worried that his shabby appearance might get him arrested for vagrancy. Bums, as he was used to calling them, were often arrested simply for being out on the street with "no visible means of support." So he made a special effort to avoid police officers, reversing direction and crossing the street several times. Soon, however, he noticed something odd about the cops. It was not that some were African American—he was quickly becoming accustomed to the new race relations—but that some were women. What were they doing in this dirty and dangerous job? he asked himself. Didn't everyone know that they did not have the brute physical strength needed to subdue drunks and dangerous criminals? Didn't this violate every standard of true woman-hood? Then he recalled the professionally dressed women he had seen earlier emerging from the gleaming office buildings. They did not look like secretaries. Evidently, women were now engaged in all sorts of jobs they had never held before.

Somewhere along the way, Reitz passed an abortion clinic. This, too, amazed him. Like homosexuality, abortion was something that existed only in the shadows. It was whispered about, but never discussed openly in polite society. Moreover, it was illegal. Rumor had it that you could get one, if you had the right connections, but it was risky in terms of both the law and the woman's health.

And so continued the adventures of Reitz van Winkle. At almost every turn he encountered new and amazing things. It seemed that the rules of society had changed completely. Old restrictions had collapsed. It was now possible to do, well, practically anything in public—and who knows what in private, Reitz thought to himself.

Eventually, Reitz located some members of his family. The van Winkles had not done well over the past forty years, but they were hardly destitute. A younger cousin, who was now in his sixties, lived in the old family mansion, which had fallen into a state of disrepair. The cousin took Reitz in and, with much excitement, introduced him to other family members. They were very curious, for they had all heard about their relative Reitz and his sudden disappearance one day in 1956. None of them really believed his story about his falling asleep for forty years, but at the same time, his complete naïveté about contemporary society seemed genuine.

Reitz was naturally fascinated by all of the new technology: the computers, CDs, and VCRs. But he also seemed utterly unaware of the new rules of life, particularly about sex, race, and gender. The younger children, his grandnephews and grandnieces, were amused to find someone so completely "out of it."

As he badgered his family with questions over the next few weeks, he gradually pieced together the story. A social revolution had occurred in America while he slept. All sorts of new things, previously forbidden, were now possible. The common denominator, Reitz concluded, was a revolution in rights. Everything seemed to revolve around the right to do this or the right to do that. You could see dirty movies anytime you wanted, or even kiss someone of the same sex in public. And African Americans (Reitz was still slow in learning the new terminology) could do almost anything they wanted as well.

THE RIGHTS REVOLUTION

Our fable about Reitz van Winkle dramatizes the fact that something dramatic happened in American society over the past forty years. Our daily lives are very different as a result of the explosive growth of a set of individual rights. At a formal level, these rights are defined in a vast body of court decisions and federal, state, and local laws. The real revolution in American life, however, goes much deeper and involves a profound change in what we expect out of life, how we define ourselves, how we treat others and expect them to treat us, and what we demand of government.

Many of our most cherished assumptions about personal liberty are a product of the rights revolution. And yet these assumptions, indeed the rights revolution itself, are under attack. A number of critics argue that the rights revolution has destroyed community in America, cultivating an unhealthy set of values and undermining the fabric of daily life.

My reply—and the central theme of this book—is that the growth of rights has enlarged and enriched the dimensions of community in America, fulfilling the core values of American democracy. The purpose of this book is to offer a proper historical perspective on this great change. This includes, first, restoring some awareness of the conditions of American life in the recent past—the year, for example, when our imaginary Reitz van Winkle fell asleep. Second, it includes describing the positive contributions of the growth of rights to the development of community in America.

This book is an interpretive analysis of recent American history, an essay on the social history of rights in modern America. Although it deals with matters of law, it is not an exercise in legal history in the conventional sense. It offers, for example, no fine-grained analysis of First Amendment law or of the law of privacy. There are many excellent treatments of current law in all its ramifications on these and other aspects of the rights revolution. While they are extremely valuable on their own terms, they do not address the broader question of the impact of law on society. That is what this book is about. It attempts to explain the new culture of rights in America and what it means to the way we live.

By the same token, this book is not an exercise in the philosophy of law. I find much of the literature in that field too abstract and removed from the reality of American life. I prefer what the eminent law professor Ronald Dworkin calls "philosophy from the inside out."[2] He objects to much of the current writing by political philosophers, social theorists, "deconstructionists," and others because these writers begin with general theories and then proceed to the specific applications. He prefers to begin with particular controversies and construct broader theories in response to them. This book proceeds in a similar "from the inside out" fashion. It begins with the controversies of recent American history and fashions a general interpretation of rights and community in response.

The organizing theme of the book is the relationship between individual rights and community. Harvard law professor Mary Ann Glendon, a leader of a movement known as *communitarianism,* makes a powerful argument that the growth of rights has undermined community.[3] Although I disagree with her conclusions, she is quite correct in observing that the rights revolution involves a profound cultural shift. Our daily discourse is pervaded by "rights talk," the habit of automatically thinking in terms of individual rights and, for example, defining most problems that arise in those terms. Lawrence Friedman, a historian of American law who views the rights revolution more favorably, captures the new culture in the title of his book *The Republic of Choice.* Contemporary society, he argues, is characterized by the expectation that we have a right to make free choices about our lives, unconstrained by government restrictions or family and traditional religious values. Our habit of thinking in terms of rights, he argues, forms "the distinctive core, the very marrow, of contemporary American civilization."[4]

Glendon believes that the new rights culture has a corrosive side that destroys community. We have become so obsessed with rights that we have lost the capacity to talk about duties and responsibilities. The movement toward greater individual liberty, she argues, has undermined the conditions that allow freedom to survive. Communitarian leader Amitai Etzioni adds that the movement toward more individual rights and "a greater measure of choice" has "undermine[d] the social order upon which liberties are ultimately based."[5]

The communitarians deserve a reply because they are not the only ones disturbed by the transformation of American society. Surprisingly, a number of well-known writers and social critics, representing all points on the political spectrum—right, left, and center—also believe that the rights revolution has undermined our institutions, promoted racial strife, and cultivated a destructive set of values. These critics, whom I call the *New Jeremiahs,* see American society on the verge of moral, social, and political collapse. The villain is the growth of a new culture of rights, of uninhibited expressive individualism. I examine their views in detail in chapter 1, emphasizing the pervasiveness of the attacks on the rights revolution.

The Origins of This Book

Several concerns prompted me to write this book. Initially, I was provoked by the appearance of a new intellectual and political movement known as *communitarianism*.[6] The communitarians argue that we give too much emphasis to individual rights and not enough to the needs of the larger community. The official Communitarian Network Platform declares, "The exclusive pursuit of private interests erodes the network of social environments on which we all depend and is destructive to our shared experiment in democratic self-government."[7] The Communitarian message appeals to a noble sentiment: that we should think more about the general well-being of society and less about our own selfish interests.

I was moved to reply to communitarianism because it posed a genuine threat to the individual rights that I cherish, have worked for and written about, and regard as perhaps the greatest achievement of our society.[8] Communitarian leaders offer some specific ideas about limiting individual rights in the area of criminal justice, a field that happens to be my main area of expertise. I know from twenty years of teaching and research that the specific ideas they have proposed—expanding police powers of search and seizure—not only would infringe on individual rights but also in no way would ensure greater public safety.[9]

As I began working on this book, however, my understanding of the challenge changed significantly. First, after an initial flurry of excitement, the communitarian movement stalled, at least in the political sphere. Amitai Etzioni's Communitarian Network has not gained any noticeable influence over public policy, despite the fact that President Bill Clinton initially indicated support for communitarianism and even appointed one Communitarian Network leader, William Galston, to his staff. If anything, public policy—notably the 1996 welfare reform law which ends the historic federal commitment to the poor—seems to be moving away from anything that might be called communitarian principles.[10]

But while the Communitarian Network seemed less of a threat, I increasingly realized that the communitarians' criticisms of individual rights were only one part of a more pervasive intellectual and political current. Questions about the role of rights in our society range from direct attacks from conservatives to a more diffuse sense of unease and doubt on the part of many moderate centrists, liberals, and even some on the political left. Criticisms of rights form an important school of thought among political philosophers and legal scholars. In short, the doubts about our prevailing rights culture are broader and deeper than the official Communitarian Network, and therefore a far more important development.

I found three aspects of the criticisms of rights particularly significant. First, it became increasingly apparent that commentators from very different political perspectives were saying many of the same things, albeit with different agendas. In various ways, conservatives, moderates, and liberals were all saying that we have gone too far in pursuing individual rights and that this has undermined the moral fabric of society and destroyed our political culture. The problem is not any particular right—the rights of criminal suspects, abortion, affirmative action—but the underlying idea that rights should be given the highest priority on matters of law and social policy. The issue is exactly what Mary Ann Glendon says it is: the pervasive culture of rights.[11]

A second, closely related and especially troubling point is the extent to which so many of the criticisms of rights ultimately lead back to the issue of civil rights. Affirmative action is the focal point of a broad attack, but it is only the tip of an iceberg that involves a more general phenomenon of "identity politics," the habit of thinking of ourselves in terms of discrete groups rather than as Americans with a common culture. This problem implicates the entire history of the modern civil rights movement. Conservatives use affirmative action to attack the assumptions underlying official civil rights policy. Liberals, deeply wedded to racial equality and the history of the civil rights movement, are profoundly ambivalent. Nonetheless, their doubts about "identity politics" and their concerns about the alleged balkanization of American society into hostile groups do implicate the civil rights movement.[12]

The possible connection between the civil rights movement and our current social problems posed an even more urgent challenge. My defense of rights began to take on a very different character in this respect. By a process of historical guilt by association, the critics were raising serious questions about the achievements and the underlying principles of one of the greatest chapters in recent American history. The task, then, was not simply to defend established rights but to reexamine and defend the impact of the civil rights movement on American history and contemporary society.

Third, I was appalled by the view of American history advanced, explicitly or implicitly, by the critics of rights. It is an idealized vision of the recent past, an America of the 1950s free of problems: no crime, no "angry" racial conflict, no hostility between the sexes, and without every imaginable issue ending up in the Supreme Court. According to Amitai Etzioni, "In the 1950s divisiveness was low and a sense of shared bonds, of community, was relatively high."[13] This is another version of the familiar "decline and fall" interpretation of American history: once we were a healthy, vibrant, and unified society, but then the courts intervened and imposed a rigid set of rules that undermined the fabric of society. This view rests, however, on an imagined or invented view of the past.[14] It is ideology masquerading as history, and becomes a blunt instrument for advancing a specific political agenda.[15]

In Defense of the Rights Revolution

It may seem strange to have to defend the principle of individual rights at this late date in American history. Why should it be necessary to defend ideas and values that are widely shared and deeply embedded in our law and culture?[16] A defense is necessary because established assumptions are always being questioned anew. Time moves on, bringing forward new issues and new perspectives. As I have already indicated, the most important new perspective today is the lack of one—a proper historical perspective. The purpose of this book is to put the rights revolution in proper perspective.

To that end, it is necessary to describe the full meaning of the rights revolution. For the most part we understand the parts but not the whole; we see the trees but not the nature of the forest. There is a vast literature on each of the specific aspects of the rights revolution: the evolution of free speech law; the drama of the civil rights movement; the growth of women's rights and gay and lesbian rights; the idea of a right to privacy and its many implications. Go to the library, and you will find innumerable books and articles discussing these and other discrete rights.

But the rights revolution is far more than its constituent parts. Ironically, the critics see this better than anyone else. Communitarian leader Mary Ann Glendon is one of the few to understand the comprehensive nature of the new rights culture. She grasps the extent to which it pervades our thinking and our common discourse.

Unfortunately, she sees only the negative side of the story, emphasizing its destructive aspects. She is not alone in this regard, however. Chapter 1 surveys the views of a variety of critics from across the political spectrum, emphasizing the extent to which they are all troubled by aspects of the rights revolution. Chapter 2 attempts to describe the pervasiveness of the new rights culture and the extent to which it has become part of the "everydayness" of our lives.

The communitarian perspective on rights provides a framework for chapters 3, 4, and 5. My central argument is that the growth of rights, far from being a destructive force, has expanded and enriched the meaning of community in America. Chapter 3 examines several aspects of the role of rights with regard to exclusion and inclusion in American society. Some of the examples discussed are rather obvious, as in the role of the civil rights movement in ending formal racial segregation. Others are less obvious but equally important. The two religion clauses of the First Amendment—the establishment clause and the free exercise clause—are usually thought of in rather narrow terms. Working in tandem, however, they have played a major role in defining the terms of community in America: that all groups, no matter how obnoxious, are legitimate members, and that no one religious group shall be favored over others.

Chapter 3 also addresses the issue of "identity politics." One of the leading criticisms of the rights revolution is that it has fostered a divisive group consciousness in America, allegedly creating conflict rather than harmony. The great villain here, of course, is affirmative action and all other forms of group-based preferences. I argue in reply that group-based divisions were imposed on American society by the creators of the old forms of discrimination: from racial segregation to sexist forms of discrimination, and the silencing of gay and lesbian people, to name only three examples. In the current bitter national debate, critics of affirmative action have successfully, but without historical justification, advanced the idea that the advocates of that policy introduced group consciousness in America.

Chapter 4 examines the role of First Amendment rights in ensuring meaningful participation for historically excluded groups. The basic premise can be stated simply: to speak is to participate; to be censored is to be silenced and excluded. The critics of rights see only the more extreme aspects of expressive individualism: the right to wear publicly a T-shirt with an offensive slogan. They do not see the deeper communitarian values implicit in free speech rights: the obligation to tolerate and to hear those ideas we do not like.

Chapter 5 explores less obvious but equally important aspects of the impact of the rights revolution on community in America. It describes the famous Willowbrook case, a legal challenge to appalling conditions in the New York state hospital for the mentally retarded that had a billiard ball effect. The placement of thousands of severely mentally retarded children in community-based facilities ran headlong into neighborhood-based attempts at housing discrimination. It also imposed new burdens on public schools, which were forced to meet the educational needs of handicapped children. The side effects of the Willowbrook litigation raised new issues regarding the dimensions of community in America and the costs of maintaining a truly inclusive society.

The fundamental point raised in each of these three chapters, one the critics of rights fail to see, is that each right carries with it a corollary obligation. The freedom to speak includes the obligation to hear. One person's right to equal treatment carries with it the obligation of many others not to discriminate and exclude. Someone's right to privacy—in family and sexual matters, for example—means that you and I cannot use the coercive power of the law to impose our standards on others. A healthier balance of rights and obligations is the essential feature of the new rights culture.

Chapter 6 critically examines the views of the Communitarian Network, the organized voice of communitarianism. It considers the specific proposals offered in the organization's official platform, along with the published views of the network's leaders, notably Amitai Etzioni and Mary Ann Glendon. While the communitarians do indeed address a number of serious problems in American society—the decline of civility in public life, the debasement of the political process—their proposed remedies are woefully inadequate. Instead of concrete alternatives, they tend to offer vague rhetoric and soothing generalities. Worse, on a number of important issues they evade the difficult issues that their own criticisms raise.

Perhaps the greatest intellectual failure of the communitarians is their failure to define what they mean by "community." In their hands the word becomes a mantra, invoked uncritically as a solution to all problems. As I argue in chapter 6, however, community has several meanings. Many people think of community in terms of residential neighborhoods. Others think in terms of religious, racial, and cultural groups that transcend geographic boundaries: the Jewish community, the African American community, the intellectual community, and so on. Some define community in regional terms, as in the old "southern way of life." Still others prefer a national sense of community, as in the American way of life or the proverbial "American dream." Finally, there are those who envision an international community of peoples, particularly with reference to international standards of human rights.

The problem, of course, is that these different definitions often conflict with each other. Neighborhood-based definitions of community have historically been the mainspring of housing discrimination and the effort to exclude certain racial or religious groups. Religious definitions of community conflict with a national definition, most notably where members of particular sects conscientiously object on religious grounds to certain national laws. And we should not forget that one infamous regional definition of community, the "southern way of life," was the rationale for institutionalized racial segregation. Finally, with respect to an international community, people in many other countries object to the effort to impose essentially American notions of rights on their culture. Separation of church and state, and the right to dissent from the official state religion are anathema in many, if not most, cultures.

Given these conflicts, it is useless to invoke the word "community" as the communitarians do without specifying what it means, and addressing and resolving the conflicts. The rights revolution, in my view, has in fact offered a definition of community, one that is grounded in the principles of inclusion and tolerance. Those are the values advanced by a strong commitment to freedom of speech, privacy, and other civil libertarian values. There is no doubt that these principles often conflict with some definitions of community. But with respect to residential housing, for example, there is no doubt in my mind that discrimination for the purposes of protecting property values or an alleged neighborhood way of life is an invalid definition of community.

The issue, in short, is not "rights" versus "community" at all. It is rather a question of what vision of community we seek to establish, and how the development of various rights contributes to that end. Some definitions of community, it must be stated forthrightly, are less worthy than others. The civil libertarian values of the rights revolution represent the preferable vision of community.

THE RIGHTS REVOLUTION

Chapter One
THE PROBLEM OF RIGHTS

JUSTICE THOMAS'S INDICTMENT

"THE CRISIS IN American society today," thundered Supreme Court Justice Clarence Thomas, is a result of the "judicial rights revolution."[1] Our streets are overrun with crime, drug abuse is rampant, and teenage pregnancy is epidemic. These and other problems are symptoms of a pervasive collapse of individual responsibility in contemporary society. And who is to blame for this disaster? The courts—or, to be more precise, activist liberal federal judges. "Why is there no discipline in our schools?" "Why are so many of our streets rife with drug bazaars?" He places the blame on judicial activism on behalf of rights.

The collapse of moral standards, Thomas continued, is the result of a "fundamental transformation" of the law that began forty years ago. What started as a well-intentioned, necessary, and long-overdue pursuit of civil rights for African Americans ended up instead harming those people. Judicial efforts to end racial discrimination encouraged African Americans to define themselves as victims. Over time this reduced them to a "crippling dependency" on the courts and on government. The habit of blaming everything on discrimination undermined the sense of personal responsibility and produced a culture of "victimhood."

THE NEW AMERICAN JEREMIAHS

Justice Thomas delivered his indictment of judicial activism at a conference entitled "The Rights Revolution," sponsored by the conservative Federalist Society.[2] It is no surprise to find conservatives attacking judicial activism. They have been doing so through the entire history of civil rights and civil liberties in this century. Other leading conservatives share Thomas's view that American society is on the verge of moral, social, and political collapse. Robert H. Bork, unsuccessful nominee for the U.S. Supreme Court in 1987 and now a prominent conservative spokesperson, believes "there are aspects of almost every branch of our culture that are worse than ever before and . . . the rot is spreading."[3] Fellow conservative William J. Bennett argues, "Over the past three decades we have experienced substantial regression. Today the forces of social decomposition are challenging—and in some instances, overtaking—the forces of social composition."[4]

What is surprising, however, is the extent to which similar views have been expressed in recent years by people with very different political perspectives. A broad array of social critics, whom I call the *New American Jeremiahs*, see evidence of social disaster everywhere.

• *Crime.* The rate of violent crime in the United States, already higher than that in European countries, tripled between the early 1960s and the 1970s. Even with the drop in crime in recent years, no other industrialized country has such high rates of murder and robbery. The 1994 murder rate of 9 per 100,000 is still almost ten times that of England and other European countries, and almost four times that of Canada.

• *Drugs.* Illegal drug use in America is widespread. One aspect of this problem is the crack epidemic that, beginning in the mid-1980s, devastated inner-city neighborhoods with open-air drug markets, violent drug gangs, and random drive-by shootings. Meanwhile, drug use among all teenagers, regardless of race or class, turned upward in the mid-1990s, a trend that ran counter to the long-term decline in the general population.

• *Teenage pregnancy.* Illegitimate births have soared since the early 1960s. In 1960, slightly more than 5 percent of all births occurred out of wedlock; by the 1990s, the number was nearly 30 percent, and for African Americans about 66 percent. The vast majority of these births involve teenage mothers.

• *Divorce.* The divorce rate increased two and a half times since the 1960s, to the point where about half of all marriages end in divorce.

• *The debasement of national politics.* Voter participation in national elections has steadily declined. Only half of all voting-age people voted in the 1992 presidential election, and only 36 percent voted in the 1994 congressional election. Many people believe this decline reflects a profound alienation from the political system and disgust at the influence of special interest groups, especially large financial contributors. The media, meanwhile, have reduced debates over important issues to empty "sound bites."

• *Increased racial strife.* Despite the historic gains of the civil rights movement in the 1960s, there appears to be an increase in racial and ethnic strife. In the 1980s there was a rash of shocking racist incidents on college campuses, including some of the most prestigious universities in the country. Critics of affirmative action believe that instead of eliminating race discrimination it has only exacerbated racial tensions, dividing whites and blacks over the issue of racial preferences.

• *The collapse of civility.* If you visit your local shopping mall, you will undoubtedly encounter someone wearing a T-shirt proclaiming "Shit Happens" or some equally crude slogan. On your way to or from the mall, you will probably see a bumper sticker with a similar declaration. Everywhere in daily life, we routinely encounter words and pictures that were once forbidden and would have resulted in an arrest.

• *The decline of personal responsibility.* People, it seems, want to avoid responsibility for their actions, preferring to blame their fate on something that was done to them: discrimination, bad parents, and so on.[5]

• *Loss of a common national identity.* The noted liberal historian Arthur M. Schlesinger, Jr., believes we are losing our sense of a common national identity.[6] He and others see the culprit as not only the rise of ethnic and racial identity but also a more pervasive balkanization of society into identity groups. Too many people think of themselves first as women, gays, handicapped, and so on, and only secondarily as Americans with a shared set of values.

• *Moral decay.* All of these problems are signs of a deeper moral decay. Crime, drug abuse, teenage pregnancy, and excuse making are but symptoms of a more general collapse of the standards of personal responsibility necessary for sustaining a healthy society.[7]

Blaming Rights
Jeremiads about the alleged moral decline of American society, and calls for a religious revival to stem it, are deeply ingrained traditions in our history. No sooner had the Puritans established the first English colonies in the New World than their leaders began issuing dire

warnings about the collapse of moral values. The historian Perry Miller observed, "In the 1640s there commenced in the sermons of New England a lament over the waning of primitive zeal and the consequent atrophy of public morals, which swelled to an incessant chant within forty years. By 1680 there seems to have been hardly any other theme for discourse."[8] Miller could very well have been describing public discourse of the 1980s and 1990s.

It would be easy to dismiss the New Jeremiahs as simply the latest version of an old and tired theme in American history, but such a response would fail to address the very real problems affecting American society. Conservatives have spoken more directly to these problems than have liberals over the past twenty years, and as a result have succeeded in shaping the national political agenda. To a great extent, they have defined the cause of those problems in the terms expressed by Justice Thomas: too much judicial activism on behalf of rights and a consequent decline in personal responsibility. In short, the problem is the new rights culture in America.

This chapter examines the various criticisms of rights expressed by commentators from across the political spectrum. My main point is to emphasize the extent to which people representing very different political points of view share similar concerns.

When I refer to "rights" in this context, I mean the core features of American constitutional law: the commitment to individual liberty as embodied in the First Amendment, equality, due process of law, and a right to privacy; the principle that rights should be applied in a universalistic and content-neutral fashion; and the principle that there should be no restrictions on individual liberty apart from some compelling government interest. One issue illustrates the special character of the American approach to rights. Virtually every other country has laws restricting racial or religious hate speech; only the United States affords broad protection to such offensive speech.[9]

One of the particularly troubling aspects of the New Jeremiahs is the extent to which they, like Justice Thomas, find the current crisis in American society rooted in the civil rights movement. Thomas is the only African American Supreme Court justice and heir to the seat previously occupied by Thurgood Marshall. As general counsel for the National Association for the Advancement of Colored People (NAACP) through the 1940s and 1950s, Marshall was the key attorney in the hugely successful constitutional attack on race discrimination.[10] It is one thing for a prominent African American to criticize some aspect of civil rights policy—say, affirmative action.

But it is especially noteworthy when such a person indicts the civil rights movement itself.

As we shall see, Justice Thomas is not alone in this regard. Many of the concerns expressed by commentators from very different political perspectives are rooted in the legacy of the civil rights movement. The tangled relationship between individual rights and group rights raises a host of issues that need to be examined.

THE CONSERVATIVE ASSAULT ON RIGHTS

Conservative attacks on individual rights are nothing new. The Grand Narrative of the growth of civil rights and civil liberties in the twentieth century portrays the fight for free speech, racial equality, and other rights as a struggle against the forces of reactionary conservatives. The famous villains in this story include the fundamentalist William Jennings Bryan at the Scopes trial, Senator Joe McCarthy during the cold war, Police Chief Bull Connor of Birmingham, Alabama, and others.[11]

In passing, it is worth noting that the story of the growth of civil rights and civil liberties is indeed presented as a Grand Narrative.[12] Various chapters are told and retold as a way of teaching certain points and inculcating certain principles about rights. The story of the Scopes case, for example, reinforces the issues of religious liberty and academic freedom. The saga of the cold war, meanwhile, teaches the importance of respecting all forms of political dissent.

Legal scholars from the Critical Legal Studies and Critical Race Theorists schools of thought deserve credit for conceptualizing the history of the growth of rights as a Grand Narrative. They do so in order to criticize the substance of the dominant narrative. As they see it, the dominant narrative represents only one point of view and ignores the perspective of the powerless, particularly racial and ethnic minorities and women.[13] Even though I disagree with this criticism, the basic concept of a Grand Narrative is very useful in explaining how we got to where we are. All of the critics of rights are attempting to write a new Grand Narrative. Charles Lawrence, an African American legal scholar and advocate of hate-speech codes, envisions a different narrative. The communitarians are attempting to write their own narrative. The struggle over the role of rights in American society is in part a struggle to control the content of the prevailing Grand Narrative and, by extension, to shape future policy.

Robert Bork and Judicial Activism

Robert Bork gained an enduring place in American history in 1987 when the U.S. Senate rejected his nomination for the Supreme Court. The battle over Bork was only one chapter in a larger and continuing political struggle over the role of the Court in American society. Bork's critics portrayed him as someone who, as a Supreme Court justice, would vote to reverse the 1973 *Roe v. Wade* decision on the right to an abortion, along with other landmark decisions on privacy, civil rights, and civil liberties.[14] The battle over his nomination even contributed a new verb to the English language: "to Bork" means to mount a hard-hitting, if not vicious, personal attack on a public figure.[15]

Following his defeat, Bork offered a full statement of his views in a book entitled *The Tempting of America.*[16] Suffice it to say that the book confirmed the worst fears of his critics. It was an uncompromising attack on the core principles underlying the rights revolution of the past forty years.

Like Justice Thomas, Bork argues that unrestrained judicial activism has been a jurisprudential, political, and social disaster. Liberal Supreme Court justices have substituted their own political agenda for the "original meaning" of the Constitution. Thus, the entire body of rights-oriented Supreme Court decisions since the 1950s has been unprincipled, politically driven, and "results-oriented." Results-oriented liberal justices, he argues, first determine the result they want from a particular case (say, legal abortions) and then fashion a legal rationale to justify it. Such decisions are not anchored in constitutional principles but instead are the expression of the political views of those justices who happen to command a majority on the Court.

The argument that the Supreme Court has departed from the original meaning or intent of the Constitution is popular among conservative legal scholars.[17] While serving as attorney general in the Reagan administration, Edwin Meese actively promoted such an idea. Supreme Court Justice Antonin Scalia is the most vocal exponent of this view, with Justice Thomas consistently joining him. The original-meaning argument is important to our discussion of the attacks on rights because it sweeps so broadly, serving as a weapon for invalidating all aspects of the rights revolution of the past forty years.

Bork identifies the source of the problem as the justly famous 1954 Supreme Court decision in *Brown v. Board of Education,* which declared racially segregated schools unconstitutional. Although he regards *Brown* as "a great and correct decision" and "the greatest moral triumph constitutional law ever produced," he believes it "was supported by a very weak opinion."[18] He finds two fundamental flaws in it. First, it violates the intent of the framers of the Fourteenth Amendment: they did not mean it to outlaw segregated schools, which continued to exist in some northern states.[19] Second, the social science evidence regarding the psychological effect of segregation on African American students cited by the Court was mere window dressing, a pretense for justifying a result the Court had already decided on.

Bork correctly perceives that the moral authority of *Brown* emboldened the Court to go further in the direction of judicial activism. "Much of the rest of the Warren Court's history," he argues, "may be explained by the lesson it learned from its success in *Brown*."[20] That lesson, he believes, is that "the Court can do what it wishes, and there is almost no way to stop it, provided its result has a significant political constituency." Any issue that fit within the emerging "egalitarian and redistributionist" philosophy could be resolved through judicial activism.[21]

Because it was not based on sound constitutional principles, Bork continues, *Brown* has had "a calamitous effect upon the law."[22] Unprincipled judicial activism has fostered a deeper moral and political crisis that goes beyond legal relativism. By substituting its own political views for the original meaning of the Constitution, liberal activist jurisprudence taught "disrespect for the actual institutions of the American nation," especially the Constitution and the Court.[23] The implicit but nonetheless clear message is that constitutional principles do not count; all that matters is whether you want results and have the power to get them. Thus, from a slightly different angle than Justice Thomas, Bork sees a similar link between institutions, values, and behavior.

Bork also argues that judicial activism undermines the capacity for democratic self-government by denying local majorities the power to govern their own communities. Efforts to promote religious values through prayer in public schools, for example, are invalidated as violations of the separation of church and state. Attempts to maintain standards of public decency through restrictions on the sale of sexually explicit material are struck down in the name of free speech. Legislative districting plans are thrown out on grounds of race discrimination. The list goes on. As the federal courts assume greater influence over local practices, this argument goes, local communities lose their sense of sense of power and responsibility.[24]

The Tempting of America was a narrowly focused argument about trends in jurisprudence. By 1996, Bork's views had changed substantially. His more recent book, Slouching Towards Gomorrah, is a sweeping indictment of modern liberalism.[25] Previously, Bork had always been somewhat of a social liberal, favoring abortion and the Brown decision but not the Court decisions that affirmed them as constitutional rights.[26] His implicit argument was that if we would change the composition of the Supreme Court, we could reverse the earlier decisions and set American society on a proper course. The new Bork sees a total collapse of moral values and can envision salvation only through some kind of religious revival. In effect, Bork has moved from being a moderate Jeremiah to a radical one.

William Bennett and the Crisis of Values

Former secretary of education and national "drug czar" William J. Bennett emerged in the 1990s as the leading champion of "values," successfully articulating a widespread sense that American society faces a fundamental crisis of moral values. His anthology The Book of Virtues, which became an enormous best-seller, is a collection of stories (read: narratives) designed to help parents teach the proper values to their children.[27] Bennett believes that the current moral crisis primarily involves the collapse of personal responsibility and self-restraint. A new culture of self-indulgence has arisen, one with little regard for either the personal or the social consequences of certain behavior.

Bennett had previously written a little book entitled The Index of Leading Cultural Indicators.[28] A clever twist on the long-standing Index of Leading Economic Indicators used by economists, Bennett's book purports to measure the moral health of our society. Bennett offers it as a "comprehensive statistical portrait . . . of behavioral trends over the last 30 years." The book includes data on crime, drug abuse, teen pregnancy, and other social problems as evidence of a national moral decline. The Index is a classic New Jeremiah statement, filled with references to "social regression," "social decomposition," and "social pathologies."[29]

According to Bennett, the cause of our social disintegration is "a marked shift in the public's beliefs, attitudes, and priorities."[30] He cites polls indicating that "our society now places less value than before on what we owe others as a matter of moral obligation."

Instead, we place too high a value "on things like self-expression, individualism, self-realization, and personal choice."[31] In short, the problem is not one of formal legal rights but of a deeper set of cultural attitudes.

Bennett does not specifically blame the courts for the current crisis, but his argument closely parallels the arguments of those who do. Insofar as the courts have expanded the right of freedom of speech, they have cultivated the value of self-expression, giving individual liberty a higher priority than community efforts to maintain public order and civility. This right of freedom of expression, Bennett's argument runs, has degenerated into mindless self-indulgence. Along the same lines, the constitutional right to an abortion affirms the principle of free personal choice in sexual matters, which many conservatives see as cultivating an ethic of self-gratification and irresponsible sexual behavior. The result has been social chaos in their view.

In terms of the link between institutions, values, and behavior, the argument advanced by Bennett and other social conservatives closely parallels the one made by economic conservatives. The tax and social welfare policies that emerged under the New Deal in the 1930s, they argue, have cultivated destructive values and behavior.[32] High income taxes and welfare entitlements undermine the work ethic, penalizing achievement and rewarding laziness. For both social and economic conservatives, there is a close link between institutions (the courts, tax policy), values, and individual behavior. In one way or another, this same linkage is also seen as a problem by the other critics of rights we will examine.

THE REVOLT OF THE AFRICAN AMERICAN CONSERVATIVES

One of the most notable political and intellectual developments of the 1980s was the emergence of a group of prominent African American conservatives: Justice Clarence Thomas, economist Thomas Sowell, professor of English Shelby Steele, and others.[33] As a Supreme Court justice, Thomas is certainly the most famous and most powerful member of this group. The African American conservatives play a particularly important role in the assault on rights. By virtue of their race, their attacks on civil rights policy and affirmative action have special authority. They cannot be dismissed as white racists, and consequently they give legitimacy to the criticisms of affirmative action and other civil rights policies expressed by whites. Most important, insofar as they challenge the underlying assumptions of the civil rights movement, they raise questions about the broader rights culture in America.

The central argument of the African American conservatives is that official civil rights policy actually *harms* African Americans. They believe that the civil rights movement took a disastrous wrong turn in the early 1970s when it shifted from the color-blind, race-neutral, individual rights orientation of the original civil rights movement to a race-conscious group approach. Under affirmative action, group membership replaces individual merit as the standard for employment and college admissions.

Thomas Sowell and the Economics of Rights

The economist Thomas Sowell is generally recognized as the godfather of the African American conservative movement, with his 1975 book, *Race and Economics,* as the founding manifesto.[34] An enormously prolific writer, he has published many books on related subjects over the past twenty years while also writing a syndicated newspaper column.[35] In a sense, there are almost two Thomas Sowells. His newspaper columns are generally vicious, ill-tempered hatchet jobs, with little intellectual substance. His books, on the other hand, are a serious intellectual challenge to official civil rights policy. Even those who disagree with his arguments about civil rights policy (as I do) find his arguments provocative.

Sowell attacks affirmative action from the perspective of an economic conservative, arguing that it violates the principles of the free market. This is part of his general view that all forms of government intervention in the marketplace are inefficient and counterproductive, reducing economic opportunity for everyone, including minorities. Sowell argues that affirmative action is not necessary. In his rose-colored view of the marketplace, economic self-interest will always override prejudice. The employer will choose the talented African American over the less-qualified white candidate. As he declares in one of his books, "Translating subjective prejudice into overt economic discrimination is costly for profit-seeking competitive firms."[36]

This is not the place to engage Sowell's basic argument about race and the free market. Suffice it to say that it seems to be contradicted by several hundred years of history. Major-league baseball offers an obvious example. Team owners did not hire the hugely talented Josh Gibson and Satchell Paige, among others, precisely because racism trumped talent and the alleged pressure of free market competition. Other examples abound. Some historians, argue that early in the twentieth century, successful African American entrepreneurs in the service sector (particularly food preparation) were displaced by European immigrants because of racism and not because the new arrivals provided better services.

Sowell presents another version of his view that economics is more important than politics (including formal legal rights) in *Ethnic America*, a history of racial and ethnic groups in America.[37] His view of history is relentlessly upbeat: each group came, suffered through poverty and discrimination, but struggled and eventually entered the mainstream of American life. Each group made its contribution to our rich cultural diversity: the Germans gave us their music and food, the Italians did the same, and so on. According to Sowell's account, "Much of the vernacular, food, music, and other cultural characteristics of American society today were once ethnic peculiarities but are now part of the common heritage." He goes on to cite "Gershwin, the Kennedys, Andrew Carnegie, Joe DiMaggio, and O. J. Simpson" (this was written in 1981) as "American phenomena rather than ethnic figures."[38]

The challenging part of Sowell's analysis is his explanation of the relative success of different groups. Using census data on median family income, he finds that Asian Americans and Jews have been the most successful (average family income indices of 172 and 132, respectively), with Polish Americans (115) and Italian Americans (112) above the national average. The comparative failures are the Irish (103), who have been outstripped by their fellow white Catholic Europeans.[39]

Sowell makes the challenging argument that Italians and Poles have enjoyed swifter and greater success than the Irish because they have chosen the entrepreneurial route, rather than the political route favored by the Irish. In a similar fashion, Asian-Americans and Jews have succeeded socially because they built solid economic bases. Sowell believes that the comparative stagnation of the Irish in this country represents an object lesson for African Americans: business entrepreneurship, not politics, is the route to success and acceptance in America. "The paths to group advancement emphasized by black leaders have been precisely those paths rejected by Italian Americans . . . government aid and special treatment."[40]

Japanese Americans rose as a group precisely because they chose "quiet persistence" over militant political action.[41]

Among the critics of rights, Sowell gives special emphasis to the free market. Although he does not attack judicially enforced rights, his argument complements those critics who do. Like Justice Thomas and Bennett, he emphasizes the link between institutions, values, and behavior. Relying on politics and legal remedies undermines the values of self-reliance and economic entrepreneurship that are the keys to social advancement. It cultivates a culture of victimization and an expectation that advancement is something that will be granted automatically, not something to work for and achieve on one's own.

Shelby Steele and the Importance of Character

The most powerful case for the harmful effect of affirmative action on African Americans is made by Shelby Steele, a professor of English at San Jose State University. "After twenty years of implementation," he writes, "I think affirmative action has shown itself to be more bad than good." If it is allowed to continue as public policy, African Americans "now stand to lose more than they gain."[42] The title of Steele's best-selling book, *The Content of Our Character,* is taken from Martin Luther King's famous 1963 "I Have a Dream" speech, in which the great civil rights leader envisioned a day when his four children would "live in a nation where they will not be judged by the color of their skin but by the content of their character."[43] King's speech is justly famous as one of the most eloquent statements of the ideal of a color-blind society. By invoking King's speech, Steele seeks to make the point that affirmative action has departed from the ideals of the early civil rights movement.

As evidence of the failure of affirmative action, Steele cites the huge dropout rate among African American students at both his own university, San Jose State, and the elite University of California at Berkeley campus not far away. He believes that affirmative action programs admit students who lack the academic skills to succeed, and consequently the students either fail outright or drop out to avoid formal dismissal. Thus, affirmative action not only fails to achieve its nominal goal of increasing the number of minority students but also compounds the original problem by heaping a strong dose of failure on those who drop out.

Steele also points out that the gap between white and black median incomes increased during the 1970s and 1980s, the period in which affirmative action developed and spread. Following Sowell's line of reasoning, he argues that "preferential treatment does not teach skills, or educate, or instill motivation. It only passes out entitlement by color."[44] The result is a "crippling dependency" on legal remedies that do not serve the best interests of their intended clients in the long run.

The argument that affirmative action has had a "crippling" effect is one part of the idea that we have developed a culture of "victimization" in the United States, a point made by many other critics. Justice Thomas, as we have seen, believes that civil rights policy generally, and not just affirmative action, has created a sense of dependency. We will consider shortly the views of some prominent feminists and the noted civil liberties lawyer Alan Dershowitz on this issue.

Finally, Steele argues that affirmative action perpetuates racial stereotypes and aggravates racial conflict. By giving racial minorities an entitlement, it has "reburdened" American society with the old "marriage of color and preference," simply reversing the hierarchy of preference to favor minorities over whites. Group-based remedies, moreover, accentuate the sense of *difference* between groups: "What has emerged on campus in recent years . . . is a *politics of difference*, a troubling, volatile politics in which each group justifies itself, its sense of worth and its pursuit of power, through difference alone."[45] Thus, civil rights policy has the effect of heightening racial conflict and fragmenting American society even further.

The idea that affirmative action and other group-based policies have had a divisive effect on American society also troubles many people on the political left and in the center. Steele plays a particularly important role in legitimating this argument from an African American perspective, and by challenging the moral authority of official civil rights policy, he also lays the groundwork for a broader attack on rights.

There are several possible responses to the criticisms of affirmative action offered by Steele. Along with other critics of the policy, he ignores any consideration of the economic trends of the past quarter century, which many economists believe are responsible for the growth of a new underclass and the worsening situation of the black lower class in particular.[46] It is a fair criticism that affirmative action has not and cannot overcome the resulting economic hurdles, but the policy did not cause them. With respect to college admissions, Steele fails to point out that the dropout rate among African Americans, particularly males, is very high on almost all campuses, including colleges with open admissions policies. Thus, affirmative action is not the central problem with respect to graduation rates. This is not the occasion for a full-scale debate over affirmative action. My point in this chapter is to highlight the extent to which the criticisms of rights offered by conservatives are shared, in various ways, by commentators with very different political perspectives. Let us now move to the other end of the political spectrum and see how various self-professed leftists share some of the same concerns.

DISILLUSIONMENT ON THE LEFT

Some prominent members of the political left are also critical of certain aspects of the rights revolution. This may come as a surprise, since the left claims to speak for the powerless—racial and ethnic minorities, women, the poor—who have been major beneficiaries of the rights revolution. There are actually two quite distinct leftist critiques of our prevailing rights culture. One argues that we have not given enough attention to difference, while the other asserts that we have given it too much.

The Critical Race Theorists and the Hate Speech Controversy

In the 1980s, there emerged a group of legal scholars, referred to as *Critical Race Theorists,* who argued that our prevailing concept of rights had not served the interests of racial and ethnic minorities.[47] This group gained special prominence in the national debate over hate speech. In response to an apparent rise in racist incidents, a broad coalition of racial minority, female, lesbian, and gay students demanded college and university codes of conduct prohibiting offensive speech. This demand was a remarkable historical development: the first time in the history of American higher education that students, rather than administrators or alumni, had demanded controls over offensive speech.[48]

The campus speech code movement lost much of its momentum when federal district courts declared the codes at the University of Michigan and the University of Wisconsin unconstitutional violations of the First Amendment.[49] Nonetheless, the arguments raised by the Critical Race Theorists continue as a particularly important criticism of our prevailing rights culture.

The most prominent advocates of restrictive hate-speech laws are Charles Lawrence, Mari Matsuda, and Richard Delgado.[50] All three are either minorities or women, and their criticism of unrestricted free speech arises from their perspective as members of minority groups. Matsuda argues that debates over free speech need to take into account "the victim's story." Citing her own experience, she recalls the racism directed at her family and how her parents taught her to "never let anyone call me a J——p."[51]

Matsuda and other Critical Race Theorists argue that the abstract, universalistic, and content-neutral norms of contemporary free speech law, which protect racist speech, fail to take into account the special circumstances of racial and ethnic minorities. The main point is that the law is insensitive to *difference*. Protecting racist speech serves to maintain the larger racist structure of American society. Taking different racial experiences into account leads to different conclusions about freedom of speech. Victims' voices tell us that hate speech does real harm. In Delgado's phrase, these are "words that wound."[52] The racist epithet is the same as a physical assault. As Charles Lawrence III puts it, "The [racist] invective is experienced as a blow, not as a preferred idea."[53] Thus, it falls outside the scope of protected speech.

The Critical Race Theorists' argument in favor of restrictive campus speech codes closely parallels, and draws upon, the emerging law of sexual harassment.[54] Just as sexual harassment creates a "hostile environment" in the workplace, so hate speech creates an environment on campus that interferes with the educational opportunities of its victims. In this analysis, Fourteenth Amendment considerations of equality balance First Amendment considerations of free speech, justifying some limited restrictions on expression. It is important to note that the Critical Race Theorists are not hostile to a rights-oriented society per se but only to the extent that the Fourteenth Amendment has, in their view, taken a backseat to the First and other amendments.

By arguing that First Amendment law should take into account the special circumstances of racial and ethnic minorities, the Critical Race Theorists adopt a particularistic rather than a universalistic approach to constitutional law. As we will see shortly, some feminist legal scholars argue that the law needs to accommodate the special and different circumstances of women in American society.[55]

In important respects, the particularistic approach to constitutional law advocated by Critical Race Theorists and Critical Feminist Theorists is similar to traditional conservative objections to American free speech law, which also argue that the law should take into account the impact of certain kinds of speech in certain circumstances. Thus, conservatives have sought to limit criticism of the government during wartime, or to limit sexually oriented expression because of its allegedly harmful effect on public morals. (It might also be noted in passing that the Marxist left in America took the same position, arguing that fascists and racists had no right of free speech—that is, until they found themselves under assault during the cold war, at which point they sought refuge behind a different interpretation of the First Amendment.)[56] The difference—and it is an important one—is that the Critical Race Theorists and Critical Feminist Theorists are working within a framework of rights. They argue for a few narrow limits on certain established rights of free speech in order to advance other rights.

The particularistic approach to rights advocated by the left-oriented minority and feminist scholars form an important part of the mosaic of contemporary criticisms of rights. As advocates of equality, these groups represent an unexpected source of criticism. Nonetheless, they share with conservative critics to view that the dominant approach to rights is too doctrinaire and absolutist, and has unacceptable social and political consequences.

The Feminist Antipornography Crusade

Another criticism of our dominant rights culture from a left perspective involves the feminist antipornography movement, led by Catharine MacKinnon and Andrea Dworkin, whose position closely resembles that of the Critical Race Theorists. Sexually degrading material, they argue, does real harm to women, just as racial epithets do real harm to racial and ethnic minorities.[57] The prevailing norms of First Amendment law—abstract and content-neutral—protect sexually explicit expression and, by extension, help sustain the larger pattern of sexism in American society. Like the Critical Race Theorists, MacKinnon emphasizes the special circumstances of women in a sexist society. In this respect, she is a *difference* feminist, as distinct from an *equality* feminist.[58]

MacKinnon is a force to be reckoned with in terms of legal theory. She played a major role (perhaps *the* principal role) in defining sexual harassment as discrimination.[59] The Supreme Court has accepted the essentials of this argument in its decisions on sexual harassment.[60] She and Dworkin drafted a model ordinance creating a civil cause of action for women against pornographers. A woman could sue the proprietor of an adult bookstore that sold pornographic books or magazines, claiming harm and asking for monetary damages. The city of Indianapolis enacted an ordinance based on MacKinnon and Dworkin's proposal, but it was declared unconstitutional in 1985.[61]

Critics of MacKinnon and Dworkin accuse them of advancing, if only inadvertently, a conservative political agenda that is hostile to women's equality.[62] Although they vehemently deny this charge, their position on the First Amendment is similar to the traditional conservative view: that certain exceptions should be made to freedom of speech in order to prevent harm to society. If conservatives want to limit free speech in the name of public order or national security, MacKinnon and her allies want to limit it in the interests of women's equality. The underlying rationale is the same; only the definition of the best interests of society is different.

Lament for the New Left

A very different critique of rights from a left perspective has been expressed recently by former New Left activist Todd Gitlin and journalist Michael Tomasky.[63] Gitlin and Tomasky both lament the collapse of a viable left alternative in American politics. They attribute the demise of the 1960s New Left to the new phenomenon of "identity politics": the habit of relatively powerless groups—racial minorities, women, lesbians, and gays—to think in terms of their group identity rather than in broader class terms. Unlike the Critical Race Theorists and Critical Feminist Theorists, in short, they think we have given *too much* attention to difference. The particularly troubling aspect of their argument is that the phenomenon of identity politics is a direct legacy of the civil rights movement.

As one of the early leaders of Students for a Democratic Society (SDS), Gitlin has well-established left credentials. Because there is so much misunderstanding on the subject, it is important to note that when he talks about the New Left he refers to its early phase, with its humanistic, democratic orientation, as distinct from the undemocratic and often nihilistically violent left of the late 1960s (as represented by the Weathermen).[64] One of Gitlin's earlier books, *The Whole World Is Watching,* is the finest treatment of the extremely complex relationship between the news media and the political movements in the 1960s.[65]

Gitlin opens *The Twilight of Common Dreams* with an account of a battle over public school textbooks in Oakland in the early 1990s. Minority groups fought bitterly over the extent to which they were represented in the books being considered for adoption by the school board. He presents this episode as emblematic of the extent to which powerless groups abandoned the struggle over their common economic plight and instead fought among themselves over the content of textbooks.[66]

As he sees it, the fragmentation of the left into separate movements based on *identity*—African American, Hispanic, female, lesbian, gay, and so forth—since the late 1960s has destroyed any possibility of a broad-based coalition offering an alternative to American capitalism. As someone heavily influenced by Marxist thought, Gitlin can still envision an alternative political movement in America based on class rather than group identity—hence the reference to "common dreams" in the title of his book.

Gitlin does not criticize the idea of rights directly, and he undoubtedly is a strong supporter of most, if not all, of the new rights that have developed in the past quarter century: prisoners' rights, abortion rights, the rights of lesbians and gays, and so on. Nonetheless, his criticism of "identity politics" has enormous implications for the rights revolution, since so much of that revolution involves the assertion of group-oriented rights. The issue presents him—and all of us—with a profound dilemma. The civil rights movement was one of the great chapters in American history, and yet it seems to have encouraged some disastrous tendencies.

Although writing from a left perspective, Gitlin has much in common with conservatives Thomas Sowell and Shelby Steele. Like them, he sees the civil rights movement inculcating an absorption in group identity that prevents powerless people from taking the steps needed to produce real improvement in their lives. For Gitlin, those steps involve collective political action; for Sowell and Steele, they involve hard work, perseverance, and individual initiative.

The dilemma that agitates all of these observers is one of the most important and thorny problems facing contemporary American society. Put simply, how can we transcend the problem of race and move toward a color-blind society without in some way heightening racial consciousness along the way? The famous social psychologist Erving Goffman addressed this problem more than thirty years ago. In a discussion of "in-groups" and "out-groups," he noted, "When the ultimate political objective is to remove stigma from the differentness, the individual may find that his very efforts can politicize his own life, rendering it even more different from the normal life initially denied him."[67] Our political history of the last three decades suggests that Goffman understated the problem. In place of "may find" we can substitute "does find." And his perceptive comments about individuals apply with equal force to entire groups.

There is no easy resolution to this dilemma. It is at the core of the race problem that remains, despite a half century of civil rights activism, the fundamental problem facing American democracy. Moreover, it applies not just to African Americans but to all groups who seek to end discrimination: women, the handicapped, lesbian and gay people, and so on. Law professor Martha Minow offers the most subtle discussion of this problem with respect to women, the handicapped, and bilingual education in her book *Making All the Difference*. She poses the dilemma with a rhetorical question: "When does treating people differently emphasize their differences and stigmatize or hinder them on that basis? and when does treating people the same become insensitive to their difference and likely to stigmatize or hinder them on that basis?"[68] She devotes nearly four hundred pages to her answer and makes it abundantly clear that there are no simple answers to the "dilemma of difference."

Journalist Michael Tomasky voices his leftist perspective on the damaging impact of identity politics in his book *Left for Dead*. The deliberately ironic title of chapter 3, "*E Unum Pluribus* [Out of One, Many]: The Politics of Identity," dramatizes his main point.[69] The rise of group identity fragmented and eventually destroyed the left political movements of the 1960s, allowing conservatives to completely dominate the national political agenda. Tomasky concedes that while the quest for identity has had many good aspects, it has been a political disaster for the left.

Tomasky makes the extremely useful point that identity politics per se is nothing new in America. The old urban political machines that emerged in the nineteenth century "were veritable identity factories," building on and in many ways reinforcing the ethnic identities of Irish American, Polish American, Jewish American, and innumerable other groups.[70] But he argues that there is a crucial difference between the old-style machine politics and the new identity politics. The old style "amounted to little more than coalition building among different groups." In the new style, however, "people seek rights not as Americans but as members of self-identified groups."[71] This is an interesting argument, and one that historians could explore. Tomasky may be romanticizing the extent to which the rise of ethnic consciousness always pointed in the direction of coalition building. This process may in fact have been specific to the unique circumstances of New Deal politics in the 1930s. (This includes a more specific point for investigation: Why did the economic disaster of the Great Depression lead to ethnic coalition building, while the serious but far less severe economic problems of the post-1973 period seem to accentuate intergroup strife?)

My point is that Tomasky voices the same indictment of the new rights culture as do other critics. His fellow leftist Gitlin, conservatives such as Shelby Steele, and, as we shall see shortly, liberals such as Arthur Schlesinger, Jr., are all deeply troubled that rights consciousness has fostered a group consciousness that accentuates difference rather than a shared experience and destiny.

THE UNEASY LIBERALS

A number of prominent liberals are also uneasy about identity politics and other aspects of the new American rights culture. The focus of discussions is usually the policy of affirmative action, an issue that can be debated on purely constitutional grounds, with respect to reverse discrimination, and on pragmatic terms with respect to whether it achieves its intended results. Just below the surface, however, is the more troubling issue of group consciousness, and the question of whether the civil rights movement set in motion something that has increased rather than reduced group divisions in American society.

Arthur Schlesinger and the Meaning of America

The noted liberal historian Arthur M. Schlesinger, Jr., is deeply troubled by what he sees as the "disuniting of America."[72] Our society, he believes, is coming apart at the seams, and we are in danger of losing a shared sense of national identity. He warns that "a cult of ethnicity has arisen" in America. The "underlying philosophy is that America is not a nation of individuals at all but a nation of groups," defined by race, ethnicity, gender, sexual preference, and a host of other discrete identities. The liberal Schlesinger agrees with the conservative Justice Thomas that American society is losing the core values that hold it together, and he shares the concerns of the leftists Gitlin and Tomasky that identity politics divides rather than unites us.

Schlesinger's liberal credentials are impeccable. If anything, he is the epitome of the liberal scholar-activist. A longtime adviser to

Democratic Party politicians, he served on the White House staff of President John F. Kennedy and has celebrated the achievements of liberal activism and strong presidential leadership in a series of widely praised biographies of Presidents Andrew Jackson, Franklin D. Roosevelt, and Kennedy. His 1949 book, *The Vital Center,* helped to define post–World War II liberalism: strongly anti-Communist at home and abroad, while committed to fulfilling the social reform agenda of the New Deal at home.[73]

Like other liberals of his generation, Schlesinger regards the civil rights movement as one of the great achievements of recent American history. And yet, like Gitlin and Tomasky, he senses that the current balkanization of American society into a set of warring groups has its roots in the civil rights movement. Committed as he is to racial equality and the history of the civil rights movement, Schlesinger has particular trouble facing up to the implications of his own disturbing thoughts. If group-oriented thinking is suspect, doesn't this call into question the civil rights movement itself? There is no simple resolution to the dilemma posed by Goffman: that the effort to end group distinctions only heightens group consciousness. Tomasky offers the best reply—that group identity was not invented by the civil rights movement—but this only illuminates the dilemma without resolving it.

Rights and "Victimhood"

The noted art critic Robert Hughes shares Schlesinger's concerns about identity politics and adds another dimension: the so-called cult of "victimhood." In his best-selling book *The Culture of Complaint* he writes, "Thirty years ago, one of the epic processes in the assertion of human dignity started unfolding in the United States: the civil rights movement."[74] Like Schlesinger, Hughes regards the struggle for racial justice as one of the most important events in recent American history. And yet he now finds that the notion of rights has been perverted into a cult of "victimhood." Virtually everyone, he argues, now claims some right on the basis of being the member of a victimized group. "The range of victims available ten years ago—blacks, chicanos, Indians, women, homosexuals—has now expanded to include every permutation of the halt, the lame, and the short."[75]

Many others have taken up the "victimhood" theme. It is a particular favorite among conservative feminists such as Christina Hoff Sommers and Katie Roiphe, both authors of best-selling books attacking the mainstream feminist crusade for women's equality.[76] Conservative social critic Charles J. Sykes labels us a "nation of victims," while Walter K. Olson attacks antidiscrimination laws as an "excuse factory."[77] And as we have already seen, Justice Thomas, Shelby Steele, and other African American conservatives believe the civil rights movement has cultivated a sense of victimhood by relentlessly emphasizing the wrongs done to African Americans, with no emphasis on personal responsibility.

A particularly significant voice in the chorus of attacks on "victimhood" is that of Harvard law professor Alan Dershowitz. In *The Abuse Excuse,* he denounces what he sees as the growing American habit of evading personal responsibility and attempting to blame our problems on something or someone else.[78] Dershowitz occupies a unique place on this issue. As one of the most prominent civil libertarians in the country, he does not use the victimhood issue to advance a conservative, anti-rights political agenda. Unfortunately, however, *The Abuse Excuse* is primarily a collection of his newspaper columns, and he does not spell out in detail how we might limit the damaging effect of excuse making while retaining important individual rights.

Most of the "victimhood" literature is ephemeral pop sociology. Christina Hoff Sommers devotes *Who Stole Feminism?* to demolishing some of the careless and absurd allegations made by some feminists.[79] Assuming the role of investigative journalist, she attempts to track down the origins of these allegations and usually finds that there is no factual basis for them. In doing so, however, she ignores the underlying issue. She skillfully debunks the idea that Super Bowl Sunday is the worst day of the year for domestic violence, for example, but never really addresses the feminist argument that domestic violence is a serious problem.

A certain amount of hypocrisy also surrounds many of the attacks on victimhood. The people who attack African Americans, feminists, and the handicapped rights activists are discretely silent on the issue of the Holocaust. But what are the justly celebrated Holocaust Museum in Washington, the award-winning film *Schindler's List,* and various university Holocaust studies courses and programs but efforts to keep alive the memory of one group's tragic suffering? Nor has anyone challenged those Jewish community leaders who have expressed alarm over the trends in intermarriage and the possible disappearance of Jewish identity and culture.[80] If group identity has a harmful effect on American society, and if focusing on past group suffering is harmful to the group itself, then don't these same criticisms apply to Jews? The silence of the many critics of identity politics on this issue represents a hypocritical selective application of their alleged principles.

It is easy to dismiss books such as Sommers's and Sykes's as pop ephemera. Yet, when someone as strongly committed to the cause of civil rights as Robert Hughes suggests that something has gone seriously wrong with the group-based civil rights strategy, the criticisms cannot be dismissed as racist rhetoric. Moreover, the fact that Hughes's doubts closely parallel Schlesinger's and resonate with the views of Justice Thomas, Shelby Steele, and other conservatives tells us that there is a problematic relationship between the civil rights movement and the continuing racial tensions in America.

THE COMMUNITARIAN VISION

Rising liberal and moderate concerns about the role of rights in American society eventually coalesced into a movement known as *communitarianism*. In brief, communitarianism holds that in matters of law and policy we have given far too much attention to individual rights and have neglected both the needs of the larger community and the importance of individual responsibility.

The intellectual roots of communitarianism are over twenty years old and have produced a rich body of academic literature in the fields of political philosophy and law.[81] The idea burst upon the political scene in 1990 with the formation of the Communitarian Network, a nonprofit public interest group designed to influence public policy along communitarian lines. Organized by sociologist Amitai Etzioni, the Communitarian Network quickly enlisted the support of a number of prominent politicians, including then-Senator Bill Bradley, a liberal, and conservative Senator Alan Simpson. This political odd couple is only one indication of the extent to which communitarianism speaks to widely shared concerns about the state of American society.

The Communitarian Network adopted an official platform, and thus has translated its concerns into a concrete program for action. The Communitarian Network Platform calls for "restoring the moral voice" to American public life by strengthening the family, restoring order to the schools, and encouraging a commitment to the public good.[82] The Network also established a journal (*The Responsive Com-*

munity) and published position papers on topics such as organ dona-tion. Etzioni, meanwhile, has published his own manifestos, *The Spirit of Community* and *The New Golden Rule: Community and Moral-ity in a Democratic Society.*[83] We will examine the specific proposals of the communitarians in detail in chapter 6.

Communitarianism represents the most comprehensive chal-lenge to the idea that individual rights should enjoy the highest pri-ority in our scale of social values. It argues that we have emphasized individual rights at the expense of the common good; that we think too much about ourselves and not enough about others; that we talk about "me" rather than "us." As Etzioni puts it, in a communitarian society, "individual rights are to be matched with social responsibil-ities."[84] Although in their view of contemporary society and some of their policy proposals the communitarians have much in common with political conservatives, they distance themselves from the rad-ical right. They incorporated the term *responsive* in the title of their journal because they see themselves as responsive to the needs of individuals and the tradition of individual liberties in a way that the political right is not.[85]

Etzioni and Mary Ann Glendon argue that our discourse about rights is "morally incomplete" because it lacks any sense of person-al responsibility or obligation to others. They draw heavily upon an extremely influential anthropological study of Americans, *Habits of the Heart,* which claims to show that although Americans talk about individual liberty, their lives demonstrate a deep commitment to community and shared experience—a commitment for which this study argues they have no language.[86] Instead of always insisting on our rights, Glendon believes we should seek "compromise, mutual understanding, and the discovery of common ground" with people and movements we disagree with.[87]

The real villains, according to the communitarians, are the "rights absolutists," particularly the American Civil Liberties Union (ACLU), who have aggressively and relentlessly pursued a broad rights agenda. Etzioni's focus on the ACLU is justified. Over the course of more than seventy-five years, the organization has been responsible for placing rights at the center of our legal and political agenda. The ACLU has played a special role in the growth of the so-called new rights that emerged in the late 1960s: the rights of the mentally ill, prisoners, women, children, and so on.[88]

The obsessive pursuit of rights, the communitarians argue, has produced a "rights inflation" that devalues the truly important rights such as free speech and equality. The very idea of the "rights of single people," for example, cheapens the idea of free speech. (On this point, I will examine the ACLU handbook entitled *The Rights of Single People* in chapter 2.)[89] Communitarians such as Etzioni and Glendon have a deep respect for the values of free speech and equality, and it is this commitment that sets them apart from many of the other critics of rights. Glendon, for example, defines her goal as "not the abandonment, but the renewal, of our strong rights tradition."[90] As a start toward developing a healthier balance, Etzioni urges us to "put a tight lid on the manufacturing of new rights."[91]

The appeal of communitarianism lies in its ability to provide both a coherent explanation for the social problems that afflict American society and a morally compelling alternative. It sums up virtually all of the arguments expressed by the New Jeremiahs: crime, family breakdown, moral decay, loss of personal responsibility, too much litigation and judicial activism, and so on. Instead of the heavily negative tone of so many criticisms of rights, communitarianism offers a positive vision of a better society based on an appealing set of values. Its altruistic ethos of asking people to put aside their selfish concerns and work for the common good has a strong appeal among people of many political persuasions. In the end, the communitarians view the current crisis in American society in terms of a stark dichotomy between rights and community.

Mary Ann Glendon and the New "Rights Talk"
The most intellectually gifted communitarian spokesperson is Harvard law professor Mary Ann Glendon. Her book *Rights Talk* is the most articulate discussion of the extent to which the growth of rights has produced a new culture of rights.[92] Better than any other critic, she grasps the nature of the fundamental changes in our society. She argues that we think reflexively in terms of rights, defining virtually every issue that arises in those terms. Problems related to children, for example, are immediately defined in terms of "children's rights," the problems of the poor are immediately defined in terms of the "rights of the poor," and so on.

Glendon is especially perceptive in seeing how deeply the language of rights has penetrated the lives of ordinary people. Concepts and terminology that were once the exclusive province of lawyers now fall easily from the lips of nearly everyone. She believes we have almost lost the capacity to express thoughts about personal responsibility and the common good.[93] We are quick to talk about our rights, but we maintain a near-complete "silence with respect to personal, civic and collective responsibilities."[94]

The new rights culture, Glendon continues, is excessively legalistic and absolutist: legalistic in the sense that we approach every social problem as a matter of formal legal rights, and absolutist in the sense that we are unwilling to consider compromise. It is precisely the ACLU's absolutist position on separation of church and state, for example, that arouses the ire of the communitarians. This combination of legalism and absolutism "impedes compromise, mutual understanding, and the discovery of common ground."[95] In this way, the pursuit of rights undermines the development of a healthy community.

In the Law Schools: Civic Republicanism

A variation of communitarianism known as *civic republicanism* has developed among a group of legal scholars.[96] This school of thought addresses the basic purpose of the Constitution and, like the communitarians, finds that we have overemphasized individual rights. Law professor Cass Sunstein argues that the central purpose of the Constitution is not to protect rights for their own sake but to promote democratic self-governance.[97] Thus, for example, a difficult free speech question should be resolved in favor of the result that promotes "deliberative democracy." Some racist speech, he argues, can be restricted because it contributes nothing of value to the democratic process. Racial epithets, for example, "are not intended and received as contributions to social deliberation about anything."[98]

Sunstein's version of civic republicanism resembles the views of Mari Matsuda, Charles Lawrence III, and Catharine MacKinnon to the extent that it emphasizes the social impact of particular forms of expression.[99] Unlike these other views, however, civic republicanism seeks to advance not the interests of particular groups but the common good.

Civic republicanism puts particular emphasis on "civic virtue," which it defines as an active concern for the common good. This includes a willingness to take up the burdens of participating in civic life and to place the common good above self-interest. It is a value that, for civic republicans, takes precedence over the pursuit of individual rights. One recent communitarian book explores possible ways of nourishing civic virtue in families, neighborhoods, and the workplace.[100]

Civic virtue, however, has been undermined by the extremely

active role of the federal courts in enforcing individual rights. Political philosopher Michael J. Sandel argues that the result has been not the promised liberation but a pervasive sense of disempowerment, a "loss of mastery." Laws embodying community standards of decency are struck down as violations of freedom of expression; community efforts to instill religious values are invalidated as violations of the separation of church and state, and so on. Sandel explains the great "discontent" that Americans have felt about democracy, beginning in the 1970s and rising to a peak in the 1990s, in terms of this loss of community control to abstract notions of rights enforced by the courts. "Americans found to their frustration that they were losing control of the forces that governed their lives."[101] Thus, from a very different perspective, Sandel, Sunstein, and other communitarians end up very close (probably closer than they would like to admit) to Justice Clarence Thomas in their analysis of what is wrong with America. Judicial activism has undermined the basic institutions of society and cultivated a harmful set of values.

CONCLUSION: THE PROBLEMS WITH RIGHTS

American society, we are told, is on the verge of collapse. Some of the New Jeremiahs see the problem in terms of moral decay. Others see a loss of national identity and the rise of a divisive balkanization fueled by "identity politics." Still others see a loss of community as a result of a self-indulgent expressive individualism. Communitarian leader Amitai Etzioni frames the indictment of rights in stark terms: Has the enormous expansion of individual liberty and freedom of choice "undermine[d] the social order upon which liberties are ultimately based"?[102]

The common denominator uniting these various indictments is the new rights culture that has arisen over the last forty years. In various ways, conservative, liberal, and leftist critics trace our problems back to the growth of rights. They all argue that the pursuit of individual rights has become perverted into a destructive quest for group rights.

The critics reviewed in this chapter pose a serious challenge to the assumptions underlying the rights revolution. The pursuit of individual rights, instead of enhancing a free and democratic society, they argue, has debased it. My response to this challenge follows in the chapters ahead. I shall argue that these critics lack a proper historical perspective. They assume, implicitly but without justification, that all was well with American society forty years ago. They fail to see what was wrong, particularly the narrow and exclusionary definition of community that prevailed. And thus they have no appreciation of the positive contributions of the rights revolution in that regard.

Chapter Two

THE TRANSFORMATION OF AMERICAN LIFE

THE NEW FABRIC OF DAILY LIFE

SOMETHING FUNDAMENTAL has changed in American society. The change is far more profound than the readily evident superficial aspects of contemporary life: modern technology, changes in clothing and hairstyles, and suburban sprawl and urban decay. Some of the New Jeremiahs sense the depth of the transformation, noting a profound change in values and behavior. The problem with the New Jeremiahs, however, is that they focus only on certain aspects of this change—such as crime or teenage pregnancy—and see only the negative part of the larger picture.

The change we are concerned with involves the basic *fabric* of daily life. The metaphor of a fabric is useful because it suggests the intricate network of relationships that make up our lives. These changed relationships are the essence of the new rights culture created by the rights revolution.

Reitz van Winkle, whom we met in the introduction, would quickly notice the more visible aspects of the rights revolution in his walk around Atlanta: the intermingling of people of different races, the porn shops, the public display of same-sex relationships. What he could not see, and could appreciate only with the passage of time, are the more subtle changes in the way we relate to each other: the way we talk, the words we use, the words we choose not to use, the way we think about our options before we act.

Although the rights revolution is a pervasive aspect of our lives, it is an extremely elusive phenomenon. It involves the kind of broad changes in attitudes and behavior that historians find difficult to handle. Historians are skilled at dealing with the dramatic events of *public* life: wars, elections, presidencies, laws, riots, the business cycle, and other events. Although the rights revolution includes public events such as laws and court decisions, it is most important in terms of subtle but nonetheless profound changes in everyday life. We are concerned here not with the thoughts and actions of powerful social elites and decision makers but with the lives of ordinary people.

The new rights culture that has developed is one aspect of the pervasive role of law in contemporary society. As two legal scholars put it, law "is a virtually invisible factor" in our daily lives. It is "part of the taken-for-granted world," shaping our behavior in ways that we often do not fully understand.[1] Law is not merely an instrument for achieving certain purposes. Rather, it is something that shapes and defines our everyday lives, including how we think about ourselves and our relations with other people. The purpose of this chapter is to capture this "everydayness" of our rights culture. The central point of this book is that things we now take for granted were not taken for granted only a few years ago.

One example helps to illustrate the point. The 1964 Civil Rights Act is one of the most important laws ever enacted in the United States, declaring that discrimination was illegal as a matter of national policy. Historians and political scientists can easily describe the political and legislative history of the law; legal scholars explore the voluminous litigation that now surrounds it; social scientists attempt to measure the law's impact in terms of employment practices. What is missing from such studies, however, is the extent to which the law has reshaped our thinking and our habits, including the extent to which routine decisions about hiring someone, or renting an apartment, or putting together a panel for a conference are affected by considerations of possible discrimination. It is this subtle, pervasive, but nonetheless powerful long-term impact that constitutes the essence of the rights revolution.

The rights revolution poses a classic problem of trees and forests. It is easy to describe the trees of the rights revolution, and there is a vast body of literature on free speech law, the civil rights movement, the women's rights movement, and other parts of the forest. We are interested in the forest itself, however. To change metaphors for a moment, the sum is greater than the whole.

The purpose of this chapter is to attempt to convey some sense of the forest that is the rights revolution. Because it is such an elusive phenomenon, our approach here will be somewhat impressionistic. We will consider a variety of aspects of how the rights revolution has affected our lives.

ASPECTS OF THE RIGHTS REVOLUTION

The Rights Revolution in History

The rights revolution began sometime in the mid-1950s and continues into the present. A good case can be made that it began in 1937 when the Supreme Court did a historic about-face, withdrawing from the strict constitutional scrutiny of economic regulatory measures and embarking on the protection of political and civil rights.[2] From that point until sometime in the early 1960s, these changes were generally perceived as discrete developments in separate areas of the law such as free speech or civil rights. By the late 1960s, it was increasingly clear that a new and comprehensive rights culture was emerging.

Although popular folklore identifies the 1960s as the period of an explosion of individual freedom, the rights revolution did not fade away in the allegedly conservative decades that followed. In many respects, it did not reach flood tide until the 1970s and the 1980s. The Supreme Court, for example, did not affirm women's rights and the right to an abortion until the early 1970s. The gay rights movement did not really begin until the 1969 Stonewall incident—a police raid on a gay bar by that name in New York City.[3] Its major gains, including state and local laws prohibiting discrimination based on sexual preference and formal recognition of same-sex relationships for insurance benefit purposes, did not gain significant momentum until the late 1980s.[4]

Consider for a moment the night of November 5, 1968, when Richard Nixon was elected president. Liberals at the time saw this as the dawn of a new era of conservatism. In certain respects, they were correct; national politics has been far more conservative over the past thirty years. But when we consider that night from another perspective, the history of this country looks very different. As Richard Nixon was declaring himself the victor, abortion was legal in only one or two states, homosexuality was not even a subject for public discussion, there was no constitutionally protected right to burn the American flag, prisoners and persons confined in mental institutions had some privileges but few legally protected rights, and there were no Supreme Court decisions affirming women's rights. The list goes on.

The point is that in many important respects there has been a tremendous expansion of individual rights since the night Richard Nixon was elected and the dawn of an allegedly more conservative era. This expansion of rights during a period dominated by Republican presidents, in fact, is the cause of a good deal of frustration and anger among many conservatives. The latter assumed that Republican presidents would appoint conservative Supreme Court justices, who would then reverse the controversial decisions of the Court under Earl Warren.[5] The conservative counterrevolution in the Supreme Court has been somewhat limited. Nor has the Congress been willing to pass constitutional amendments outlawing abortion or permitting prayer in school. The failure of the conservative counterrevolution accounts for, among other things, Robert Bork's utterly despairing view of American society in his 1996 book, *Slouching Towards Gomorrah*. Where Bork once thought conservative justices could set things right, he now finds hope only in some kind of religious revival.[6]

The great exception to this generalization is, of course, the area of race and, to a lesser extent, crime. The present Court is clearly hostile to laws and policies embodying any form of race-based preferences. Nonetheless, it is remarkable how long it has taken the Court to reach its current position.

How do we explain the growth of rights in so many areas during this allegedly conservative era? I believe that the basic principles underlying the rights revolution—individual liberty, equality, due process of law, privacy—have penetrated deeply into American culture, to the point where they are shared by many conservatives.[7] The social conservatives who demand prayer in school are usually the first to protest government intrusion into the private lives of American citizens. The political conservatives who want to ban flag burning are, in the next breath, alarmed by what they see as threats to free speech by conservatives on college campuses. The vocal opponents of affirmative action frame their position in the language of equality and freedom from discrimination. In short, conservatives have absorbed the new rights culture and are unable to transcend it.

Rights and Constraints

The critics who attack the culture of individual rights consistently overlook the fact that each right necessarily entails a constraint. The right of freedom of speech obligates others to tolerate that speech; the right to equal opportunity entails the obligation not to discriminate. The critics of the rights revolution focus their attention on only one half of the new equation. They see only the expansion of expressive individualism: the right to shout offensive epithets, the right to a private choice in sexual activity.[8] Equally important, however, is the other side of the equation: the extent to which rights *constrain* our behavior at the same time they free us.[9] The new rights culture means that we cannot use our majoritarian power to suppress or limit what we don't like. The pro-choice community, to cite only one example, is forced to endure (that is, tolerate) the offensive rhetoric of militant pro-life activists.

Only occasionally do some of the critics sense the constraining side of the rights revolution. In a characteristic outburst attacking the growth of rights, communitarian leader Amitai Etzioni declares that *"each newly minted right generates a claim on someone."*[10] Precisely. Unfortunately, he does not explore the implications of this insight. One person's right inevitably involves a claim on others. As law professor Lawrence M. Friedman puts it, "Every right implies a duty, and every duty implies something about rights."[11] The reciprocity between freedom and constraint defines the new shape of community in America.

THE SCHOOLS AND THE WORKPLACE: TWO CASE STUDIES

The rights revolution has penetrated deeply into American society, to the point where it is part of the "taken-for-granted everydayness" of our lives. We can gain some appreciation of this by looking at two aspects of American society: the public schools and the workplace.

A Day in the Life of a High School Principal

Consider for a moment a routine week in a typical public school. The principal wants to suspend a student. Questions of constitutional law immediately arise. Is the suspension fair? Has the student received adequate due process? Is there a pattern of race discrimination in suspensions? What about the student's conduct that is in question? Is it constitutionally protected? Does it involve, say, an allegedly offensive T-shirt that raises free speech issues? Or was it an allegedly disruptive activity by African American students protesting racial discrimination in previous disciplinary actions?

A group of students, meanwhile, held a prayer meeting on school property. Did this violate the separation of church and state, or was it a constitutionally protected free exercise of religion? Did the students pray inside the building or outside? During school hours or beforehand? What about the students who prayed together during lunch period? Yet another group of students wants to have a meeting for gay and lesbian students. Can they meet in the school building? Can the principal allow them to meet after denying permission to the Bible study group? Some angry fundamentalist parents want the gay and lesbian student group disbanded. Can the principal ban the group altogether?

The science faculty, meanwhile, have created a special program for gifted students. All of the students admitted to the program are white. Is the program discriminatory? What does the principal say to the angry parents who accuse the school of race discrimination? Another school in the city tried to handle this problem with an informal affirmative-action program, guaranteeing the admission of a certain number of minority students. This approach, of course, only embroiled the school in a controversy over reverse discrimination, involving protests by parents of some white students who were not admitted to the program even though they had higher grades and test scores than some of the minority students.

In yet another development, a history teacher is rumored to be a member of a crypto-Nazi group. Some parents demand that he be fired. A militant Jewish group pickets the school board meeting. Can the school district fire the teacher? Can it even inquire into his beliefs and associations? Even if it can, is membership in an offensive group—apart from any unprofessional behavior in the classroom—sufficient grounds for termination? If not, what does the principal say to the angry Jewish and African American parents who feel that the employment of this teacher violates their right to a nonhostile educational environment?

The matter does not end. Another teacher is rumored to be a lesbian, and some parents want her fired. Yet another teacher is a prominent activist in the local pro-choice movement, and some anti-choice parents want her fired as well. A pro-life teacher has, off campus, endorsed the blockading of abortion clinics; another was even arrested in a blockade. Are these people "fit" to be public school teachers?

The New Rule-Bound Schools

We could carry this scenario further, adding more problems and complications. These are not far-fetched issues. They are not the kind of questions a law professor might invent in a constitutional law class. They are played out in the public schools every week. All of the issues described here have been litigated and are the subject of a substantial body of case law.[12] As one historian of the public schools suggests, to the traditional "three Rs" of reading, writing, and arithmetic we have added a fourth—rules, meaning judicially enforced legal rules.[13] American public schools were transformed in the quarter century between the early 1960s and the 1980s. The change in the environment of the schools—the rise in new demands for rights, the judicial enforcement of many of those claims, and the bureaucratic changes in response to the new legal rules—is but one chapter of the larger transformation of American society.

No doubt most school officials today yearn nostalgically for what they imagine to have been a simpler bygone era—a world with no belligerent students shouting about their rights, no angry African American parents calling officials racists and threatening a mass protest, no ACLU lawyer suing to eliminate the school Christmas pageant, and no elaborate due process requirements for either expelling a student or firing a teacher.

Life was undoubtedly simpler in the years before the rights revolution. Whether it was *better*, and better for *everyone* involved, is another question altogether. It is not clear that it was better for the many students summarily expelled from school. Nor was it necessarily better for the students who were agnostics, atheists, or Jews to be coerced into Christian religious exercises. And it was certainly not better for all of the African American students who were compelled to attend separate and unequal schools. The idea that things were better in the 1950s represents a classic example of nostalgic history. It is an idealized version of the past, an invented history that chooses to consider only one part of the picture—in this case, the convenience of school administrators—while ignoring others.

In our scenario of the public schools the critics of the rights revolution find confirmation for their argument that our rights-oriented litigiousness has "destabilized" schools, destroyed public education, and, as a consequence threatened the future of the country.[14] This perspective, however, focuses on only part of the story. It is undeniable that the schools have been penetrated by law, and constitutional law in particular. It is no exaggeration to say that today's public school administrator needs to be, if not an expert on the subject, at least sensitive to basic aspects of constitutional law.

Law, however, is only an instrument, and it is proper to ask what larger ends this instrument serves. Our scenario of the public schools illustrates the point that it is an instrument of the *claims* of many diverse groups and individuals. There are many different claims as well as often competing claims, such as the students who want to pray versus the parents who want a separation of church and state. As a matter of public policy, we have attempted to resolve these competing claims through principles of constitutional law. As many observers have pointed out, the United States is unique in terms of the prominent role of the Supreme Court in our daily lives. The penetration of the schools and other institutions by law has been a key element of the rights revolution.[15] The real story, however, is found in the claims that underlie this use of the law. Such claims involve a pervasive demand for equality and for individual freedom, including both freedom of personal expression and freedom from arbitrary government actions. These demands and expectations are the driving force behind the rights revolution. Law, and constitutional law in particular, is the *means* by which we have attempted to fulfill these expectations.[16]

In the Workplace

The workplace has changed no less dramatically than the public schools. There is probably no one reading this book whose thoughts and actions on the job have not been affected by the new culture of rights. Title VII of the 1964 Civil Rights Act has penetrated deep into the workplace. Decisions about hiring, promoting, disciplining, or firing an employee today involve at least some consideration of discrimination. This includes not just the decision itself but how it might be perceived as well.

Much of the public attention on employment discrimination, however, has focused narrowly on the extremely contentious issue of affirmative action. The level of public concern, and hostility, was evident in the extent to which affirmative action became a major political issue in the 1996 elections, including a referendum in California that abolished all racial preferences. Affirmative action, however, is only one means to an end. To appreciate the full impact of the rights revolution on the workplace, we need to take a comprehensive view.

The drive to rid workplaces of discrimination has affected a very broad range of on-the-job behavior. Few people reading this book will not have given careful thought to recent comments they have made—particularly whether those words might offend or be misinterpreted as offensive. Jokes we casually told just a few years ago we do not tell today, even among good friends. Many of us look at the walls of our offices in a different way than we did just a few years ago. Might that poster or cartoon give offense? The new legal concept of sexual harassment is only one aspect of this larger change.[17] Pity the poor person who organizes a committee without thinking about the proper racial, ethnic, and gender balance. In those communities where the lesbian and gay population is large, open, and politically active, their representation becomes a part of the mix.

It is popular among many conservatives to make fun of the heightened concern over "sensitivity" in today's society. And there is no shortage of absurdities and horror stories about overzealous sensitivity enforcement.[18] A student code of conduct at the University of Connecticut, for example, prohibited jokes and "inappropriate laughter" that might give offense. And there is no doubt that many of the campus speech codes represented violations of free speech and academic freedom—as the federal district courts in Michigan and Wisconsin ruled.[19]

Yet the attacks on hypersensitivity—usually by conservatives who have only recently discovered the First Amendment—are cynical and disingenuous. None of them would casually use words such as "kike" and "nigger" in public. In other words, they do recognize the legitimacy of certain standards regarding appropriate public behavior. The main point, however, is the pervasiveness of the concern about giving offense and the extension of this concern to groups that, until fairly recently, were considered fair game for public ridicule.

Like school principals, many employers and employees alike yearn nostalgically for the simpler world of the past when they did not have to calculate every employment decision in terms of potential discrimination claims, and when telling an offensive joke was no problem. Of course it was simpler. Life is always simpler when entire groups are excluded and the resulting workplace is homogeneous. One conservative critic, Walter K. Olson, argues that current employment laws "paralyze" business. His criticism of antidiscrimination laws summarizes virtually all of the points made by the New Jeremiahs about American society in general: they undermine efficiency (and thereby prevent job creation), embroil everyone in costly and debilitating litigation, and cultivate a sense of "victimhood" and a habit of excuse making that encourage irresponsibility.[20] In reading Olson's account, however, one might get the impression that no act of employment discrimination ever occurred. His view is a classic example of the romanticized version of the past, where everything was fine until all of these rights-oriented laws came along.

As is the case with the public schools, life may have been simpler for some, but it was far worse for many others. Because of the American habit of amnesia, most people today are not aware of the blatancy of discrimination in the recent past. At my own university, I found an old job announcement from 1952. The requirements for a position as film librarian in the audiovisual department included the following: "Sex—female"; "Church preference—Protestant"; "Race preference—white"; "Other specifications—Preferably single; if married, preferably no children; or children of school age."[21] By contemporary standards, the explicitness of the discrimination here is utterly astounding. It was not the least bit covert but instead was a matter of explicit policy. This was race discrimination not in the Deep South but in the Great Plains (Nebraska), as well as preference for Protestants in a heavily Catholic community (Omaha).

This 1952 job announcement dramatizes the extent to which new rules pervade the workplace, regulating previously unregulated behavior. And as with the schools, the growth of these new rules represents a set of claims by the historic victims of that behavior. To reiterate the basic point, the rights revolution involves a complex mixture of freedom and constraint. Freedom from employment discrimination for some people inescapably entails constraints on others in their ability to hire a good friend or close associate.

AN INVENTORY OF RIGHTS

Another way of describing the scope of the rights revolution is to draw up an inventory of the new rights that have arisen in recent years. How would we begin to compile such an inventory? One convenient source is the series of handbooks published by the American Civil Liberties Union. The ACLU has been one of the principal forces behind the rights revolution. In many instances it brought the cases

that established new categories of rights. Over the past quarter century, the ACLU has been the principal litigator in such areas as
women's rights, reproductive rights, prisoners' rights, and lesbian
and gay rights.[22]

The handbooks are part of the ACLU's public education effort,
designed for the general audience and written in a conversational,
question-and-answer style. The series now includes over thirty-five
titles.[23] A full list, arranged alphabetically by the group or subject,
appears in Table 2.1.

TABLE 2.1   ACLU Handbook Series

Norman Dorsen, General Editor 1973–1996.
David Carliner, Lucas Guttentag, Arthur C. Helton, and Wade J.
    Henderson, et al., *The Rights of Aliens and Refugees*, 2d ed.
    (1990).
Kenneth Norwick and Jerry Simon Chasen, *The Rights of Authors,
    Artists and Other Creative People*, 2d ed. (1992).
Burt Neuborne and Arthur Eisenberg, *The Rights of Candidates and
    Voters* (1980).
James Stark and Howard Goldstein, *The Rights of Crime Victims*
    (1985).
John A. Robertson, *The Rights of the Critically Ill* (1983).
George Annas and Barbara Katz, *The Rights of Doctors, Nurses,
    and Allied Health Professionals* (1981)
Wayne N. Outten, Robert J. Rabin, Lisa R. Lipman, *The Rights of
    Employees and Union Members*, 2d ed. (1994).
David Rudenstine, *The Rights of Ex-Offenders* (1979).
Martin Guggenheim, Alexandra Dylan Lowe, and Diane Curtis, *The
    Rights of Families* (1996).
Robert O'Neil, *The Rights of Government Employees* (1978).
Christine M. Marwick, *Your Right to Government Information* (1985).
Stephen L. Pevar, *The Rights of Indians and Tribes*, 2d ed. (1992).
Stephen Gillers, *The Rights of Lawyers and Clients* (1979).
Nan D. Hunter, Sherry E. Michaelson, and Thomas B. Stoddard,
    The Rights of Lesbians and Gay Men, 3d ed. (1992).
Bruce J. Ennis and Richard D. Emery, *The Rights of Mental
    Patients* (1978).
Robert M. Levy and Leonard Rubenstein, *The Rights of People With
    Mental Disabilities* (1990).

Paul R. Friedman, *The Rights of Mentally Retarded Persons* (1978).
Robert Rivkin and Barton F. Stichman, *The Rights of Military Personnel* (1981).
Robert Brown, *The Rights of Older Persons,* 2d ed. (1988).
Alan Sussman and Martin Guggenheim, *The Rights of Parents* (1980).
George J. Annas, *The Rights of Patients,* 2d ed. (1988).
William B. Rubenstein, Ruth Eisenberg, and Lawrence O. Gostin, *The Rights of People Who Are HIV Positive* (1997).
Kent Hull and Paul Hearne, *The Rights of Physically Handicapped People* (1981).
Gilda Brancato and Elliot E. Polebaum, *The Rights of Police Officers* (1981).
Sylvia Law, *The Rights of the Poor* (1974).
David Rudovsky, Alvin J. Bronstein, Edward I. Koren, and Julia Cade, *The Rights of Prisoners,* 4th ed. (1988).
Evan Hendricks, Trudy Hayden, and Jack Novick, *Your Right to Privacy,* 2d ed. (1990).
Evan Hendricks, *The Right to Privacy* (1980).
Joel M. Gora, David Goldberger, Gary M. Stern, and Morton Halperin, *The Right to Protest* (1991).
Robert M. O'Neil, *The Rights of Public Employees,* 2d ed. (1993).
Laughlin McDonald and John A. Powell, *The Rights of Racial Minorities,* 2d ed. (1993).
Barry Lynn, Marc D. Stern, and Oliver S. Thomas, *The Right to Religious Liberty,* 2nd ed. (1995).
Joel M. Gora, *The Rights of Reporters* (1974).
Mitchell Bernard, Ellen Levine, Stefan Presser, and Marianne Stecich, *The Rights of Single People* (1985).
Alan Levine, et al., *The Rights of Students,* 3d ed. (1988).
Oliver Rosengart, *The Rights of Suspects* (1974).
David Rubin and Steven Greenhouse, *The Rights of Teachers,* 2d ed. (1984).
Richard E. Blumberg and James R. Grow, *The Rights of Tenants* (1978).
Clyde Summers and Robert Rabin, *The Rights of Union Members* (1981).
David Addlestone et al., *The Rights of Veterans* (1978).
Susan Deller Ross, Isabelle Katz Pinzler, Deborah A. Ellis, and Kary L. Moss, *The Rights of Women,* 3d ed. (1993).
Alan Sussman and Martin Guggenheim, *The Rights of Young People,* 2d ed. (1985).

Reflections on the Inventory of Rights

Several aspects of the list of books in Table 2.1 deserve comment. The sheer number and scope of new rights is impressive. Moreover, the list moves far beyond the traditional rights enumerated in the Bill of Rights (free speech, due process, etc.) to include the rights of discrete *groups*. These are what many critics refer to as the "new" rights. They represent the legal aspect of group thinking and "identity politics."[24]

All of these new rights emerged in the late 1960s or early 1970s.[25] Forty years ago, few people thought that mental patients or the poor had legal rights. Many of these notions of rights were unimaginable at that time. In this respect they represent an intellectual, political, and legal revolution in how we conceptualize rights. Others were imaginable—women's rights, for example—but had little substance in terms of the law.

The list gives some idea of the broad impact of the rights revolution on social institutions: schools, hospitals, the military, and so on. Conservatives look over the list and find confirmation of their belief that crime is rampant because suspects have too many rights, that our schools are in chaos because students have too many rights, that our health system is in crisis, at least in part, because both patients and health professionals are claiming rights. One particular new right is regarded by conservatives as a direct threat to the foundations of society: childrens' rights. The idea that children have legally enforceable grave rights vis-à-vis their parents threatens the most private of institutions, the family, and strikes at the very foundation of parental authority.[26]

Rights Inflation?

The ACLU list is fodder for critics such as communitarian leaders Amitai Etzioni and Mary Ann Glendon, who believe there has been an uncontrolled "rights inflation." In their view, the creation of a vast new array of rights devalues the traditional rights of free speech and equality.[27] Many people find it absurd that single people should claim rights. Conservatives such as columnist George Will deplore what they see as the constant "minting" of new rights.[28] Etzioni wants to stop the process and calls for a "moratorium" on the "manufacturing of new rights."[29]

The argument about rights inflation deserves a reply. Are there no limits to who can claim rights? Is there any end to this process of creating new rights? One noted legal scholar has suggested that trees and other parts of the natural environment have some rights.[30] A quick glance at recent history, however, reveals that the rhetoric about an endless "minting" of new rights is wildly hyperbolic. The Supreme Court has not recognized any significant new rights since about the mid-1970s. In the 1986 *Bowers v. Hardwick* decision, it explicitly declined to rule that homosexual activity was protected by the right to privacy.[31] (The 1996 decision striking down a Colorado state constitutional amendment prohibiting gay rights ordinances, however, may signal a change in the Court's position.)[32] The only major new advance in the area of rights has been the Court's acceptance of the concept of sexual harassment in the 1986 *Meritor* decision.[33] Even that was not a "new" right but an extension of an established right, protection from sex discrimination, to include particular forms of behavior.

In short, since the mid-1970s the Supreme Court has not been wildly inventing new rights, but has exercised the judicial restraint that was expected of the conservative Republican-appointed justices who now dominate the Court. The communitarians' rhetoric about an uncontrolled "rights inflation" is hysterical and simply not supported by the actual trends in the Supreme Court. The rights revolution does, however, have an expansive dynamic, as basic concepts of rights such as equal protection or privacy develop and reach into new areas of society.

Rights Radicalism?

Another popular criticism of the new rights is that they represent dangerously radical concepts of rights. In fact, many of these new rights are far less radical than they might appear. In this regard, it is worth taking a close look at the ACLU handbook *The Rights of Single People*.[34] Many critics would cite basic premise of the book as a perfect example of the absurdity of the new rights culture. If single people have "rights," is there any group that cannot lay claim to its own set of specially defined rights?

When we actually read the handbook on the rights of single people, we find that it is far from revolutionary. Essentially, it is a restatement of existing laws as they might apply to someone who is single. Chapter 2 on criminal law covers issues related to cohabitation, fornication, and sodomy (behavior that is still a crime in many states, and not too long ago was a crime in virtually every state), rape by an ex-husband (an act that was traditionally not regarded as criminal), and protection orders against threatened violence (an area of domestic violence law that has changed dramatically in recent years). Chapter 3 on housing covers restrictions on zoning and apartment leases, the sale of housing, and eligibility for public housing (areas where there has been a range of both de jure and de facto discrimination against single people). Chapter 4 covers employment discrimination law as it relates to people who are single, divorced, cohabiting, or with custody of a child (another area of both de jure and de facto discrimination against people who are unmarried or divorced). In short, the handbook hardly defines or creates any "new" right.

The question of the rights of single people also offers some perspective on the issue of "identity politics." The critics of rights argue that defining oneself as a single person, as opposed to a member of the larger community, is a perfect example of the fragmentation of society as a consequence of the rights revolution. It elevates difference over commonality, separateness over community. Yet, as all of the issues discussed in *The Rights of Single People* indicate, the identification of single people as a special class, subject to special treatment, originated with others: the landlord who refused to rent the apartment, the judge who denied custody of the child, and so on. Criticizing single people for asserting their rights in the face of such discrimination is a classic example of "blaming the victim." It is unfair to blame a group of people who had a special identity, and restrictions, imposed on them for referring to themselves in those terms when they seek to eliminate those restrictions.

The same point can be made with respect to race, gender, sexual preference, and other group identities that have been criticized as a destructive identity politics. In each case, the group was labeled by others and was subject to discrimination. The group rarely if ever claimed the label in the first instance.

Our inventory of the rights revolution based on the ACLU handbooks leads us to the following conclusions. First, it highlights the dramatic change that has occurred in the law and in public consciousness since the mid-1960s. Second, it indicates the growth of group-oriented rights. Third, it suggests that there has not been an uncontrolled rights "inflation" in recent years. Fourth and finally, the group orientation to rights is fundamentally a reactive phenomenon, a response to externally imposed identities and disabilities.

THE IRONY OF ANTI-RIGHTS RIGHTS TALK

Another indication of the pervasiveness of rights consciousness in American society today is the extent to which some of the most vociferous opponents of certain rights use the language of rights themselves. As I mentioned earlier, opponents of affirmative action use the traditional rhetoric of the civil rights movement regarding equal opportunity. Opponents of abortion define the issue in terms of a *right* to life. For over twenty years, they have fought to define the fetus as a person with all the attendant constitutional *rights*. Right-to-life activists invoke the imagery of the civil rights movement, equating their crusade with Martin Luther King's nonviolent direct-action movement. They portray *Roe v. Wade* as a modern-day *Dred Scott* decision that denies personhood to an entire class of people.[35]

The right-to-life zealots do not seem to appreciate the irony of how they frame their argument. Despite their fury at the Supreme Court for establishing a right to abortion, they have, willy-nilly, embraced the entire framework of constitutionally protected rights. They simply want a different result—whether through reversal of *Roe*, a constitutional amendment, or a human life statute—that would protect the *rights* of this particular group, the unborn.

An excellent example of how critics of rights have absorbed the language of rights is a *Harper's* magazine symposium on the idea of a "Bill of Duties."[36] This is a popular idea among conservative rights critics. Robert Bork, for example, calls for a Bill of Personal Responsibilities to balance the Bill of Rights.[37] Participants in the *Harper's* symposium promptly took up the issue of children, particularly the fact that so many suffer because parents, especially fathers, fail to meet their responsibilities of care and financial support. In the midst of the discussion, however, law professor Christopher Stone pointed out that the participants viewed the issue in terms of *children's rights*. Even when they attempted to talk about parental responsibility, they framed the issue in terms of childrens' *right* to care and financial support.[38]

The inability of even critics of rights to transcend the rights framework is revealing and critically important to the issues under discussion in this book. It confirms Mary Ann Glendon's argument about the pervasiveness of "rights talk" and the inability of people to think and talk in other terms.[39] The *Harper's* symposium is particularly revealing because even participants who wanted to talk about duties found themselves as caught up in the web of rights talk as the people they criticize.

AN INTERNATIONAL PERSPECTIVE

The current debate over rights and community in the United States is extraordinarily provincial. The New Jeremiahs who see our society in a state of moral and social collapse implicitly argue that this condition is unique to the United States. The related assumption is that the source of the problem is our unique approach to individual rights. Among the critics, only Mary Ann Glendon, who has published a comparative study of trends in divorce and abortion law, has any appreciation of international developments.[40]

Provincialism is nothing new in this country. Americans are notorious not just for their lack of historical perspective but also for their lack of awareness about the rest of the world. The idea of "American exceptionalism" has a long history. The French observer Alexis de Tocqueville, author of the classic *Democracy in America*, first published in 1835, was not the first to suggest that American society had cultivated a unique set of ideas and habits.[41] The alleged loss of a common (and implicitly unique) American identity is what provokes so much concern about "multiculturalism" and "identity politics."[42]

It is certainly true that the United States is very different from other countries on many of the issues we have considered. No other industrialized country has violent crime rates that begin to compare with ours. Our race problem and the recent civil rights movement give our history a unique dimension. And in no other country does the equivalent of our Supreme Court play such a prominent role in public affairs.

Nonetheless, a comparative approach to the issue of rights offers a fresh perspective on the issues at hand. A quick look at international trends related to human rights suggests that the rise of a rights consciousness is not unique to the United States. In fact, it seems that our concern with rights and the particular approach we take to them have been extremely influential around the world.

The International Human Rights Movement

In the area of international law, one of the most important developments since World War II has been the appearance of an international human rights movement. A direct response to the Holocaust, this movement has sought to define basic principles of human rights and to create legal structures to enforce them. The principles are now embodied in over forty declarations, covenants, and conventions on human rights.[43]

The international human rights movement represents a revolution in international law. Prior to World War II, international law governed relations *between* nations. What any country did within its own borders to its own people was its own business. The new human rights movement seeks, for the first time, to regulate the *internal* practices of nations regarding how they treat their own people.

A quick glance at the principal international human rights documents reveals that they have a distinctly American flavor. They are modeled on the American Bill of Rights in three basic respects. First, they define human rights in terms of *individual* rights, not, significantly, in terms of communal or collective rights. Second, they are *written* declarations of rights, following the American model of a written Constitution rather than the British model of an unwritten one. Third, with a few notable exceptions, the *enumerated rights* are identical to those in the American Bill of Rights: freedom of speech, due process, and so on.

As some commentators have pointed out, notions of rights have been a major American export.[44] We might facetiously suggest that they have been a more significant export than mainframe computers, jet aircraft, and Hollywood movies. Moreover, the international "trade" in rights is very one-sided. As Mary Ann Glendon points out, people from other countries have borrowed American ideas about rights, but Americans have borrowed very little from other countries.[45] As I will discuss shortly, I believe there is a reason for this one-sided trade.

The American influence on the international human rights movement poses a challenging question for many critics of rights in this country. If the United States has gone so far off the track with respect to rights, why have activists and legal scholars around the world been so eager to borrow our notions of rights? Why have Americans borrowed so little from the rest of the world? There are answers to these questions, but first let us take a closer look at the principal international human rights documents.

The Universal Declaration of Human Rights
The 1948 Universal Declaration of Human Rights is the founding statement on human rights, and serving as the inspiration and

model for virtually all of the subsequent documents. The core principle of this declaration is that "all human beings are born free and equal in dignity and rights" (Article 1; excerpts from this and other key sections are found in Table 2.2). The declaration then proceeds to enumerate the specific rights that flow from this. These include the "right to life, liberty and the security of person" (Article 3); freedom from slavery (Article 4) and torture (Article 5); and equality before the law (Articles 6 and 7).

The Universal Declaration of Human Rights borrows most of its enumerated rights from the U.S. Bill of Rights. These include the full range of First Amendment rights (freedom of thought, conscience, religion, expression, and assembly); due process rights (freedom from cruel punishment, arbitrary arrest, detention, or exile, the right to a fair public trial, a presumption of innocence, and so on); equal protection of the law (including freedom from discrimination based on race, gender, age, or religion). The basic elements of the Universal Declaration are fully compatible with the *Policy Guide* of the ACLU, a compilation of all the official policies of the organization on individual rights.

TABLE 2.2   Excerpts from the Universal Declaration of Human Rights

Article 1

All human beings are born free and equal in dignity and rights. They are endowed with reason and conscience and should act towards one another in a spirit of brotherhood.

Article 2

Everyone is entitled to all the rights and freedoms set forth in this Declaration, without distinction of any kind, such as race, colour, sex, language, religion, political or other opinion, national or social origin, property, birth or other status.

Furthermore, no distinction shall be made on the basis of political, jurisdictional or international status of the country or territory to which a person belongs, whether it be independent, trust, non-self-governing or under any other limitation of sovereignty.

Article 3

Everyone has the right to life, liberty and security of person.

. . .

Article 7

All are equal before the law and are entitled without any discrimination to equal protection of the law. All are entitled to equal protection against any discrimination in violation of this Declaration and against any incitement to such discrimination.

. . .

Article 9

No one shall be subjected to arbitrary arrest, detention or exile.

. . .

Article 11

1. Everyone charged with a penal offence has the right to be presumed innocent until proved guilty according to law in a public trial at which he has had all the guarantees necessary for his defence.

. . .

Article 12

No one shall be subjected to arbitrary interference with his privacy, family, home or correspondence, nor to attacks upon his honour and reputation. Everyone has the right to the protection of the law against such interference or attacks.

Article 13

1. Everyone has the right to freedom of movement and residence within the borders of each state.

2. Everyone has the right to leave any country, including his own, and to return to his country.

. . .

Article 16

1. Men and women of full age, without any limitation due to race, nationality or religion, have the right to marry and to found a family. They are entitled to equal rights as to marriage, during marriage and at its dissolution.

2. Marriage shall be entered into only with the free and full consent of the intending spouses.

3. The family is the natural and fundamental group unit of society and is entitled to protection by society and the State.

Article 17
1. Everyone has the right to own property alone as well as in association with others.

2. No one shall be arbitrarily deprived of his property.

Article 18
Everyone has the right to freedom of thought, conscience and religion; this right includes freedom to change his religion or belief, and freedom, either alone or in community with others and in public or private, to manifest his religion or belief in teaching, practice, worship and observance.

Article 19
Everyone has the right to freedom of opinion and expression; this right includes freedom to hold opinions without interference and to seek, receive and impart information and ideas through any media and regardless of frontiers.

Article 20
1. Everyone has the right to freedom of peaceful assembly and association.

2. No one may be compelled to belong to an association.

. . .

Article 22
Everyone, as a member of society, has the right to social security and is entitled to realization, through national effort and international cooperation and in accordance with the organization and resources of each State, of the economic, social and cultural rights indispensable for his dignity and the free development of his personality.

Article 23
1. Everyone has the right to work, to free choice of employment, to just and favourable conditions of work and to protection against unemployment.

2. Everyone, without any discrimination, has the right to equal pay for equal work.

3. Everyone who works has the right to just and favourable remuneration ensuring for himself and his family an existence worthy of human dignity, and supplemented, if necessary, by other means of social protection.

4. Everyone has the right to form and to join trade unions for the protection of his interests.

Article 24

Everyone has the right to rest and leisure, including reasonable limitation of working hours and periodic holidays with pay.

Article 25

1. Everyone has the right to a standard of living adequate for the health and well-being of himself and of his family, including food, clothing, housing and medical care and necessary social services, and the right to security in the event of unemployment, sickness, disability, widowhood, old age or other lack of livelihood in circumstances beyond his control.

2. Motherhood and childhood are entitled to special care and assistance. All children, whether born in or out of wedlock, shall enjoy the same social protection.

Article 26

1. Everyone has the right to education. Education shall be free, at least in the elementary and fundamental stages. Elementary education shall be compulsory. Technical and professional education shall be made generally available and higher education shall be equally accessible to all on the basis of merit.

2. Education shall be directed to the full development of the human personality and to the strengthening of respect for human rights and fundamental freedoms. It shall promote understanding, tolerance and friendship among all nations, racial or religious groups, and shall further the activities of the United Nations for the maintenance of peace.

3. Parents have a prior right to choose the kind of education that shall be given to their children.

. . .

Article 29

1. Everyone has duties to the community in which alone the free and full development of his personality is possible.

2. In the exercise of his rights and freedoms, everyone shall be subject only to such limitations as are determined by law solely for the purpose of securing due recognition and respect for the rights and freedoms of others and of meeting the just requirements of morality, public order and the general welfare in a democratic society.

3. These rights and freedoms may in no case be exercised contrary to the purposes and principles of the United Nations.

The Case of Religious Liberty

Perhaps the best example of the American influence is the protection of religious dissent. Article 18 of the Universal Declaration of Human Rights guarantees an individual the freedom "to manifest his religion or belief in teaching, practice, worship and observance," and to do so "in public or private." This principle is more fully developed in the 1981 Declaration on the Elimination of All Forms of Intolerance and of Discrimination Based on Religion or Belief.[46] Article 1 of that document states that "everyone shall have the right to freedom of thought, conscience, and religion." Article 2 states that "no one shall be subject to discrimination . . . on grounds of religion or other beliefs." Article 5 affirms the priority of the family over the state in controlling childrens' religious education: no child shall "be compelled to receive teaching on religion or belief against the wishes of his parents."[47]

The right of religious liberty, including open dissent from any official state religion, is now deeply ingrained in American popular culture. The 1997 Supreme Court decision striking down the Religious Freedom Restoration Act (RFRA) was denounced by a broad spectrum of religious and political leaders (just as the 1993 RFRA itself was supported by a broad coalition of otherwise unlikely allies). We Americans, however, tend to forget how unique this idea is. It is a special feature of the Anglo-American tradition of religious dissent, and one that Americans have pursued more vigorously than has England. At the same time, few Americans who celebrate religious dissent appreciate how recently we have translated the abstract principle into actual practice. (A lengthier discussion of this issue appears in chapter 3.) Through recorded human history, the

dominant practice has been conformity to official religious orthodoxy, including unity between church and state, suppression of dissent, and the right of the state to compel adherence to official belief.
The current upsurge of Islamic fundamentalism, with its demand
for a religious-based civil law, is more consistent with past history.

On the extremely volatile point of religious dissent, then, the
international human rights movement follows the American model,
asserting a legally enforceable individual right over and against the
state and majority will. It specifically rejects any collective, communal, or communitarian alternative. The provisions of the 1981 Declaration on the Elimination of All Forms of Intolerance regarding
parental authority represents, in essence, the main thrust of American church-state law, particularly the body of case law prohibiting
religious exercises in school.

In passing it is worth noting that in the late 1990s conservatives
suddenly took up the issue of religious freedom around the world,
demanding that the federal government protest the persecution of
Christians in other countries. In short, the very groups that loudly
oppose the rights revolution in this country, and its attempt to
secure freedom and equality for historically oppressed groups, now
demand government intervention to protect the rights of what they
believe to be an oppressed group.

The Case of the Rights of Children

Another example is the issue of childrens' rights. For many conservatives this is a truly terrifying idea.[48] As I have already mentioned,
many conservatives believe that it threatens the very foundations of
a well-ordered society, with the law (in the form of civil liberties
lawyers) invading the sanctity of the family and setting children
against their parents. The idea that children can challenge parental
authority—and find support for such challenges in court—is at the
root of the collapse of traditional values and the rampant problems
of teenage drug use and illegitimacy. Better than anything else, for
conservatives it symbolizes the madness of our pursuit of rights.

An international perspective, however, reveals that the idea of
childrens' rights is not unique to the United States, and is certainly
not the exclusive province of a small group of radical activist
lawyers. The idea that children have rights and that those rights
should be protected through the formal apparatus of the law is an
international movement that originated long before the 1960s.

The 1948 Universal Declaration of Human Rights gave this idea passing mention, asserting that "motherhood and childhood are entitled to special care and assistance" (Article 25[2]). In 1959 the United Nations elaborated on this general point by adopting the Declaration of the Rights of the Child. The UN Human Rights Commission began work on a Convention on the Rights of the Child in 1979, and a final version was adopted by the UN General Assembly ten years later.[49]

Like the other international human rights documents, the 1989 Convention on the Rights of the Child has a thoroughly American flavor. With only a few exceptions, it is quite consistent with the provisions of the Bill of Rights and the policies of the ACLU. Its basic premise is that children have legally enforceable rights. It declares that "in accordance with the principles proclaimed in the Charter of the United Nations," it recognizes "the equal and inalienable rights of all members of the human family." The specific rights enjoyed by children are those belonging to everyone: equality, freedom from discrimination, freedom from arbitrary and excessive punishment, freedom of speech, assembly, and religious expression.

Article 12, for example, affirms the child's freedom of speech: "the child who is capable of forming his or her own views" shall be assured "the right to express those views freely in all matters affecting the child." Article 13 asserts that the child has a right to express himself or herself "either orally, in writing, or in print" in the "media of the child's choice." Neither of these two sections contains any wording indicating that the child's freedom of expression may be limited by parental authority. The right asserted here is far broader than freedom of expression. The underlying principle is the competence of the child to make independent judgments. In the context of world history, this is a radical notion indeed. The fact that it enjoys the imprimatur of the United Nations suggests that it is hardly a unique American concept.

Article 3 of the Convention on the Rights of the Child declares that decisions affecting the welfare of children, by public and private agencies, shall give "primary consideration" to "the best interests of the child." This concept is well developed in American law. Article 24 provides a specific application of this principle by declaring that all states shall take appropriate steps to abolish "traditional practices prejudicial to the health of children." Presumably, this would apply to the practice of clitorectomy, a subject that has become a major international human rights controversy. The Article 34 prohibition on child sexual abuse might also apply. Assuming that a particular family embraces clitorectomy or some other traditional practice, the Convention on the Rights of the Child is a direct challenge to parental authority.

In short, the Convention on the Rights of the Child suggests that the basic precepts of the American rights revolution are part of an international movement. It is impossible, therefore, to blame American developments on a small group of elite radical lawyers, as critics of the rights revolution often do. It is important to add that the idea of childrens' rights arouses at least as much opposition, if not more, in other cultures.[50] In many other countries the idea is an even greater threat to traditional patterns of family authority. The point here is that the supposed "culture war" involving different standards of morality and family authority, which is alleged to be tearing the United States apart, is in fact not unique to this country.[51]

International Variations on Human Rights

There are some important differences between the international human rights statements and the prevailing law of individual rights in the United States. The most important one relates to economic rights. The Universal Declaration of Human Rights, for example, guarantees the right to "social security" (Article 22); "work" (Article 23); a trade union (Article 23); "rest and leisure" (Article 24); an "adequate" standard of living (Article 25); and an education (Article 26). Similar guarantees of economic rights are contained in documents specifically related to social and economic issues and various regional statements, such as the 1948 American Declaration of the Rights and Duties of Man. Article 14 declares that "every person has the right to work"; Article 16 asserts that "every person has the right to social security which will protect him from the consequences of unemployment, old age [or any other circumstances] that make it physically or mentally impossible for him to earn a living."

The American approach to rights emphasizes political and civil rights, to the exclusion of economic rights. The commitment to this approach is so strong that for almost thirty years even the allegedly radical ACLU has consistently rejected proposals from a substantial minority of its own members that it incorporate economic rights into its official policies.[52]

The Universal Declaration of Human Rights defines a right of privacy that is different from that in American law. It defines an individual's privacy as freedom from "arbitrary interference with his privacy, family, home or correspondence" (Article 12). The declaration's protection of "honor and reputation" conflicts with much of American law on freedom of speech. At the same time, the Universal Declaration does not define privacy in terms of reproductive rights as has the United States Supreme Court. The 1969 American Convention on Human Rights, in fact, specifically states that life begins "from the moment of conception."[53]

Finally, and most important, the Universal Declaration of Human Rights, along with every other international human rights statement, specifically permits certain limitations on rights. Article 29 states that "everyone has duties to the community in which alone the free and full development of his personality is possible." To this end, rights can be limited "for the purpose of securing due recognition and respect for the rights and freedoms of others and of meeting the just requirements of morality, public order and the general welfare in a democratic society."[54] Virtually identical language appears in almost all of the international human rights statements. The 1969 American Convention on Human Rights declares, "The rights of each person are limited by the rights of others, by the security of all, and by the just demands of the general welfare, in a democratic society."

The course of American constitutional law since the 1930s represents a steady rejection of these rationales for limiting individual rights. Mary Ann Glendon is off the mark when she observes that Americans have not considered international standards of balancing rights and responsibilities. Quite the contrary, we have considered such principles and rejected them.[55] The balancing principles she finds in the international documents have been duly considered and rejected over the course of several decades of social conflict and litigation. The American preference for rights emerged in large part out of a recognition of the undesirable consequences of limitations imposed in the name of the general welfare.

We will address this issue in greater detail in chapter 6, which examines the specific proposals offered by communitarians. For the moment, it is important to note the strong American flavor in the international human rights movement. The differences are less important than the similarities, particularly the priority of individual rights, the enumeration of rights in written documents, and the borrowing of specific rights such as free speech and freedom of religious conscience.

The extent of American influence on the international human rights movement puts our own rights revolution in a fresh light. It suggests, first, that the United States is far from unique. The concern for human rights is a worldwide phenomenon. The United States may lie at one extreme on some imaginary continuum, but the differences with other industrial countries are differences of degree and not of kind. Second, the fact that other countries have borrowed so heavily suggests that there is a powerful appeal in the American approach to individual rights.

The Case of Affirmative Action

Although affirmative action as a means of eliminating discrimination is not specifically mentioned in international human rights documents, an international perspective on this highly controversial issue supports my general argument that the American approach to rights is not unique.

Affirmative action, according to so many critics, is the worst aspect of our new rights culture. It is said to be divisive, creating a new system of racial preferences, contrary to the principles embedded in the Constitution, and a perversion of the original and worthy ideals of the civil rights movement. Yet the bitter political and legal controversy over affirmative action in this country is especially parochial. It is presented as something unique to the United States, arising out of the special circumstances of the American race problem, and expressing the special demands of the civil rights establishment.

Ironically, the best evidence refuting this view comes from Thomas Sowell, one of the leading critics of affirmative action. His book *Preferential Policies: An International Perspective* opens with the statement that "what is called 'affirmative action' in the United States is part of a much larger phenomenon found in many countries around the world."[56] Sowell goes on to describe government programs giving preferences to the untouchables in India, the Maoris in New Zealand, the Bumiputeras in Malaysia, and Central Asians in the former Soviet Union.

India's untouchables represent one of the most extreme examples of an outcast group. They were literally not to touch members of the dominant groups; in some places, they were not even allowed to let their *shadow* fall upon a member of the dominant Hindu caste. Discrimination against the untouchables was officially outlawed by Article 17 of the 1949 Constitution, but as in the United States with African Americans, it persisted. India then adopted a series of preferential programs designed to elevate the status of the old untouchables. These included admission quotas at all levels of education, special scholarships (representing over half of all money spent on behalf of untouchables), quotas for government positions, and special land distribution programs.

The first preferential programs were adopted in the late 1940s, following India's independence from colonial rule. Although scheduled to expire in 1959, they were extended for another ten years, and then extended again in 1969 and 1980. Sowell's main argument is that these policies have failed to achieve their intended results. He cites abundant data on the lack of progress of untouchables in education and employment. This failure, in fact, is one of the main reasons the policies have repeatedly been extended. Sowell also argues that these preferential policies have had a number of destructive consequences, such as lowering of standards in higher education in order to fill quotas. His arguments have been a major influence in shaping the opposition to affirmative action in the United States.

My purpose here is not to enter into the debate with Sowell over affirmative action. Suffice it to say that he makes a powerful argument, and that others have replied at the appropriate level. My point here is simply to put the American debate over affirmative action in perspective. Sowell's evidence clearly indicates that the American situation is not unique. In fact, it is significant that India's policies predated affirmative action in the United States by about twenty years.

Whatever the merits of affirmative action, American policy is part of a broad international effort to eliminate discrimination against historically outcast groups. Sowell himself acknowledges that, given the long history of discrimination in the world, "the idea of treating people alike . . . is historically recent and unusual."[57] The rights revolution in the United States, then, is not unique. Although it has certainly manifested itself in ways that are unique to this country, it is part of a broad international concern for promoting equality.

CONCLUSION

This chapter ends by repeating its original point: something fundamental has changed in the United States over the past forty years. We call this change the *rights revolution,* and its product is a new rights culture that pervades every aspect of our daily lives. Although elusive, it is omnipresent. On this basic point, both the critics and the defenders of the rights revolution agree.

The purpose of this chapter has been to describe somewhat impressionistically the various dimensions of the rights revolution. I have attempted to describe how it has reshaped the public schools and the workplace, how it dominates the thinking of even those who seek to transcend it, and how it is an international phenomenon and not unique to the United States. The three chapters that follow explore the impact of the growth of rights on particular issues and institutions. The basic argument is that the rights revolution has redefined the meaning of community in America and created a new set of rules for how we live together.

Chapter Three

BELONGING TO AMERICA: RIGHTS AND MEMBERSHIP

"NO DOGS OR JEWS"

It was a poignant moment in the hearings to confirm Ruth Bader Ginsburg for a seat on the U.S. Supreme Court, one of the most powerful positions in the country. She recalled an incident from her childhood in which her family, on a vacation trip through Pennsylvania, passed a hotel with a sign reading "No Dogs or Jews."[1]

This episode dramatizes in a very personal and painful way the issue of rights and membership in America. It serves as an ugly reminder of the history of prejudice and discrimination. In the America of the 1950s, a time often recalled today as one of harmony and tranquillity, even the vilest expressions of prejudice were publicly displayed. Hotels and vacation resorts across the country openly barred Jews, sometimes advertising for "Christian" guests. The leading colleges and universities maintained exclusionary quotas limiting the number of Jewish students. Many employers openly refused to hire Jews.[2] Women were barred from the country clubs where men golfed and conducted business. And, of course, de jure segregation prevailed throughout the South, with separate schools, and even public drinking fountains designated "White" and "Colored."

The Ginsburg hearings were not the first time the issue of discrimination had arisen in a recent Supreme Court nomination hearing. Seven years earlier it was revealed that Justice William Rehnquist, then being nominated for chief justice, owned New

England vacation property with a restrictive covenant forbidding sale of the property to Jews.[3] Although the Supreme Court had declared such covenants unconstitutional in 1948, many remained on legal documents, in many cases ignored as a relic from the past but in others enforced covertly.[4]

Ruth Bader Ginsburg's life history included another tale about discrimination. In 1960, Supreme Court Justice Felix Frankfurter refused to hire her as a clerk because she was a woman, even though she had graduated first in her class at Columbia University School of Law. Later, as director of the ACLU Women's Rights Project, she was the principal architect of a new body of women's rights law that began to dismantle sex discrimination. Organizing the cases, formulating the new legal arguments, drafting the briefs, and arguing the cases, she won five of the six cases she brought before the Supreme Court—the same Court that would not hire her as a clerk but on which she would later sit as a full justice.[5]

Ginsburg's life story offers a glimpse into the dramatic transformation of American society as a result of the rights revolution. Doors have in fact opened since the 1950s for many Americans: Jews, women, African Americans, and others. To be sure, these doors are still far from completely open, and they did not open voluntarily. They were forced open through the vigorous and sustained pursuit of rights. The battle has been fought in the courts, in the streets, and in the court of public opinion. People who had been denied full membership in American society, and been subject to public humiliation as had been young Ruth Bader Ginsburg and her family, have won at least some grudging acceptance. Ginsburg's story is only one of many in the larger drama of the struggle over rights and membership in the American community.

RIGHTS, MEMBERSHIP, AND COMMUNITY

Without membership there is no community. This simple proposition forms the basic argument of both this chapter and the entire book. As political philosopher Michael Walzer puts it, "The primary good we distribute to one another is membership in some human community."[6] The person who is less than a full member, who faces some barriers to full participation or is excluded altogether, cannot enjoy any of the specific rights, privileges, and opportunities that a society offers. Walzer explains that "it is only as members some-where that men and women can hope to share in all the other social goods—security, wealth, honor, office, and power—that communal life makes possible."[7]

The social goods Walzer refers to include freedom of speech, the free exercise of religion, the right to due process of law, and all the other political and civil rights. I would add that these rights are not simply goods that are enjoyed *upon* achieving membership, but are the *means* by which membership itself is achieved. Merely to exercise a right is to stake a claim of membership. By forcing others to respond, the claim alters existing relationships in the community. The paradigmatic political act of the 1960s was not the lawsuit but the demonstration: the sit-in, the freedom ride, the march. When the four African American students sat in at the Woolworth's lunch counter in Greensboro, North Carolina, on February 1, 1960, they altered southern communities almost instantly. Suddenly, they were no longer passive, silent, and powerless but instead were active members of the community. And through their act of sitting in, in a forbidden place, they forced the dominant white power structure to respond. It is no wonder that the sit-ins had such an electrifying effect on the nation.[8]

Gay and lesbian rights demonstrations have a similar impact: a silent and invisible minority suddenly becomes visible. Homosexuality was long referred to as "the love that dare not speak its name." In that context, a public act asserts both an identity and a claim to membership. The act of asserting one's identity as a lesbian or gay person is known as "coming out." A demonstration or other public act does not guarantee full membership, but at a minimum it forces those who would prefer to deny the existence of such a group to acknowledge its existence.[9]

The examples of both the segregated South and gays and lesbians illustrate a basic but often forgotten aspect of community. As a practical matter, "community" of one sort or another is a fact of life. We inhabit the same physical space and interact with each other in various ways. The question is not whether we have some kind of relationship with each other but the *terms* of that relationship. Is it coercive, with only one side imposing the terms? Or is it an equal, participative one, with both sides having a voice in the process?[10]

It is important to emphasize this point because most of the

writing on the issue of rights and community quietly slides over the difficult questions related to the community side of the equation. There is a vast literature on the problems related to the rights side of the equation: the scope of free speech, the relationship between church and state, the meaning of due process, and so on. There has been far less written on the community side of the equation.[11] In particular, the communitarian critics of rights have tended to take "community" as a given—and a problem-free given at that.

This chapter explores some of the ways in which the boundaries of community in America have been profoundly reshaped by the rights revolution. It examines four specific episodes in modern American history, which I have selected to illustrate particular themes. The first two examples involve the religion clauses of the First Amendment: the free exercise clause and the establishment clause. They are relevant here not just because religion has always been a volatile issue in this country but also because we do not normally think of these aspects of constitutional law as contributing to the development of community. Establishment clause controversies are typically portrayed as being hostile to community values. The story is now a familiar one: some parents, assisted by the ACLU, sue to have the Christmas pageant barred from their child's elementary school. Public outrage accompanies the case. Once again, the "grinches" are stealing Christmas. The story is presented as yet another case of an obnoxious person (or persons) using the courts to prevent the community from expressing its values. Instead of wholesome religious values, the argument goes, we have division, conflict, and litigation. My argument is that, contrary to the popular view, important communal values are embedded in the issue of separation of church and state.

The third example in this chapter, on the other hand, is an obvious one. The impact of the civil rights movement on the elimination of barriers to full membership seems almost self-evident. Nonetheless, it is so central to our recent history and the argument of this book that it bears repeating.

The fourth example is also a relatively obvious one, but it merits reconsideration in the context of a discussion over rights and membership. The internment of the Japanese Americans during World War II is a cautionary tale for those who, in the name of the common good, object to the "absolutist" pursuit of rights.

MEMBERSHIP FOR THE OBNOXIOUS

National Crisis over the Jehovah's Witnesses

Newton Cantwell was something of a fanatic. Aggressive and obnoxious, he tried to impress his religious views on others, including people he knew would be offended. He was also a terrible bigot who made a habit of publicly attacking the Catholic Church, describing it as a "harlot" and a "racket." Cantwell's obnoxious and often offensive behavior brought him trouble with the law on several occasions. Two cases, including one that bears his family name, reached the Supreme Court of the United States. *Cantwell v. Connecticut* (1940) remains a landmark in the history of the free exercise of religion in America.[12] For our purposes here, it is important because it redefined the meaning of membership in the American community with respect to small and obnoxious religious sects.

Cantwell was a member of the Jehovah's Witnesses (officially the Watchtower Bible and Tract Society). Prior to the mid-1930s, the Witnesses were just another of the many small sects that dot the American religious landscape.[13] Under the leadership of Joseph Rutherford, however, they underwent an ideological and organizational transformation in the 1930s. Rutherford centralized control of the organization and heightened the group's self-image as the true chosen people of God. As the chosen people, they had a special mission to convert the heathen. Thus, each member was a minister with a duty to go forth and seek converts.

The Witnesses' worldview became increasingly paranoiac and conspiratorial as the 1930s progressed (an outlook that was only reinforced by the hostility and repression their activities provoked). Satan worked in fiendish ways, they believed, and his most evil trick was to disguise himself in the garb of religion. Hence, all other religions were false. It followed logically that the largest church, the Roman Catholic Church, was the most sinister evil of all. The Witnesses produced a vicious anti-Catholic diatribe, *Enemies*, that denounced the Church as a "racket," and an old "harlot" with a "long and bloody record as [an] inquisitionist." *Enemies* was published both as a book and as a record that individual Witnesses, in the course of their proselytizing activities, would play on portable hand-cranked record players.[14]

Taking the message in *Enemies* at face value, it is fair to say that the Witnesses were hate mongers. To put it in contemporary terms, they were a hate group spewing forth hate speech. Their attacks on Catholics were no less vicious than, say, the standard anti-Semitic diatribes. In the context of the 1930s, the Witnesses assumed a special place in American society compared with other hate groups. There were many domestic Nazi groups (the Silver Shirts, the White Shirts, the Khaki Shirts, and others), but most were small, ragtag organizations led by obvious crackpots.[15] The Ku Klux Klan was still a powerful force in many areas but was not as large and violent as it had been in the 1920s. The Witnesses were different by virtue of their aggressive proselytizing. Unlike either the domestic Nazis or the KKK, they sought out and confronted millions of ordinary Americans in face-to-face encounters.[16]

To convert the heathen, the Witnesses descended en masse on entire communities, in what they called their "locust" technique. They canvased door-to-door and conducted "street-corner witnessing." (In the 1950s, the Witnesses underwent another change, dropping both the offensive parts of their message and their more aggressive proselytizing.) These tactics were irritating to many Americans and obviously offensive to Catholics in particular. Broadcasting *Enemies* on a portable record player in a predominantly Catholic neighborhood was understandably regarded as a deliberate affront.

The combination of the Witnesses' hateful message and obnoxious behavior provoked a bitter, hostile reaction across the country. Local communities tried to restrict their activities with an array of laws limiting the distribution of literature, restricting the right to hold meetings, outlawing door-to-door canvasing, taxing the sale of their literature, and so on.[17] Some of their street-corner witnessing tactics provoked angry reactions that escalated into violence. Often, the Witnesses and not their antagonists were arrested, charged with breach of the peace or some other common-law crime.

By 1939 the conflict over the Witnesses had escalated into a national emergency.[18] Some Americans were impatient with the law and organized vigilante attacks on the Witnesses. A wave of violence swept the country, reaching its peak in the spring of 1940. A mob of twenty-five hundred people burned down a Witnesses Kingdom Hall in Maine. The entire adult population of Litchfield, Illinois, reportedly turned out to attack a Witness gathering. In Nebraska, one member of the sect was kidnapped and castrated. Vigilante mobs in Louisiana chased Witness gatherings out of the state.

Public hostility to the Witnesses was only intensified by the controversy over saluting the American flag, which on grounds of religious conscience, Witnesses refused to do. For adults, this was rarely a problem, but an increasing number of schools instituted compulsory flag salute exercises for all students. With the rise of Nazism and Japanese aggression in Asia, and with the world evidently headed for another global conflict, patriotic fervor in the United States rose dramatically. Local communities saw compulsory flag saluting as a way to instill patriotism in their children. The Witnesses, who were already being persecuted in Nazi Germany, viewed this as a direct threat to their beliefs and intensified their opposition to flag saluting. This stance, in turn, only heightened their status as pariahs in the eyes of most Americans.[19]

The many confrontations between Witnesses and local officials produced forty-five Supreme Court cases between 1938 and 1955, of which the Witnesses won thirty-six. These decisions were a critical part of the revolution in constitutional law that fashioned the first significant protections of free speech in America. Only the NAACP made a greater contribution, as a group, to the growth of civil liberties law in American history.[20] One of the most important of these cases involved Newton Cantwell.

Cantwell Before the Court

Enemies brought Newton Cantwell before the Supreme Court. He and his two sons, Jesse and Russell, had been proselytizing in New Haven, Connecticut, on April 26, 1938. Cassius Street, where the incident in question occurred, was in a neighborhood estimated to be 90 percent Catholic. The anti-Catholic vitriol emanating from the Cantwells' portable record player provoked a hostile response. People they stopped were offended. One said he was "tempted to strike Cantwell unless he went away." The Cantwells promptly packed up their books and record player and moved on. No violence occurred.[21] All three members of the family were arrested and convicted on a variety of charges, including violating the state law requiring them to obtain a permit to solicit money, and inciting a breach of the peace.

When the Supreme Court ruled on the Cantwells' appeal in 1940, it held that their activities were protected by the free exercise clause of the First Amendment. The requirement that they obtain a permit from the secretary of the Public Welfare Council, who had complete discretion to determine what was a bona fide religion, was "a censorship of religion." The conviction for inciting a breach of the peace was also overturned. No family member had committed or threatened any violent act. With respect to the allegedly offensive content of their message, the Court delivered one of the enduring affirmations of freedom of belief, one that gave liberty a clear preference over public order. The unanimous opinion held that "in the realm of religious faith, and in that of political belief, sharp differences arise." Some religious groups would inevitably resort to "exaggeration" and even "vilification" of other faiths. Nonetheless, the right to express one's views, no matter how offensive, was an "essential" condition of a free society.[22]

With respect to constitutional law, *Cantwell* marked the beginning of the modern law on the free exercise of religion.[23] The Court not only took an expansive view of religious activity, and protected it against charges of offensiveness, but also incorporated the free exercise clause into the due process clause of the Fourteenth Amendment, making it applicable to the states. Perhaps even more important, however, was the broader message of the decision regarding the meaning of community in a diverse society.

New Rules for Membership in the American Community

In the context of the national controversy over the Witnesses in 1940, the implications of *Cantwell* reached far beyond the specific holding in the decision itself. Constitutional protection for the obnoxious and offensive under the free exercise clause of the First Amendment represented a new set of rules about the place of religious groups in America. The underlying principle was tolerance. The Supreme Court concluded its opinion in *Cantwell* by noting that constitutional liberties "shield many types of life, character, opinion and beliefs."[24] It quickly added, "Nowhere is this shield more necessary than in our own country for a people composed of many races and of many creeds." The explicit recognition of the diversity of American society, and the conflict that inevitably arises from that diversity, represented a new theme in American constitutional law. It rested, in turn, on a new understanding of the nature of American society itself and the role of law in it.

The majority could not use the law to restrict a group's activities, no matter how obnoxious or offensive it might be. Nor could the state use seemingly neutral laws with an apparently worthy purpose. The Connecticut licensing law under which the Cantwells were convicted was designed to protect the public against fraud by unscrupulous operators. Nonetheless, it vested in a government official the power to determine, in advance of any actual activity, what constituted a genuine religion. By the same token, the Court ruled in other Witness cases that local communities could not restrict their activity through seemingly benign laws on littering, door-to-door canvasing, and the like.

The most eloquent statement of the principle of tolerance, even for hated groups, arose out of the second Supreme Court case involving the Witnesses' refusal to salute the flag. In the 1943 *Barnette* decision, the Court reversed its earlier decision in *Gobitis* and affirmed the right of Jehovah's Witness children to refuse to participate in compulsory flag salute exercises. In one of the greatest passages about individual liberty in the entire history of the Court, Justice Robert Jackson wrote, "If there is any fixed star in our constitutional constellation, it is that no official, high or petty, can prescribe what shall be orthodox in politics, nationalism, religion, or other matters of opinion."[25]

The timing of the *Barnette* decision added to its message about the meaning of democracy. The United States was in the midst of a two-front world war, with victory far from certain, and the Court rendered its decision on June 14, Flag Day. The message was unequivocal: even in wartime, dissenting minorities had the right not to salute the symbol of national unity. The core principle of constitutional democracy was not in forced conformity to a national symbol but in tolerance for all members of the community.

The underlying principle of tolerance in *Cantwell* and *Barnette* represented a genuine revolution in the place of religion in American life. Despite the national mythology about religious freedom, the real history of religion in America is one of intolerance and persecution. The Puritans came to the New World seeking religious freedom for themselves but brooked no dissent within their own ranks. They brutally persecuted the Quakers because of their unorthodox beliefs[26] and attempted to suppress Roger Williams, who eventually fled to Rhode Island to secure his own religious freedom.

The persecution and flight of Roger Williams was repeated on a larger scale in the case of the Mormons, who were driven out of New York, Ohio, Missouri, and Illinois by massive hostility, including vigilante violence. Joseph Smith, founder of the sect, was murdered in an Illinois jail in 1844, probably by officers of the state militia who had been called out to suppress the Mormons. They eventually found refuge in the territory of Utah.[27]

As the stories of Roger Williams and the Mormons indicate, Americans developed the habit of resolving religious differences by separating. Beginning in the colonial era, Puritan congregations settled their theological disputes by splitting. The dissenting minority moved and established a new community—where it could enforce a religious conformity of its own. The geographic expanse of the continent facilitated this pattern of separation. Later, in urban America, residential segregation kept Protestants, Catholics, and Jews apart.

Throughout this long period, which constitutes most of American history, there was no constitutional doctrine protecting religious diversity. The free exercise clause of the First Amendment was, for all practical purposes, a nullity. Untrammeled majoritarianism prevailed. The majority could limit whatever it found dangerous or merely offensive. "Community" existed only in the sense that diverse groups of people lived in close proximity, but not in the sense of mutual respect and tolerance.

Cantwell and *Barnette* set the United States on a very different path, in the direction of tolerance and inclusiveness. The Court's new role with respect to religion was only one aspect of its historic reversal on constitutional law in 1937.[28] Just as it dramatically withdrew from an active role in scrutinizing the constitutionality of economic regulatory measures—thereby ending its confrontation with the Congress and the White House—so it took up the task of protecting the rights of the unpopular and the powerless. The Court articulated the principles that guided its new concern with rights in an odd place: a footnote in an otherwise unremarkable case, *United States v. Carolene Products* in 1938.[29] The Court announced that it would give special attention to laws "directed at particular religious, or national, or racial minorities," along with "prejudice against discrete and insular minorities" that interferes with the political processes of democracy.

Embedded in this legalese was the clear declaration that the unpopular and the powerless were entitled to full membership in the American community, and that the Court would protect them when and if the other processes of democracy failed. Most of the rights revolution over the next half century involved fleshing out the meaning of the *Carolene Products* footnote. By affirming the rights of the unpopular and the powerless, the Court was at the same time imposing constraints upon the majority, constraints that compel it to tolerate those it dislikes. Rights in this context have no meaning apart from the constraining side of the equation. The Court, of course, has no real enforcement powers of it own; it can assert constitutional principles, but it must rely on other agencies to enforce them. To the extent that the free exercise of religion has any practical meaning today, it is almost entirely due to the voluntary compliance of innumerable government officials. Government, Justice Louis Brandeis once said, is "the potent, the omnipresent teacher."[30] On this issue, the government, in the form of the Supreme Court, has sought to teach a new set of rules about membership in the American community.

SCHOOL PRAYER AND THE SYMBOLS OF MEMBERSHIP

Joe Roth's Family

In 1989, Joe Roth reached the pinnacle of success. As the new head of production at 20th Century Fox, he was the proverbial mogul, with all the accompanying power and perks (he subsequently moved on to equally powerful positions with other studios). He had the power to "green-light" the production of a movie and was regularly on the phone with the biggest stars and power brokers of the entertainment world. By the mid-1990s, after a series of changes in the film industry, Roth was established as a top executive at the highly successful Disney studio.

Joe Roth did not always enjoy such status and power. As a teenager he was taunted, ostracized, and physically attacked by fellow students. His family received vicious hate mail; someone burned a cross on their lawn, and a bomb was planted in their basement. These attacks occurred in an otherwise placid middle-class suburb on Long Island, New York.[31]

The Roths were the target of these attacks because they were among the plaintiffs in a suit challenging the official prayer in New York State public schools. The Regents Prayer that opened each school day was rather weak tea. In an attempt to offend as few people as possible, it was thoroughly nondenominational and drained of all reference to any specific creed or denomination. The entire prayer read: "Almighty God, we acknowledge our dependence upon Thee, and we beg Thy blessings upon us, our parents, our teachers, and our Country." New York officials drafted this version in the wake of a series of challenges to earlier in-school religious exercises that were both sectarian and compulsory.[32] It was a desperate effort at achieving some kind of compromise, by providing some religion but nothing too specific.

The case involving the Roths, *Engel v. Vitale*, was decided by the Supreme Court in 1962. The Court ruled that the Regents Prayer violated the First Amendment prohibition against an establishment of religion. Justice Hugo Black wrote that there could be "no doubt" that recitation of this prayer was "a religious activity" in violation of the First Amendment. The fact that the prayer was nondenominational and that recitation was voluntary did not "free it from the limitations of the Establishment Clause."[33] The following year the Court took another dramatic step toward separating church and state by ruling that in-school Bible reading was also unconstitutional.[34]

In the turbulent history of the Warren Court, *Engel v. Vitale* remains one of the three or four most controversial decisions.[35] It provoked a storm of controversy and a national debate over religion in the schools that still rages more than thirty years later. Religious leaders and conservative politicians denounced it in the strongest terms. Linking it with other decisions by the Warren Court, they accused the Court of kicking religion out of the schools and putting Communists in. Southern segregationists gave the charge a different twist, accusing the Court of kicking Christ out and "putting the niggers in."

Engel produced a flood of proposed constitutional amendments to permit prayer in school. Given the apparent mood in Congress and in the country at large, it seemed that an amendment would easily win adoption. None ever did, however. One of the most surprising political developments over the last thirty-five years, which political observers fail to appreciate, has been the consistent failure of religious conservatives to gain a constitutional amendment permitting school prayer. Even after Ronald Reagan was swept into power in a conservative tidal wave, he could not deliver on his promise of a prayer amendment. And in 1994, Republican leader Newt Gingrich omitted school prayer altogether from his famous Contract with America.[36]

The question of why the allegedly powerful religious forces have failed in their effort to restore prayer to the schools is an extremely important matter.[37] Before suggesting an answer, let us examine the role of the establishment clause from the perspective of community in America.

Prayer, the Schools, and Community

Advocates of in-school prayer have always justified it as a whole-some activity that inculcates religious values, including respect for authority and habits of discipline and self-control.[38] Conservatives and many of the communitarians mentioned in chapter 1 argue that the elimination of prayer and other religious exercises from the schools is one of the principal causes of America's moral decline. As William J. Bennett sees it, the removal of religion from the public schools has "de-valued" society, contributing to both the deterioration in the quality of public education and the rise in crime, drug abuse, and teenage pregnancy.[39] Robert H. Bork reiterates the point made by many other conservatives, that we have been living off the borrowed "moral capital" of the nineteenth century and will soon pay a steep price for having failed to replenish it.[40] Neoconservative religious leaders such as Robert John Neuhaus, an Episcopalian priest who converted to Catholicism late in life, complain that the courts have banished religion from the "public square" of American life, and in the process have drained our civic life of the morally enriching voice of religion.[41] Yale law professor Stephen Carter, a thoughtful and deeply religious legal scholar, argues that the establishment clause has trivialized religion.[42]

As communitarians Mary Ann Glendon and Amitai Etzioni see it, the "radical individualists" in the ACLU have imposed their abstract notions of rights—in this case the separation of church and state— on society at the expense of the wholesome community-oriented values of the majority.[43] Thus, the annual story about the ACLU "grinches" blocking the school Christmas pageant is a paradigm for the larger impact of the rights revolution on American society.

As Joe Roth's experience illustrates, however, in-school prayer was far from a benign practice that enhanced the well-being of everyone. Injecting religion into the public schools tended to stigmatize those who were not Christian and aggravate existing religious conflicts.

Nor was Joe Roth the only child to suffer, emotionally and physically, from the controversy over religion in the schools during the post–World War II years. Terry McCollum was beaten up when his mother, Vashti McCollum, challenged the released-time program in the Champaign, Illinois, schools. Released time was one of the compromises designed to accommodate religion and public education, allowing students to be released from regular classes for religious instruction. Even before he was physically assaulted, Terry McCollum suffered the emotional strain of being forced to sit alone in an empty room while other students received their religious instruction. On one occasion, when that room was being used, he was forced to sit out in the hall. Students and teachers passing by assumed he was there for misbehavior.[44]

The New York State released-time program attempted to separate religious instruction from the school by having the students take their religion classes off school grounds. Leah Cunn, from Brooklyn, was only one of the students and teachers who testified that the program heightened religious tensions, making everyone aware of differences in beliefs and backgrounds. Cunn herself was called "Christ killer" and "dirty Jew" by other students.[45] Law professor Jesse H. Choper opens his recent defense of the establishment clause with a personal note on his "first experience" with religion in school as a seventh grader, when he was compelled to attend a daily chapel meeting where the Bible was read. Because the ceremony was "contrary to [his] religious training and belief," he stood silent throughout.[46]

The attacks on Joe Roth, Terry McCollum, and Leah Cunn sprang from a deep emotional response to the lawsuits brought by their parents. The issues at stake were far broader than the fine points of First Amendment law. Everyone understood, at least emotionally if not intellectually, that the real issues involved the public symbols of what it means to be an American, which groups are defined as fully American, and who controls the public symbols. School prayer, in short, was a far from wholesome activity. It was a vital symbol of power and control.

The principal effect of *Engel* (and the many other decisions regarding separation of church and state that preceded and followed it) was to *dis*establish Protestantism as the quasi-official religion of the United States. Protestants had dominated American culture, politics, and law since the first European settlements.[47] Even after the immigration of millions of Catholics and Jews in the late nineteenth and early twentieth centuries transformed the United States into a heterogeneous society, the Protestant elite dominated American politics and culture. As historian Arthur M. Schlesinger, Jr., recently put it, "For better or for worse, American history has been shaped more than anything else by British tradition and culture."[48]

Anglo-Saxon hegemony provoked a long and bitter "culture war" between different ethnic and religious groups. The political commentators who see contemporary American society racked by conflict over cultural values—on the issues of abortion, homosexuality, religion in the schools—lack historical perspective. Conflict over the proper standards of morality and public behavior has a long history in this country.[49]

In the nineteenth century, the principal battleground involved the consumption of alcoholic beverages. The Protestant elite embraced temperance (and later Prohibition) as a badge of self-control and self-improvement. The person who controlled his or her drinking, or abstained completely, was both morally superior and more likely to succeed in life. Temperance advocates sought to impose this value on the Irish and German immigrants whom they thought drank too much. Charles Loring Brace's 1872 book *The Dangerous Classes*, with its condemnation of the drinking, family breakdown, unemployment, and crime among immigrants, reads very much like contemporary descriptions of the underclass.[50] The original temperance movement relied primarily on moral suasion and voluntary restraint, although it did include legal controls over the time and place of drinking. When they concluded that voluntarism did not work, the antidrinking forces embraced the coercive approach of Prohibition.[51]

The public schools were another battleground. Until the post–World War II era, however, the Protestant majority held sway. Among other things, it simply took for granted that the public schools were an instrument for advancing its own values. Schlesinger argues that "American history was long written in the interests of white Anglo-Saxon Protestant males."[52] A crucial part of this agenda was the assumption that Protestant Christian doctrine was properly a part of the public school curriculum. The great American educator Horace Mann fought diligently against sectarian control of the schools, but his goal was to make sure that no one Protestant denomination controlled them. He firmly believed that religion was not only a permissible but an essential element of the curriculum.[53]

Among other things, Protestant hegemony over the schools prompted American Catholics to develop an extensive network of parochial schools. Catholics understood full well that the public schools were being used to impose an alien set of religious values.[54] In the 1920s, two efforts to suppress cultural diversity led to two Supreme Court decisions that set the stage for the modern concept of a right to privacy. As part of the hysteria surrounding World War I, Nebraska outlawed teaching the German language; the Supreme Court invalidated that law in *Meyer v. Nebraska*.[55] Meanwhile, in a referendum sponsored by the Ku Klux Klan, Oregon voters outlawed private religious schools altogether; the Court invalidated that law in *Pierce v. Society of Sisters*.[56] Although the two decisions predated the civil liberties revolution that began in the late 1930s and embraced none of the modern rhetoric about cultural diversity, their practical impact was clear: the majority could not coerce cultural minority groups into submitting to a common (read: communal) public school curriculum.

Control of the public school curriculum was a straightforward exercise in majority rule. The majoritarian view of democracy holds that the majority of the community is free to shape the curriculum and other school policies. Until the intervention of the Supreme Court, there were few, if any, legal constraints on this aspect of majority rule. The *Meyer* and *Pierce* decisions were early straws in the wind. The famous Scopes "Monkey Trial" in 1925, involving a Tennessee law prohibiting the teaching of evolution, might have forced the issue because it raised the question of whether the majority could prohibit the teaching of any idea, not just one with religious implications. Unfortunately, the case was resolved on minor technicalities, and no Supreme Court test case developed.[57]

As an aside, we might note that majoritarianism was a game that everyone could play with respect to the public schools. One of the curious chapters in the history of American education involves the so-called captive schools that existed throughout the 1950s. Because of immigration patterns, some rural areas were almost exclusively Catholic. The residents established parochial schools early on and, at some point, simply merged them into the public schools. Education continued much as before, except that the nuns and priests were now paid by public tax dollars. With the parents and taxpayers overwhelmingly Catholic, and local Protestants reluctant to challenge their hegemony, no one raised any objections. And until the Supreme Court introduced the wall of separation doctrine in 1947, there was no constitutional basis for a challenge.[58] The captive schools were an oddity that proved the general rule. Whichever group constituted a majority in a given locality could use that power to control the curriculum and, through it, promote its own religion.

The 1962 school prayer decision, together with the many establishment clause cases that followed, effectively disestablished Protestantism as the unofficial religion of America. By ending Protestant hegemony, the principle of separation of church and state dictates equality among religious groups. No one religion can use its political power to claim control over public institutions. This mandated equality represented the new rule governing the relations between religious groups in America.

The advocates of school prayer have always stressed its positive effect on public morality. They fail to appreciate the symbolic message conveyed by ceremonial activities in schools and other public agencies. Prayer conveys a message about legitimacy, saying that certain religious beliefs have official sanction and that the members of that faith have a higher status in the community than people with different beliefs. Supreme Court Justice Sandra Day O'Connor eloquently articulated this issue in a 1984 grave case involving a crèche in front of the Pawtucket, Rhode Island, courthouse. Although the Court's decision was a curiously mixed one, O'Connor explained what is at stake in any form of government sponsorship of religion: "Endorsement sends a message to non-adherents that they are outsiders, not full members of the political community, and an accompanying message to adherents that they are insiders, favored members of the political community."[59]

The battle over prayer in the public schools has been so long and bitter because it touches the raw nerve of what it means to be an American. And so it was with Joe Roth, Terry McCollum, and Leah Cunn in the 1950s and early 1960s. They and their parents understood that the prevailing religious exercises in the schools sent the message that they were not full members of the community.

As a final observation, it is important to note the relationship between the two religion clauses of the First Amendment in rewriting the rules of community in America. As Jesse H. Choper explains, the establishment clause and the free exercise clause are "mutually supportive" in "protecting religious liberty."[60] Just as constitutional protection of free exercise of religion embodies the principle that no religious group may be excluded from full and equal participation in the community, so the principle of separation of church and state says that no group shall enjoy special favored status. Together, the two religion clauses define the new rules of membership in the American community.

It is impossible, in this regard, not to note the divisive conflicts in Russia and Israel in recent years over church-state issues. Russia in 1997 enacted a new law that gives preference to certain "traditional" religions and imposes various restrictions on others. Most

observers believe the law is designed to protect the Russian Orthodox Church from the aggressive, and rather successful, proselytizing
by the Mormons and other evangelical Protestant denominations.
Israel, meanwhile, is in turmoil over the preferred place occupied by
the Orthodox rabbinical establishment. Their attempt to disallow
conversions performed by Reform and Conservative rabbis has
deeply offended American Jews. These recent events in Russia and
Israel seem to reaffirm the wisdom of not allowing any particular
religious group to wield special political privileges if the goal is to
maintain a tolerant and inclusive society.

RACE DISCRIMINATION AND MEMBERSHIP

This Little Light of Ours: Fannie Lou Hamer

Fannie Lou Hamer only wanted to register to vote. For her attempt
to exercise the most basic democratic right, she was evicted from her
home, fired from her job, and then, on June 9, 1963, arrested on
trumped-up charges and mercilessly beaten in jail.[61]

Hamer is one of the folk heroes of the civil rights movement. She
is the subject of a full biography, and her story has become part of
the standard history of the southern civil rights movement. An
impoverished sharecropper in Ruleville, Mississippi, she was one of
the first African Americans in the state to respond to the initial
voting rights efforts in 1962. At the time, only 155 of the 13,524
eligible African Americans in Sunflower County—home to the
implacable segregationist U.S. Senator James O. Eastland—were registered to vote. In 1955, shortly after the *Brown* decision declaring
segregated schools unconstitutional, Senator Eastland advised his
constituents that they not only did not have to obey the court's
decision but were actually obligated to disobey.[62]

The beating Hamer received in the Winona, Mississippi, jail was
especially savage. Such was the totality of white supremacy that the
jailer was able to make another black prisoner actually do it. Hamer
recalled that he "beat me until he give out." She was not able to lie
on her back for weeks afterward. Under rising political pressure from
civil rights forces, the Justice Department indicted the sheriff, the
police chief, and three others involved in the incident; they were
acquitted by an all-white jury. Denied the vote, African Americans
had no voice in the Mississippi criminal justice system. Nor was the
beating the only physical brutality inflicted on Fannie Lou Hamer.

Two years earlier, at age forty-three, she had been sterilized without her knowledge or consent.

Fannie Lou Hamer's story is only one of literally thousands that could illustrate our point here. Race discrimination represents the most blatant denial of community in American history. Disenfranchisement of African American voters in the South became institutionalized and systematic in the 1890s and continued until the federal Voting Rights Act of 1965. The nonenfranchisement of women lasted longer but was never accompanied by anything like the Ku Klux Klan–led reign of terror that occurred in the South during the Jim Crow era. Fannie Lou Hamer's story dramatizes the impact of disenfranchisement on ordinary people, especially their utter helplessness in the face of official lawlessness.

The language of the Jim Crow era perfectly expresses the implications of discrimination for membership. The legal doctrine of "separate but equal" conveys with brutal eloquence the message of forced exclusion. At the risk of pointing out the obvious, this was certainly not a voluntary separateness, such as the case of a religious sect that chooses to live apart from the mainstream of society. This was an enforced exclusion, established by law and supplemented by vigilante violence. Nor was there ever anything more than pretense about the "equal" half of segregationist doctrine. The public schools and every other aspect of life under the racial caste system were completely unequal.

Civil Rights and the American Community

The history of the civil rights movement offers a valuable perspective on the current status of race relations in America. On the one hand, it highlights how much has been achieved in terms of the most elemental aspects of membership in the community: the eradication of de jure segregation in schools and other public facilities, the end of voter disenfranchisement, and, with the 1964 Civil Rights Act, the establishment of nondiscrimination as official U.S. policy. It is laughable for anyone to seriously argue that anything approximating community existed with respect to race relations prior to the mid-1960s.

An appreciation of civil rights history also reminds us of how much has not been accomplished, and how far we still are from the dream of true equality. Many observers, in fact, believe that race relations had actually worsened by the mid-1990s. The civil rights movement had lost most of its momentum and was on the defensive. In a series of decisions on legislative districting and employment, the Supreme Court had invalidated programs involving preferential treatment based on race.[63] Opposition to affirmative action emerged as a potent issue in the political realm. Symptomatic of the movement's plight was the embarrassing disarray of the NAACP in 1994–95, as it teetered on the brink of bankruptcy. A group of prominent conservative African American thinkers—Thomas Sowell, Shelby Steele, and others—argue that the civil rights movement suffers from an even more debilitating intellectual bankruptcy. They challenge the core assumptions that guided the civil rights movement for half a century and argue that the movement's program actually harms rather than helps African Americans by creating a culture of dependency.[64]

At the same time, the African American community faces an apparent rise in old-fashioned racism. The most alarming development of the 1980s was the outburst of blatantly racist incidents on college and university campuses. Some of the more highly publicized incidents were notable not just for their viciousness but also because they occurred at some of the best public and private institutions: Smith, Brown, the University of Wisconsin, and others. These events were a sobering development for everyone who had optimistically assumed that education was the best antidote to racism.[65] And in 1996 there was a rash of church burnings, many of which appeared to be cases of racially motivated arson against African American churches.

Many of the critics of rights examined in chapter 1 argue that the culture of rights is in part responsible for the resurgence of racism. Placing so much emphasis on racial and ethnic identity has fragmented society and aggravated racial divisions. Affirmative action in employment and education, meanwhile, by seeking preferential treatment on the basis of race, has played a particularly insidious role in poisoning race relations. "Identity politics," the child of the civil rights movement, has become the major obstacle to progress for the African American community.

This view of contemporary race relations suffers from a deeply flawed sense of history. The Kerner Commission, appointed to investigate the urban riots of the 1960s, perpetuated this perspective in its 1968 report. In the most widely quoted phrase, the commission declared, "This is our basic conclusion: Our nation is moving toward two societies, one black, one white—separate and unequal."[66] To say that we *are becoming* more group-conscious and more divided assumes that we were once a harmonious and well-integrated society. As the history of the civil rights movement indicates, nothing could be further from the truth. We were in fact a segregated society, separated by both law and informal practice, for many years.

To a great extent, this mystification of history is an attempt to deny the legacy of racism and racial segregation. The racial divisions in American society are far deeper than whatever was prescribed by law or practiced as a matter of custom. Out of this separateness we created different cultures. To those white Americans who imagine that we were once a unified common culture, we can only ask if they have ever attended an African American church service or listened to blues and jazz. African American religion and music developed their unique traditions because African American people themselves were forcibly separated from the mainstream of American life, in violation of any reasonable definition of community. There are similarly distinct traditions of food, humor, and spoken English. To say that we were not separate is to imagine a fantasized American history.[67]

Most important, the history of the civil rights movement highlights the extent to which the issue of identity politics is far more complex than its critics are willing to admit. There is no doubt that it has many negative aspects, notably the cult of victimhood, in which individuals evade responsibility for their own behavior and blame their fate on external forces. But as was suggested in the discussion of the rights of single people in chapter 2, a separate racial identity is not something that originated with the African American community. It was a consequence of the prejudice, discrimination, and exclusion that were imposed on that community. Insofar as it has been the mainspring of civil rights activity, moreover, that separate identity has played the principal role in dismantling the system of exclusion and the creation of a more equal and inclusive community.

We are left with a virtually insoluble dilemma: the sense of separateness, which is the legacy of our history, is a necessary condition for undoing that separateness. This is the dilemma we have been wrestling with—in the courts, the legislatures, and the political arena—over affirmative action: how to build a color-blind society through color-conscious laws and policies. We again confront the dilemma posed by Erving Goffman, which was discussed in chapter 1: that efforts to remove the stigma of differentness only heighten consciousness of that very differentness.[68]

Nan D. Hunter, former director of the ACLU Lesbian and Gay Rights Project, explains how this dilemma affects homosexuals. "Many of the thorniest challenges" facing the lesbian and gay rights movement, she observes, "will come in trying to subvert categorical modes of thinking about sexuality and sexual orientation, *while still taking advantage of a civil rights heritage that is grounded in identity politics*" (emphasis added).[69] She quickly notes that "breaking the gridlock of identity politics is no easy task." There is an inherent tension between the desire to end the "imprisoning category" and "the need to defend those persons who are disadvantaged because they bear the group label." Her comments are as relevant to race discrimination, sex discrimination, and every other category involved in the modern rights revolution as they are to discrimination against lesbians and gay men.

The answer to the dilemma posed by Nan Hunter is not clear. A sense of the history of the civil rights movement certainly suggests one inappropriate answer. To demand that people abandon their sense of separate identity is folly. Certainly with respect to race, that sense is a deeply rooted phenomenon that is not going to go away. Our current problem, in fact, is not that we have too much separate identity but that we have too much separateness as a matter of daily life: too much prejudice, discrimination, and inequality.

THE TRAGEDY OF THE JAPANESE AMERICANS

Wars always pose the severest tests of a society's fundamental values. The forced relocation and internment of the Japanese Americans during World War II is widely regarded as one of the greatest tragedies in American history. About 120,000 people, including 70,000 bona fide American citizens, were evacuated from the West Coast, under threat of arrest if they refused to go, and confined in a series of government-run "relocation centers"—a polite euphemism for concentration camps. In addition to the loss of fundamental liberties, the Japanese Americans lost an estimated $400 million in personal property as they were forced to sell businesses, farms, and other property under emergency conditions. None of the 120,000 were accused of any crime. They were evacuated and interned solely because of their race.[70]

The tragedy of the Japanese Americans is a sordid stain on American history. As early as 1945, a public opinion backlash set in, and increasing numbers of Americans recognized that a horrible tragedy had been perpetrated. Almost no one today attempts to justify the government's actions. One measure of the backlash is the fact that no legal scholar has written anything attempting to justify the Supreme Court decisions upholding the constitutionality of the government's action.[71] The two principal decisions, *Hirabayashi* and *Korematsu*, are jurisprudential orphans, in the same category with the equally notorious *Dred Scott* decision of 1857 denying the citizenship of African American slaves. In 1988, Congress provided some measure of redress through the Civil Liberties Act, which gave each surviving internee $20,000.[72]

The internment of the Japanese Americans is a cautionary tale for those who believe that individual rights have been pushed too far and that we need a healthier balance between rights and responsibilities. The word "responsibilities" has an appealing ring, implying voluntary restraint by individuals. In actual practice, however, rights are balanced against coercive government action. It is worth reconsidering the Japanese American tragedy in light of this balancing question.

When President Franklin D. Roosevelt issued Executive Order 9066 on February 19, 1942, neither he nor any of his immediate advisers contemplated concentration camps. Issued as a war-time measure, the order authorized the secretary of war or military officials under his command to designate military zones and to exclude "any and all persons" from them. It did not specifically mention the Japanese Americans. The details were left up to military authorities, and in this respect Executive Order 9066 was a wholesale delegation to the military of authority over the civilian population.

In retrospect, one of the most shocking aspects of the entire story is how few people protested the gross violation of fundamental civil liberties. Across the country, all of the traditional defenders of minorities, liberals and leftists alike, turned their backs on the Japanese Americans. All accepted the argument that the war effort was the highest priority and it was necessary to support the commander in chief. Earl Warren, whose name is now synonymous with judicial protection of individual rights, was then attorney general of California and strongly supported removal of the Japanese Americans. He urged the federal government to act because California did not have legal authority to do so.[73] Without any question, racial

prejudice played a principal role in reinforcing the war effort rationale. It is impossible to imagine any equivalent action being taken
against German Americans, if, for example, the Germans had
bombed an East Coast city.

The only people to rally to the defense of the Japanese Americans
were a few religious groups (although mainly local churches rather
than national denominations), a handful of individual lawyers, and
the ACLU.[74] Even the Quakers, who supported the Japanese Americans more than any other religious group, limited their role to
easing the suffering of the evacuees. And the ACLU, which immediately denounced Roosevelt's executive order and handled two of the
four cases that reached the Supreme Court, did so only in the face of
strong internal opposition.[75]

Concentration camps resulted because neither President Roosevelt nor any of his advisers considered the practical problems of
implementing the relocation. What do you do with 120,000 people
once you have ordered them "removed"? Not surprisingly, given the
combination of long-standing racism and wartime hysteria, the governors of midwestern states loudly objected to taking them. With no
other obvious alternative, the federal government created its own
series of "relocation centers." In another of the euphemisms that
characterized the entire affair, Roosevelt's Executive Order 9102 created the War Relocation Authority, and charged it with responsibility for the "maintenance and supervision" of the evacuees. WRA
regulations made it a crime to leave a relocation center, thereby
turning the Japanese Americans into prisoners. As one dissenting
Supreme Court justice pointed out, Fred Korematsu had the choice
of being arrested for not reporting for relocation or being confined
against his will in a relocation center. Obviously, this was no choice
at all.[76]

The Japanese Americans in the Supreme Court

The treatment of the Japanese Americans is not only one of the
most shameful episodes in all of American history but also a startling chapter in the history of the Supreme Court. The Court decisions in *Hirabayashi* and *Korematsu* upholding the constitutionality
of the program are notable in two respects. First, the Court showed
extraordinary deference to military authority. Second, the justices
went to great lengths to rule on the narrowest possible grounds and
to avoid considering the larger implications of the government's
program. Thus, in *Hirabayashi*, the Court ruled narrowly on Gordon

Hirabayashi's violation of a curfew.[77] In *Korematsu*, it ruled on Fred Korematsu's failure to report to a relocation center but did not consider the consequences of reporting.[78]

Especially startling in the light of history was the role of the famous civil libertarians on the Court, Justices William O. Douglas and Hugo L. Black. Both accepted and aggressively justified the government's rationale. In his *Hirabayashi* opinion, Douglas deferred to the military. "We cannot sit in judgment on the military requirements of that hour [following Pearl Harbor]," he wrote. He argued, "We must credit the military with as much good faith . . . as we would any other public official," adding that "we cannot possibly know all the facts which lay behind that decision." As a matter of fact, as scholar-lawyer Peter Irons found, the military willfully suppressed information indicating that a massive relocation was not necessary.[79] In *Korematsu*, Justice Hugo Black reiterated the deference to military necessity and callously declared that "hardships are a part of war, and war an aggregation of hardships."

Justice Frank Murphy was alone in *Hirabayashi* in condemning the obvious racism of the government's action. In a concurring opinion that was virtually a dissent, he pointed out that the curfew created "two classes of citizens" and left one of them with less constitutional protection than the other. The power of the war emergency rationale is evident in the extraordinary pressures that other justices placed on Murphy not to issue a formal dissent. Given the national crisis, they argued, it was important for the Court to both support the commander in chief and show a united front.[80]

By the time *Korematsu* was decided a year and a half after *Hirabayashi*, the mood among the justices had changed dramatically. With time to reflect on the implications of the evacuation and internment, four justices now dissented.

The Test of Extreme Situations
The tragedy of the Japanese Americans poses the issue of membership in stark terms. The terminology of the government's program —"exclusion" orders—communicated in a perversely eloquent fashion the message that certain people may be set apart and excluded from full membership in the community. From a community perspective, the terminology was as starkly eloquent as the old "separate but equal" doctrine. The real test of a society's commitment to inclusion is whether it can maintain it in times of great stress. Wars, both hot and cold, have historically brought to bear the strongest

pressures to make special exceptions to established standards.

There are many who would argue that we have learned our lesson from this tragic episode, and that it couldn't happen again. At least two current controversies, however, suggest that such a possibility is not so remote. Some prominent conservatives have proposed rounding up and/or tattooing persons who are HIV-positive. True, this idea has been widely denounced. But imagine, for a moment, if AIDS were to spread more rapidly into the heterosexual population than it has. In the early stages of the epidemic, in the mid-1980s, there were dire forecasts to this effect. It is easy to imagine the panic that would surge through middle-class America, and equally easy to imagine proposals for extraordinary measures such as confinement or public identification winning support.

The second example is even closer to reality. A broad segment of the public has demonized immigrants as a threat to our national health, claiming they take away jobs from "real" Americans and swamp public resources such as education and welfare. The anti-immigrant hysteria has moved far beyond the traditional calls for restricting immigration (an idea that goes back to the turn of the century) to include denial of various government benefits. By the summer of 1996, it had reached the point of denying eligibility for welfare to the children of *legal* immigrants. This is one long and disturbing step in the direction of defining an entire class of people for exclusion based on their alleged threat to the national interest.

In this context, the following question arises: What principles and standards do we have to prevent the exclusion of demonized groups in the midst of popular hysteria? This brings us to the arguments advanced by some critics of the rights revolution for balancing rights.

Communitarian leader Mary Ann Glendon offers the most specific suggestion for how we might properly balance rights and responsibilities, citing existing international human rights declarations.[81] The 1948 Universal Declaration of Human Rights, which is the model for the nearly fifty subsequent documents, states that individual rights can be restricted in the interests of the "just requirements of morality, public order and the general welfare in a democratic society."[82] Along the same lines, the 1966 International Covenant on Civil and Political Rights balances individual rights against the "interests of national security or public safety, public order (*ordre public*), the protection of public health or morals or the protection of the rights and freedom of others."[83] Similar language appears in virtually all of the other international human rights documents.

It should be immediately apparent that the evacuation and internment of the Japanese Americans could be readily justified in terms of these exceptions. The attack on Pearl Harbor was seen as posing a threat to "national security" and "public safety." The pivot upon which the Supreme Court upheld the government in *Hirabayashi* and *Korematsu* was the national military emergency, specifically the threat of sabotage in the wake of Pearl Harbor. Once the Court accepted the national security rationale, all other safeguards of individual rights collapsed. In his majority opinion in *Hirabayashi*, Justice Harlan Fiske Stone argued that the program "must be appraised in light of the conditions" that prevailed in the wake of Pearl Harbor. These special conditions included the evidence of the "solidarity" of the Japanese Americans and their failure to fully assimilate into American society.

Such rationales open the door to gross violation of rights in the future. Communitarians will reply that it won't happen, that we have learned our lesson from the Japanese American tragedy. But the fact remains that it *did* happen. The ultimate lesson of that earlier tragedy is the importance of maintaining the strictest limits on the power of the government to infringe on the rights of citizens. Communitarians and others object to the "absolutist" quality of our approach to individual rights, insisting that it is too extreme and uncompromising, that it fails to take into account the needs of the community in special circumstances. But that is precisely the kind of thinking that justified the evacuation and internment of the Japanese Americans. The best guarantee of an inclusive community, where the full membership of every group is protected, is a vigilant, absolutist approach to individual rights.

CONCLUSION: RIGHTS AND MEMBERSHIP

As Michael Walzer argues, membership in the community is the primary good that we distribute to one another. Without full membership, none of the rights we claim to cherish have any meaning. The episodes from American history covered in this chapter indicate that the pursuit of rights has moved American society in the direction of a more inclusive community. The argument that rights have undermined community is based on a deeply flawed historical perspective, one that idealizes the past and sees only the negative aspects of contemporary society. The critics of rights argue that the new rights culture has cultivated unhealthy values, primarily a self-indulgent, expressive individualism and a divisive group consciousness. To the contrary, however, the rights revolution has cultivated the values of tolerance and equality, producing a more inclusive community.

Chapter Four
SPEAKING AND BELONGING: FREE SPEECH AND COMMUNITY

BANNED IN BOSTON

MARGARET SANGER was banned in Boston. Mayor James Curley, one of the most colorful figures in American political history, denied the birth control pioneer permission to speak in 1923 simply because she advocated contraception. As far as Curley was concerned, "birth control" was nothing more than a euphemism for murder, and anyone who advocated violent crime forfeited his or her right of free speech.[1]

The issues at stake in the Boston confrontation extended far beyond the immediate one of birth control. In their own ways, both Sanger and Curley understood that birth control was directly related to the broader issue of women's role in American society. Sanger believed that control over conception was a crucial step toward freedom and independence for women. Mayor Curley understood as well that women's autonomy in this area threatened the patriarchal structure of society. Instinctively, he banned Sanger's speech.

Speech, Power, and Community
The 1923 confrontation between Sanger and Mayor Curley dramatizes the theme of this chapter: that free speech is a crucial condition of membership in the community. We can state it as a simple proposition: *to speak is to belong*. To speak is to be heard, and thus to become an active member of the community. Conversely, to be denied the right to speak is to be excluded from the most elemental aspect of membership. Censorship does more than suppress

an idea; it denies the speaker the right to participate in the affairs of the community.

The right to freedom of speech is more than one of the benefits of membership in the community. It may well be *the* essential precondition for achieving the capacity to enjoy all other rights and responsibilities of full membership. Or, as law professor Kenneth L. Karst puts it, "the principle of equality, understood as an equal right to speak and to participate in the affairs of the community, is part of the 'central meaning of the First Amendment.'"[2]

Michael Walzer argues that membership is the primary social good we bestow on people.[3] His formulation is too passive, however. Most often, the right to speak is demanded by the outcast or powerless groups; it is their way of asserting their membership. From this perspective, it is not surprising that the paradigmatic actions of the 1960s were expressive acts: sit-ins, marches, and demonstrations. These acts were demands to be heard, on the part of an entire class of people (as in African Americans in the South) or the advocates of certain ideas (as in opposition to the war in Vietnam). First Amendment protection of such expressive activity was crucial to the survival of movements that ultimately blossomed into broader social and political activity.

Homosexuality has traditionally been referred to as "the love that dare not speak its name."[4] As so many lesbian and gay activists have argued, the silencing of all references to homosexuality has the effect of rendering homosexuals invisible, of denying their very existence. William Rubenstein, former director of the ACLU Lesbian and Gay Rights Project, maintains that "the experience of lesbians and gay men in the United States is centrally one of silence."[5] Free speech for gays and lesbians has been instrumental in achieving some initial level of visibility, legitimacy as human beings, and status as participating members of the community. Rubenstein has argued that the First Amendment has done far more for gay rights than the equal protection clause.[6]

This chapter examines the relationship between free speech and community. It does not pretend to be a full discussion of First Amendment law, a subject that has been examined in detail in a steady stream of books by leading scholars.[7] Instead, it focuses on the specific question of the relationship between free speech and community. As in the previous chapter, the argument here is illustrated by selected episodes from modern American history involving the women's rights, civil rights, and gay rights movements.

The argument in this chapter replies to two major criticisms of rights. The first is that unlimited free speech is the enemy of equality. This criticism has arisen in two areas. Catharine MacKinnon and some other feminists argue that First Amendment protection of pornography sustains the oppression of women.[8] Along the same lines, Charles M. Lawrence III, Mari Matsuda, Richard Delgado, and other law professors who belong to the Critical Legal Studies movement argue that free speech for racists and other exponents of hate speech perpetuates racial inequality.[9] Similarly, some people argue that Nazis should not be protected by the First Amendment because advocating genocide falls outside the bounds of civilized discourse.[10] In short, this criticism holds that the prevailing absolutist, content-neutral approach to free speech perpetuates inequality and prevents the development of an inclusive community. This chapter argues, to the contrary, that the protection of allegedly offensive speech has been central to the growth of a more inclusive community in America.

The second criticism of rights is that uninhibited free speech corrodes community by undermining standards of public civility. This might be referred to as the "shit happens" problem. Most readers of this book will have had the experience of encountering a T-shirt or bumper sticker proclaiming "Shit Happens" or some other vulgar epithet. Many people not only find such things offensive but also believe that our inability to limit such expression in public corrodes the public sphere of community. Critics of rights such as Mary Ann Glendon argue that this is a classic example of the triumph of radical self-expression over regard for others and an appreciation of the needs of the good of the community,[11] or, as communitarian philosophers put it, the triumph of right over good.[12] In a discussion of extreme antiabortion rhetoric, this chapter argues that extreme and even offensive expression is a necessary part of defining the boundaries of community.

SANGER, CENSORSHIP, AND SEX

Censoring Sanger

Although famous as a colorful and corrupt machine politician who eventually went to prison for some of his illegal activities, Boston's Mayor James Curley was no fool. In fact, he had a rather well-developed theory of the First Amendment, declaring himself a "stout stickler" for free speech.[13] As he explained to James Codman, head of the local ACLU chapter, the First Amendment protected political speech but not the advocacy of violent crime. For this reason, he also banned the Ku Klux Klan from holding meetings in Boston in 1923. He cited the Klan's notorious reputation for acts of violence and, consequently, deemed it a secret criminal conspiracy rather than a legitimate political organization. (It is worth noting that Curley's argument on this point was identical to one made by many legal scholars during the cold war with respect to the Communist Party. Communists had forfeited their free speech rights because they were a secret, violence-prone conspiracy.)[14]

Sanger's troubles were not confined to Boston; she was also banned in Albany, Syracuse, and other cities.[15] Her most highly publicized conflicts occurred in New York City. She was arrested in 1914 on multiple charges that carried a combined maximum penalty of forty-five years in prison, and again in 1916 immediately after she opened the first public birth control clinic in the United States. A year later her short educational film, *Birth Control*, was also banned in New York City.[16] When the New York police prevented her from giving a speech in 1921, one officer explained that they were acting on orders from "the archbishop." The police raided her birth control clinic in 1929, arresting all eight members of the staff and seizing all patient records.[17]

The suppression of birth control advocacy was fundamentally an issue of power. All of the early birth control advocates—Sanger, Elizabeth Gurley Flynn, Emma Goldman, Mary Ware Dennett— understood that control over reproduction was central to women's equality. When Goldman took up the issue of birth control in the June 1914 issue of her magazine *The Woman Rebel,* even using the words "birth control" was considered dangerously radical. Two years later she devoted the entire May 1916 issue of her new magazine, *Mother Earth,* to the subject. She wrote that the underlying issue was "a change in the relation of the sexes," which involved "a war for a seat at the table of life on the part of the people, the masses who create and who build the world."[18] Sanger told pathetic stories of the women who flocked to her clinic in the predominantly Jewish and Italian neighborhood of Brownsville in Brooklyn. One told her, "My husband has a weak heart and works only four days a week. He gets twelve dollars, and we can barely live on it now. We have enough children."[19] Birth control was the key to control over the whole of their lives.

For their part, Mayor Curley and the other officials who suppressed public discussion of birth control understood the issue just
as clearly. Information was power, and ignorance was powerless-
ness. It was precisely because of the explosive implications of information about birth control and sexuality that so many of the important women's rights issues between the 1920s and the 1960s
involved censorship of sexually related materials.[20] During the
long period between the advent of women's suffrage in 1920 and
the rebirth of the women's rights movement in the mid-1960s—a
period when feminism lost much of its political force—the most
important women's rights issues were First Amendment challenges
to censorship.

At the national level, the 1873 Comstock Law was the primary
instrument of censorship. Named for the famed moral crusader
Anthony Comstock, the law declared "unmailable" "every article or
thing designed, adapted, or intended for preventing conception
or producing abortion," "every article, instrument, substance, drug,
medicine, or thing . . . for preventing conception," and "every written or printed card, letter, circular, book, pamphlet, advertisement,
or notice of any kind" intended for that purpose.[21] The U.S Customs
Bureau, meanwhile, vigilantly enforced a federal law that banned
the importation of any written material, instrument, or drug "for
the prevention of conception."

The turning point in terms of both the law and public opinion
came in 1929 when federal officials entrapped and prosecuted Mary
Ware Dennett for mailing her sex education pamphlet, "The Sex
Side of Life."[22] The pamphlet, which Dennett had originally written
for her own children because she could find no other information, simply described human sexuality in the most general terms.
Although not the least bit erotic, it nonetheless violated the terms of
the Comstock Law. Dennett's conviction became a national cause
célèbre, provoking the first national effort to end censorship of sexually related material. Even the ACLU had been somewhat squea-
mish about sex until then, but it was galvanized to organize a major
effort on Dennett's behalf. ACLU General Counsel Morris L. Ernst
represented her in court and won a reversal of her conviction on
appeal. In an important index of changing attitudes toward sexuality and birth control, a number of prominent and wealthy individuals across the country joined her defense committee.[23]

Ernst, who served for many years as general counsel for both the
ACLU and Planned Parenthood, took the lead in the campaign

against censorship. He handled virtually all of the landmark court cases and wrote an influential series of books on censorship for a general audience. He was the first, and for many years the only, attorney litigating cases in the area of reproductive rights. In his most famous case, he overturned the government's ban on James Joyce's novel *Ulysses*, one of the greatest novels in the English language.[24]

Today, the censorship cases over birth control and other aspects of sexuality seem quaint and almost comical. Ernst's successful effort to end the Customs Bureau ban on a book on female sexuality by the British physician Dr. Marie Stopes produced an important 1931 decision with the improbable title of *United States v.* Married Love.[25] *Married Love* was anything but obscene, containing little in the way of specific detail about sex. Its enormous popularity was due entirely to the fact that it simply acknowledged female sexuality and advised readers that a healthy marital sex life was a good thing.[26]

Five years after *Married Love* was allowed into the country, Ernst made another major breakthrough in a case ending the government's ban on birth control devices sent to a physician. The 1936 case had the title *United States v. One Package Containing 120, More or Less, Rubber Pessaries to Prevent Conception.*

The gradual dismantling of censorship of birth control information and devices represented one of the major aspects of the fight for women's rights in the 1930s. By the time of World War II, birth control had won a modest degree of legitimacy in the public sphere. Attempts to ban Sanger's speeches disappeared, and, far from appearing as a radical, she drew her support from the social elite, including the medical profession. By 1940 there were over five hundred birth control clinics operating across the country.[27]

These developments set the stage for the final assault on birth control restrictions, which produced the landmark Supreme Court decision in *Griswold v. Connecticut* striking down a Connecticut law outlawing the distribution of contraceptive devices. *Griswold* ended one long chapter in the history of sexuality but, by affirming a constitutional right of privacy, opened a new and even more controversial one. *Griswold*, in turn, provided the legal foundation for the 1973 decision in *Roe v. Wade* affirming a right to abortion.[28]

Virtually all feminists regard *Roe* as the single most important court decision on behalf of women's rights (although many would have preferred an equality rather than a privacy rationale for the decision). It is impossible to separate *Roe* from the fifty-year struggle over the censorship of discussions of sexuality that preceded it. The decision was the logical culmination of Margaret Sanger's free speech battle with Mayor Curley in 1923. The freedom to discuss control over fertility ultimately helped to change public attitudes about sex, birth control, and the rights of women.

The role of the First Amendment in this process was crucial. Ideas do have consequences, and, from his perspective, Mayor Curley's instincts were correct. If you allow people to discuss this issue, many of them might be persuaded. The role of free speech in the early years of modern feminism cannot be underestimated. As Nadine Strossen, president of the ACLU, has put it, "Free speech consistently has been an important ally of the women's rights movement," and "censorship consistently has been its enemy."[29] In this respect, the right of free speech has altered the boundaries of community in America, invalidating the power of one group (in this case, men) to silence and disempower other groups (in this case, women).

The First and the Fourteenth Amendments: MacKinnon's Amnesia

The critical role of the First Amendment in the struggle for women's rights is ignored by a number of prominent feminist legal scholars. Most notably, Catharine MacKinnon, leader of the feminist anti-pornography movement, regards the First Amendment as the enemy of women's rights. In her most provocative treatise, *Only Words*, she declares unequivocally, "The law of equality and the law of freedom of speech are on a collision course in this country." "Until this moment," she continues, "the constitutional doctrine of free speech has developed without taking equality seriously."[30] By protecting sexually explicit material that depicts women in a degrading light, she argues, the First Amendment sustains the larger structure of women's inequality.

MacKinnon's interpretation of the history of the First Amendment is an astonishing example of historical amnesia. Margaret Sanger, Mary Ware Dennett, and the other birth control pioneers simply vanish. Nor does she exhibit any awareness of the struggles of the 1920s and 1930s and the Supreme Court's decisions in *Griswold* and *Roe*. Her view of the First Amendment, in fact, parallels Mayor Curley's in important and disturbing respects. She and Curley both argue that certain categories of speech can be classified as dangerous and threatening to the well-being of the community. Curley, implicitly if not explicitly, understood the sexual political issues that were at stake. He would exercise the power of censorship to maintain a patriarchal society. MacKinnon seems oblivious to both the historical record and the ways in which the power to censor that she endorses can be used in ways that are inimical to the interests of women.

As the vast majority of feminists understand, the attempt to censor sexually oriented materials continues and often has a clearly sexist bias. The views of the majority of feminists can be gleaned from the amicus brief filed by the Feminist Anti-Censorship Task Force (FACT) opposing the Indianapolis antipornography ordinance.[31]

THE FIRST AMENDMENT AND
THE CIVIL RIGHTS MOVEMENT

Eleanor Holmes Norton said it simply and directly: "There was always the First Amendment." Repeatedly in the history of the civil rights movement, the First Amendment has provided a crucial element of protection for individual leaders, organizations, and the idea of racial equality itself. Norton knows the history of the civil rights movement from firsthand experience. She presently is U.S. representative from the District of Columbia, with a record of civil rights work that extends back over three decades. She was a volunteer lawyer in the 1964 Mississippi Summer Project, assistant legal director for the ACLU, commissioner of human rights for New York City, chair of the U.S. Equal Employment Opportunity Commission, and then professor of law at Georgetown University.[32]

Norton's first important ACLU case involved a fundamental test of free speech principles. New York City Mayor John Lindsay denied presidential candidate George Wallace, an avowed segregationist, a permit to speak at Shea Stadium in 1968. A liberal with a strong civil rights record, Lindsay feared that Wallace's speech would inflame tensions in the already racially divided city. There had been a race riot in 1964, and a bitter referendum over a civilian review board had polarized voters along racial lines in 1966.[33] Lindsay's solution to the problem was to deny Wallace a permit to speak.

New at her job with the ACLU, Norton got the case by sheer chance. For years afterward she regaled African American audiences with her account of how Wallace's aides responded when they met their ACLU attorney on the courthouse steps. For the ACLU it was a routine free speech case: affirming First Amendment rights where the speech was offensive to the majority. For Norton herself it was an early test of defending the rights of "the thought we hate."

Even though she was just beginning her legal career, Norton was well aware of how important the First Amendment had been to the civil rights movement. The most numerous and obvious cases involved either offensive speech or mass demonstrations. In the first set of cases an African American protester typically was arrested for disturbing the peace because he called a police officer a "mother-fucker" or some other epithet. In 1972 the Supreme Court ruled on three separate "motherfucker" cases. All involved offensive language by African American protesters, and in all three cases the Court overturned their convictions.[34] (More recently, in the year and half in which the University of Michigan campus speech code was in effect, twenty African American students were charged with offensive speech, while no white students were ever charged with racist speech.)[35]

In the second set of cases, a variety of charges—trespassing, unlawful assembly, riot—were available to authorities who wanted to shut down a demonstration. Rarely, if ever, were white protesters arrested under similar conditions. One of the rarely told stories of the civil rights movement was the long and bitter battle over open housing in Chicago, where African American families moving into previously all-white families were greeted by mob violence. Nor did southern authorities arrest whites who physically attacked African American sit-ins or pickets.

On this issue, the lesson of the civil rights movement was abundantly clear. The idea that some forms of expression could be limited because they were "offensive," "disruptive," or a "threat to public order" was a broad license for authorities to suppress challenges to the established order. The broadest possible protection to offensive speech kept the avenues of protest open.

In this respect, protests against racism and segregation were a central aspect of the historic role of the civil rights movement in redefining the boundaries of the American community: challenging the exclusion of African Americans and demanding full membership. Although the civil rights movement has not achieved full equality in America, it is impossible to imagine the very real gains that have been made without the contributions of the First Amendment.

The speech and assembly cases are, with the benefit of historical hindsight, relatively easy ones. Less well known are another series of cases involving attacks on the NAACP as an organization.[36] They are particularly important not just because they illustrate the expansive interpretation of the Bill of Rights that has been so characteristic of the rights revolution, but as important examples of how the expansive interpretation of rights has redefined the terms of membership in the American community.

The NAACP Cases

In the wake of the landmark 1954 *Brown v. Board of Education,* southern states launched a massive counterattack on school desegregation, the Supreme Court, and the civil rights movement. Southern politicians organized a campaign of "massive resistance" to school desegregation.[37] On September 12, 1958, Governor J. Lindsay Almond of Virginia ordered all the schools in Warren County closed rather than allow them to be integrated under a court order. Later he closed white high schools in Charlottesville and Norfolk. His assumption apparently was that no education for anyone was preferable to racially integrated education. In 1956, 101 southern members of Congress signed the so-called Southern Manifesto denouncing the Supreme Court and promising "to use all lawful means" to reverse the decision.[38] The Ku Klux Klan was revived, beginning a third chapter in its long and violent history.[39] Klan-led vigilante violence increased, and there was a concerted effort to silence moderate white voices, often by driving them out of the South altogether.

A separate line of attack was directed at the NAACP as an organization. Not only had the NAACP argued and won *Brown,* but at that time it was usually the only organized civil rights voice in southern communities. To destroy the NAACP was to cripple civil rights activity. To this end, southern states enacted a variety of laws designed to restrict the organization's activities, either directly or indirectly. Some were direct and crude, such as an Arkansas law that banned NAACP members from public employment. Others were more subtle; one, for example, required public employees to disclose all organizations to which they belonged. The result was a series of Supreme Court cases between 1958 and 1963 that have become known as the "NAACP cases."[40]

The first NAACP case to reach the Supreme Court involved an Alabama law requiring out-of-state corporations to register with the secretary of state. Under the law, state officials demanded to see the NAACP's records, including its membership list. The NAACP supplied most of the requested records but withheld the membership list. Alabama officials took the NAACP into state court, where it was held in contempt, fined $10,000 (with the fine increasing to $100,000), and enjoined it from operating in the state.[41]

There was no secret about the real purpose of disclosing the Alabama NAACP membership list. In the context of southern hostility to court-ordered school desegregation, individual NAACP members would be exposed to harassment, including Klan-led violence. On its face, the law was a neutral and seemingly worthy regulatory measure designed to protect Alabama citizens against unscrupulous operators. In the polarized racial context of the school desegregation issue, however, the practical effect of the law was far from neutral.

The Supreme Court invalidated the Alabama law, taking full account of the context and the likely consequences of the membership disclosure requirement. Writing for a unanimous Court, the conservative Justice John Marshall Harlan wrote that there was an "uncontroverted showing that on past occasions revelation of the identity of its rank-and-file members has exposed these members to economic reprisal, loss of employment, threat of physical coercion, and other manifestations of public hostility."[42]

In upholding the NAACP, the Court fashioned a new principle of freedom of association under the First Amendment. Group association was essential to "effective advocacy of public and private points of view." Compelled disclosure, Harlan continued, was likely to "affect adversely the ability of petitioner and its members to pursue their collective effort to foster beliefs which they admittedly have the right to advocate."[43] Nor were these just any beliefs. The NAACP's principal belief was racial equality, an idea that was a direct threat to the structure of southern society. As the Court clearly recognized, inhibiting the expression of that belief was a way of maintaining the status quo and limiting the membership in the community.

The Court extended the principle of freedom of association in subsequent NAACP cases. An Arkansas law requiring public school teachers to disclose the names of all the organizations they belonged to or had contributed to in the past five years raised even more difficult constitutional questions. The law served a legitimate public purpose—determining the fitness of schoolteachers—and was not specifically directed at the NAACP or any other civil rights organization. (The law, however, replaced a previous one that had barred NAACP members from public employment in Arkansas; the real intent of the law was not hard to see.)[44]

As it did with the earlier Alabama requirement, the Supreme Court responded to the Arkansas law in a subtle and creative way. Once again upholding the NAACP, it held that the underlying purpose of the law was valid but the means were excessive. An overly broad inquiry into private political behavior threatened to "stifle fundamental personal liberties." The government could pursue its legitimate interests, but only through the "least restrictive alternative."

In yet another 1963 NAACP case, the Court put serious limits on the ability of legislative investigating committees to inquire into political beliefs and associations—a protection it had consistently refused to do in a long series of cases involving Communists and suspected Communists.[45] (A number of observers have suggested, somewhat cynically, that it was only the moral authority of the civil rights movement that caused the Court to establish First Amendment protections that it had been unwilling to create in similar Communist-related cases.)[46]

Speech, Association, and Community

The new freedom of association that arose from the NAACP cases offers a different perspective on the issue of rights and community. The NAACP cases are a classic example of the creative and expansive interpretation of the Bill of Rights that has characterized the rights revolution. The word "association" does not appear in the First Amendment. This is precisely the point that enrages conservative critics of the Supreme Court. They see the creation of such concepts as an example of judicial "legislating." The idea that the Court should limit itself to the "original meaning" of the Constitution is their strategy for ending this kind of judicial activism. The NAACP cases, however, illustrate the extent to which the denial of full membership or of active participation in the community can be accomplished in many subtle and indirect ways (as in the southern "fitness" standards for public school teachers). The historic role of the First Amendment, interpreted and adapted to meet current issues, has been to prevent these kinds of subtle restrictions.

Postscript: The Klan's African American Lawyer

A civil rights controversy in the 1990s offers an instructive postscript to the NAACP cases. In response to an apparent upsurge in racist violence, the Texas Commission on Human Rights launched an investigation into the Knights of the Ku Klux Klan and subpoenaed its membership roster, mailing list, and financial records. This sweeping request implicated all of the rights established in the earlier NAACP cases. The Klan sought help from the Texas ACLU affiliate, which readily accepted the case and assigned it to one of its cooperating attorneys, Anthony P. Griffin.[47]

The case quickly attracted national attention because Griffin is an African American and was then general counsel for the Texas chapter of the NAACP. (It is not unusual in those parts of the country where the civil rights bar is relatively small for one attorney to work simultaneously with a variety of rights groups—the ACLU, the NAACP, reproductive rights groups, and so on.) Griffin followed the example of Eleanor Holmes Norton thirty years earlier by honoring the principle that the First Amendment protects everyone, including advocates of the thought we hate. The NAACP took a very different view of this case and, outraged that Griffin was defending the Klan, promptly dismissed him as its general counsel.[48]

The entire case was fraught with ironies. The Klan, hateful as it might be, invoked the principle of freedom of association that had been established in cases involving its social and political opposite, the NAACP. For its part, the NAACP chose to forget its own proud history and to oppose one of its great contributions to constitutional law. A further irony lay in the fact that, in deciding the first NAACP case, *NAACP v. Alabama,* the Court had to pretend that it was not overruling a 1928 decision involving the KKK.[49] *Bryant v. Zimmerman* involved a New York state law requiring the Klan to register and disclose, among other things, its membership list. New York cited the Klan's record of violence, and the Supreme Court upheld the law as a reasonable regulation. Although the Alabama law was essentially identical to the old New York statute, the Court managed to make a distinction (although a rather unpersuasive one). There was also little doubt that the New York law had the same purpose as the Alabama law: to single out certain groups and expose their members to public embarrassment or worse—all for the purpose of restricting an idea deemed contrary to the public interest. Had the Court adhered to the earlier *Bryant* decision, the consequences for the NAACP and the civil rights movement would have been catastrophic.

The various KKK and NAACP cases illustrate the importance of a principled and content-neutral approach to rights. Once we decide that some groups may be singled out as being less than full members of the community—in the form of restrictions that expose them to harassment—we endorse a principle that may return to haunt something we cherish. In various ways, the critics of contemporary First Amendment law who seek exceptions based on the alleged harm of certain forms of speech—racist, sexist, homophobic—would take us down that road.

It is indeed true, as the Critical Race Theorists argue, that current First Amendment law protects members of the Klan and other racists.[50] But the same legal principle that protects the Klan also protected the NAACP in the 1950s and continues to protect militant African American spokespersons today. To suppress the Klan is to risk suppressing a militant minority leader whose ideas may ultimately prove valuable. This presents us with a choice in which both alternatives involve certain risks. The lesson of history would seem to be that in terms of building a more inclusive community we are far better off choosing the risk of more rather than less speech.

COMING OUT AND COMING IN: LESBIANS, GAY MEN, FREE SPEECH, AND MEMBERSHIP

"Socially Abhorrent Activities"

The governor of New Hampshire directed the president and trustees of the University of New Hampshire in 1973 to "rid your campuses of socially abhorrent activities" and spend not one more dollar of public funds on them. The cause of this outburst was a dance sponsored by the Gay Student's Organization (GSO) on campus. The GSO had been quietly recognized as an official student organization, and a November 7, 1973, dance had occurred without incident. News media coverage of the dance, however, inflamed the governor, and he directed the trustees to "reconsider" its position on the GSO. One month later, the GSO sponsored a play on campus. The university approved the play but not a planned social event afterward. During and after the play, some individuals not associated with the GSO distributed some pro-homosexual literature that was characterized by some people as "extremist." That was the last straw for the governor, who ordered the university to ban all "socially abhorrent activities."[51]

Facing the loss of its official status as a recognized organization and a ban on all future activities, the GSO took the university to court, charging violation of its First Amendment rights. The First Circuit Court of Appeals went directly to the heart of the issue by asking whether "group activity promoting values so far beyond the pale of the wider community's values is also beyond the boundaries of the First Amendment."[52] The language of the court's rhetorical question framed the issue of rights and membership perfectly. The very phrase "beyond the pale" says that there are some groups or activities that can be excluded from full membership in the community.

The court then pinpointed the problem posed by its own rhetorical question. "How," it asked, "are the deeply felt values of the community to be identified?" Citing the abortion controversy, it noted that there were deep divisions within the community regarding the correct values. The same was true with respect to socialism, conscientious objection to military service, vivisection, and the building of more oil refineries. The court concluded that it was "unable to devise a tolerable standard" that would define the values of the community and distinguish between permissible and impermissible speech. It then directed the university to recognize the GSO and not restrict any of its activities merely because of the ideas and values it represented.

The University of New Hampshire case was one of a number of college and university cases involving recognition of lesbian and gay student organizations. William Rubenstein, former director of the ACLU Lesbian and Gay Rights Project, points out that the students won nearly all of these cases. More important, he argues that the victories conveyed a message "of vindication, triumph, [and] equality."[53] It is worth noting that the circuit court's opinion in the University of New Hampshire case frequently cited the NAACP freedom of association cases. This is simply one of many examples of where the southern civil rights movement bequeathed a body of constitutional law that has benefited other people and groups.[54]

The importance of the First Amendment for lesbian and gay people can hardly be underestimated. For virtually the entire first twenty-five years of the gay rights movement, the greatest victories have been in First Amendment cases. Rubenstein, whose ACLU project has handled virtually all of the important litigation, explains that "the First Amendment has been the only consistent friend of lesbian and gay rights litigators."[55] Cases argued on equal protection grounds were consistently unsuccessful. And in 1986, in the celebrated *Bowers v. Hardwick* case, the U.S. Supreme Court refused to invalidate a Georgia sodomy law and rejected the idea that sexual activity between two adults of the same sex was protected by the constitutional right to privacy. Gays and lesbians have won almost no important cases on equal protection grounds.[56] (The 1996 decision in *Romer v. Evans,* challenging an anti–gay rights constitutional amendment in Colorado, suggests that the Court might now be receptive to equal protection claims by lesbians and gays.)[57]

Censorship Versus Membership

Censorship has been the paradigmatic experience for lesbian and gay people in the United States and elsewhere—paradigmatic because it is an act of *silencing,* of reducing people to an invisible status in the community. The defining moment for gay people has been the act of "coming out," of publicly identifying one's sexual orientation. Rubenstein notes that speech or some other form of expression is crucial to lesbian and gay people because, unlike people of color, women, the disabled, or other disadvantaged groups, they cannot otherwise be identified. Censorship plays a critical role in suppressing homosexuality: Censorship means silence, invisibility, nonexistence, and nonmembership in the community.

The traditional phrase "coming out" becomes, in the terms of this book, a process of "coming in": of entering the community. It involves a reciprocal process of an individual acknowledging his or her own sexual identity and having that identity acknowledged by the community at large. What was true for the university community in the University of New Hampshire case and others is also true in the larger context of society: official recognition means admission as a member of the community.

This membership, moreover, is a necessary prelude to activity on every other issue that affects or might conceivably affect lesbian and gay people. When the Gay Activists Alliance applied for incorporation in New York State in 1972, for example, it was initially rejected on the grounds that its purpose was to promote activities that were contrary to existing sodomy law in the state. In overruling this denial, a state court ruled that "it is not unlawful for any individual or group of individuals to peaceably agitate for the repeal of any law."[58] And so it is on innumerable other issues: censorship in the arts, AIDS, same-sex marriages, and others. To be able to work publicly on these issues requires that you first have some legitimate status.

Giving Offense

The attempt by various universities, in response to community political pressure, to deny recognition to lesbian and gay student groups offers a valuable perspective on the current controversy over hate speech. Some lesbian and gay activists have joined the Critical Race Theorists and Critical Feminist Theorists in calling for restrictions on offensive homophobic speech. They argue that homophobic speech insults and injures its targets and creates a hostile environment that interferes with the educational opportunities of lesbian and gay students. Along with the Critical Race Theorists, these gay activists argue that by protecting offensive speech, the content-neutral approach to the First Amendment sustains the larger structure of prejudice and discrimination in society. Restricting offensive speech represents a Fourteenth Amendment approach to equal protection, which, in this instance, should prevail over a strict interpretation of the First Amendment.[59]

In response to these demands, a number of universities in the 1980s adopted campus speech codes that restricted offensive speech, some of which included sexual orientation. The University of Michigan speech code was one. The Michigan code, along with that at the University of Wisconsin, was declared unconstitutional under the First Amendment, and the movement for restrictive campus speech codes quickly faded.[60]

The idea of restricting homophobic speech rests on the premise that such speech gives offense, and in particular offends the (egalitarian) values of the university community. But, of course, it was precisely the idea that homosexuality per se offends the values of New Hampshire citizens that prompted the governor to demand that the university deny recognition to the GSO. The point would seem rather obvious: if the main criterion is whether something gives offense to someone or some group, then the question of who gets to speak is nothing more than a matter of power politics. It would seem to be equally obvious that, in any such contest, minority groups (whether racial or sexual) are likely to lose. By removing speech from these political wars, and guaranteeing recognition to all groups regardless of whether they offend someone, the First Amendment is the best guarantee of equality. As Rubenstein puts it, "The First Amendment is not just about free speech, then, but includes within it a narrative of equal rights."[61]

IS THE FETUS A MEMBER OF THE COMMUNITY?
THE SOCIAL VALUE OF OFFENSIVE SPEECH

The scene is now a familiar one. Angry demonstrators outside an abortion clinic scream "Murderer!" and "Baby-killer!" Their targets are the young pregnant women seeking abortions, the clinic staff, and the doctors. Confrontations of this sort, some large, some small, occur every week across the country, as they have for over twenty years.

The rhetoric of the antiabortion movement is extreme, vicious, and personal. We can properly call it "hate speech," as that phrase is now commonly understood. It targets specific individuals, is intended to harass, and causes emotional stress. In the phrase popularized by law professor Richard Delgado, these are definitely "words that wound."[62] Strictly speaking, it might be libelous to call a doctor or a pregnant woman a "murderer," given the fact that an abortion is a legal procedure.

Extreme antiabortion rhetoric raises a fundamental question about the relationship of free speech to community: What is the social value of shouting "Murderer!"? Cass Sunstein, writing from a civic republican perspective, argues that epithets contribute nothing of value to the public dialogue that is crucial to democratic self-government, and therefore should not enjoy First Amendment protection.[63]

Along similar lines, Mary Ann Glendon deplores the "strident" and "absolutist" quality of our rights rhetoric, which polarizes and precludes the possibility of mutual understanding and political compromise.[64] The language of the militant right-to-life movement is nothing if not strident, absolutist, and polarizing.

The relevant question is whether restricting these extreme forms of antiabortion expression promotes a healthier, more inclusive community. (To be fair, we should note that there is a wide range of opinion even among communitarians and civic republicans on this issue. Sunstein endorses restrictions on "epithets." Glendon and Amitai Etzioni, on the other hand, do not recommend censorship. And the Communitarian Network Platform specifically affirms the importance of the First Amendment and rejects any form of censorship.)[65]

My answer is that extreme antiabortion rhetoric has great social and political value. (This is limited to the purely expressive activities and does not apply to criminal acts of trespass and vandalism.) I say this even though I am an uncompromising defender of abortion rights. The immediate costs—the angry confrontations, the bitter rhetoric, the social divisions, the personal hurt felt by its targets— are indeed very real, but they are outweighed by larger considerations. The value in shouting "Murderer!" lies in its role in defining the boundaries of community.[66]

Shouting "Murderer!": Defining the Boundaries of Community

The core idea motivating the right-to-life movement is the passionate belief that the fetus is a person. From this first premise it follows logically that abortion is murder. To terminate a pregnancy is to take a human life. This view arises from deeply felt religious conviction. At least some members of all of the major religions—Protestants, Catholics, Jews, Muslims—find doctrinal justification for their opposition to abortion.[67] In a broader sense, the antiabortion view represents a moral vision of the good society based on the principle that all human life should be protected. The fetus, moreover, merits special vigilance because it is the most defenseless form of life. Pro-choice activists do not disagree on the importance of valuing human life; they disagree over whether the fetus represents a person within the meaning of the law.

Neither the Supreme Court nor the Congress has accepted the right-to-life view about when life begins. Despite the promises of President Ronald Reagan and other Republican Party leaders, Congress refused to seriously consider a constitutional amendment to ban abortion in the early 1980s. The issue was effectively buried on a procedural vote in the Senate in September 1982 and was never revived. And with the 1992 *Casey* decision, the Supreme Court reaffirmed *Roe*'s basic guarantee of a right to an abortion.[68] Significantly, two conservative justices, Sandra Day O'Connor and Anthony Kennedy, provided both the key votes and the intellectual leadership in the decision. Thus, despite a quarter of a century of vigorous protest and a massive and in many respects highly successful political effort, abortion remains a legal medical procedure. To be sure, there are many procedural restrictions on obtaining an abortion (limits on public funding, parental notification, etc.), but abortion per se remains legal some twenty years after *Roe*.

The continued legality of abortion and the failure of conservative politicians to deliver on their promises to outlaw it define the context for the militant antiabortion activities, including the vicious rhetoric. Right-to-life activists see a holocaust: a million and a half "murders" every year in the United States alone. Abortion is now the most frequently performed surgical procedure. The gravity of the moral evil and the seeming indifference of the majority of the country drive antiabortion activists, or at least those on the fringe of the movement, to extreme measures.

Historically, the initial challenge facing people of conscience who believe that a great moral evil exists is to arouse the conscience of others. The opponents of slavery, war, and nuclear weapons instinctively know this. The basic problem, as they see it, is the indifference and moral insensitivity of others. Passionate, uncompromising, and often vitriolic speech becomes a weapon to prick the conscience, awaken the public, and mobilize political support. Supreme Court Justice William O. Douglas eloquently described this process in 1949 when we wrote that free speech "may indeed best serve its high purpose when it induces a condition of unrest, creates dissatisfaction with conditions as they are, or even stirs people to anger."[69] And there can be little doubt that much antiabortion rhetoric stirs people to anger—that is in fact the point.

Shouting "Murderer!" serves a high social and political purpose by attempting to alert the public to a grave moral crisis. Specifically, it asks the public to define the fetus as human life and as a person entitled to the full protection of the law. With respect to the question of community, there is no more important issue than the question of who (or what) is a member of that community. The right-to-lifers are trying to focus that debate on the unborn. If their language is extreme, it is because they see public indifference to this great moral crisis. It is from this perspective that we should consider proposals to limit extreme speech, including epithets, in the name of community.

The Limits of Moderation

Cass Sunstein, writing from a civic republican perspective, argues that the true Madisonian purpose of the First Amendment is to promote the process of self-government. Thus it protects only speech that contributes to "deliberative democracy."[70] Although he does not specifically discuss antiabortion rhetoric, he does argue that certain forms of hate speech, especially offensive epithets, can and should be restricted. He explains, "Standing by themselves, or accompanied by little else, epithets are not intended and received as contributions to social deliberation about anything." Therefore, "it should be permissible for government to build on the basic case of the epithet in order to regulate certain categories of hate speech."[71]

In this analysis, Sunstein is thinking about racial epithets, such as a bigoted white student shouting "Nigger!" at an African American student on campus. At first glance, this argument seems persuasive. It is difficult to find some social value there. But the epithet "murderer," which is no less painful to its target, does have some social and political value. To argue to suppress a right-to-lifer's epithet on the grounds that it has no social value is to effectively silence a political movement. The only alternative is for Sunstein to distinguish between "good" and "bad" epithets. As a practical matter, this is an impossible task. Among other things, it introduces an element of political subjectivity into First Amendment analysis.

The Supreme Court has, in fact, recognized the importance of emotionally charged epithets in free speech. It is found in Justice John Marshall Harlan's opinion in *Cohen v. California* (1971), the famous "Fuck the Draft" case arising out of opposition to the Vietnam War. Paul Cohen walked through the Los Angeles courthouse with "Fuck the Draft" emblazoned on his jacket and was arrested for disturbing the peace. The Supreme Court overturned his conviction. Justice Harlan wrote that speech communicates not just ideas but "otherwise inexpressible emotions as well." The "emotive function," he explained, "may often be the more important element of the overall message sought to be communicated."[72] Cohen's protest would have had substantially less impact if he had been limited to saying "Stop the Draft" or "I Don't Like the Draft." Justice Harlan's opinion recognized that to limit the emotional impact is to limit the scope and potential effect of speech.

One of the chants popular among opponents of the Vietnam War was "Hey, hey, LBJ, how many kids did you kill today?" Since it accused the president of the United States of being a murderer, it is the closest equivalent to the antiabortion "murderer" epithet. Such an allegation leveled against the president is a serious accusation. It was clearly an epithet designed to insult and injure. President Lyndon Johnson himself, who undoubtedly thought he was carrying out his oath of office as best he could, probably took great offense. But, in the terms of the *Cohen* decision, the very offensiveness of the "Hey, hey, LBJ" chant was an essential part of the message. It was designed to get peoples' attention, to awaken them to a grave moral evil, and to recast the terms of the debate over the Vietnam War.

In a similar fashion, it is the emotionally charged aspect of antiabortion epithets that is designed to get our attention and, possibly, change the moral and legal boundaries of society.

The attention-getting aspect of offensive speech has a broad educative function in a democratic process. We can appreciate this in both personal and political terms. My own experience in thinking about abortion and the question of a right to privacy is probably similar to that of many other Americans. As a college student in the early 1960s, I never thought about the question of when life begins. I never asked whether it begins at the moment of conception, at birth, or at some other point. The question did not come up in private conversation, in public debate, or in class. The question of when life begins is certainly an important one, arguably one of the most important ones we can ask about human existence. It is also a terribly complex one, standing at the intersection of morality, philosophy, and science. Clearly, my college education failed insofar as it ignored this question.

For the last twenty years, however, I have thought about this question a lot, for the simple reason that the right-to-life movement has forced all of us to think about it. The militant activism and strident rhetoric of the antiabortion movement have succeeded where my college education failed.

The public opinion polls indicate that, for all its activity, the right-to-life movement has had almost no impact on attitudes toward abortion. Only about 20 percent of the public believe that abortion is wrong in any and all instances. That percentage has not changed in more than twenty years. This is in marked contrast, for example, to the dramatic change in public attitudes toward birth control between the 1920s and the 1940s. Margaret Sanger's issue went from an unmentionable and often censored subject to one that was generally accepted by the majority of Americans. In this respect, free speech for birth control advocates opened the channels of communication and facilitated social and political change.

Offensive Speech and the Moral Vision of the Good Society

Extreme antiabortion rhetoric also poses a serious problem for communitarian critics of rights, such as Mary Ann Glendon and Amitai Etzioni, who want to restore a "moral vision" to American political life.[73] The Communitarian Network Platform declares that our prevailing "language of rights is morally incomplete," lacking any reference to the values of "responsibility" and "duty" that are necessary for maintaining a healthy community.[74] In the place of "radical individualism," the Platform seeks to cultivate the "rich resources of moral voices" that lie in our culture and history.

Applying these precepts to the antiabortion movement creates all sorts of problems for communitarians. Abortion opponents are clearly moved by a moral vision of the good society, one in which all life is protected. They challenge the "radical individualism" that justifies abortion as a matter of private choice, and that Glendon and other communitarians object to so strenuously. At the same time, however, the antiabortion movement represents everything about contemporary rights culture that the communitarians condemn: strident rhetoric ("murderer"), simplistic framing of the issues ("life begins at conception"), an unwillingness to compromise ("no exception for rape or incest"), the lack of civility, and the lack of compassion for people in times of distress (the single pregnant woman).

The communitarians want to have it both ways. They want a moral vision, but not necessarily *that* particular vision, or one that is expressed that way. Both the communitarian and the civic republican positions are elitist and arrogant. They talk in grand, although somewhat vague, terms about restoring a moral vision to our politics, revitalizing public discourse, and strengthening the wellsprings of democracy (which, in their view, have been weakened by judicial interposition). The right-to-life movement is nothing if not an expression of these goals. Yet the communitarians and civic republicans often say that you are not doing it quite the right way: you are too strident, too uncompromising, and too insistent on rights (in this case the rights of the fetus).

The elitist notion that not all speech contributes to the democratic process can be traced back to Alexander Meiklejohn, one of the giants in the field of First Amendment theory.[75] Meiklejohn focused primarily on the role of free speech in the democratic process of self-government. But he argued that "the First Amendment . . . is not the guardian of unregulated talkativeness. It does not require that, on every occasion, every citizen shall take part in public debate." And in an often-quoted phrase, he concluded, "What is essential is not that everyone shall speak, but that everything worth saying shall be said."[76] But as law professor Kenneth Karst has pointed out, the fatal flaw here is that some authority would be required to rule on when "everything worth saying" has in fact been said. More seriously, it would authorize some authority to rule that certain speech is not worth saying.[77]

Another troubling aspect of the communitarian position is that it trivializes the moral vision of the right-to-life movement. By asking everyone to lower their voices, to tone down their rhetoric, and to seek compromise, the communitarians do not take seriously the sincere belief that the fetus is human life. It is extraordinarily arrogant to advise people who passionately believe that abortion is murder to compromise that principle. Glendon is the strongest advocate of this approach, but one wonders if she has really tried it with militant abortion opponents. Would she ask opponents of the death penalty to compromise their moral vision about the sanctity of life?

In his most recent communitarian manifesto Amitai Etzioni outlines the "Rules of Engagement for Values Talk." In debating important social and political issues, we should not demonize the other side, "not affront the[ir] deepest moral commitments," use "less of the language of rights and more of that of needs, wants, and interests," and, finally, "leave some issues out of the debate."[78] This is a truly astonishing set of rules. In effect, they say, let's not talk about anything serious. If you really believe the other side is committing murder (abortion, war, genocide), you are morally compelled to accuse them of that. Demonizing the other side is in fact a way of framing the debate in moral terms. And if we leave some issues out of the debate, presumably the most difficult and sensitive ones, what is there to debate? It would be interesting to see Etzioni apply retroactively his own rules of engagement to a debate with Nazi leaders in the late 1930s.

The same criticism applies to Cass Sunstein's concept of deliberative democracy.[79] What do we deliberate about? What issues are on the agenda of democracy? To suggest that some ideas or some modes of expression are not legitimate is to impose arbitrary limits on that process. At best, it is arrogant and elitist; at worst, it is the position taken by every repressive regime in history. In a similar fashion, Columbia law professor Kent Greenawalt tries to square the circle in his recent book, *Fighting Words*. First he argues that epithets intended primarily to humiliate should not be protected by the First Amendment. But in the next breath he holds that certain "abusive words" should be protected when they have some "general public significance."[80] To repeat our question: Who is to decide which abusive and insulting words have this public significance? The antiabortion militant would certainly argue, and I would agree, that shouting "Murderer!" has that public significance.

We might ask how Glendon and Sunstein would have responded to earlier social and political movements. A century and a half ago, would they have counseled abolitionists to lower their voices and moderate their opposition to slavery? It was precisely the intransigent moral fervor of the abolitionists that forced the country to confront the issue of slavery. Can there have been any political dialogue in our history more important to the definition of our community? In the early 1960s, would they have advised civil rights groups to be less militant in challenging segregated lunch counters? It was the massive and uncompromising character of the sit-ins and other civil rights demonstrations that forced the country to deal with Jim Crow in the early 1960s. Does Glendon advise opponents of the death penalty to be less extreme in denouncing capital punishment as "legalized murder"? Should they instead seek some compromise "middle ground"? Perhaps Glendon could explain where the middle ground between executions and no executions lies. Perhaps she could explain to death penalty opponents why they should compromise on the issue of life. Should pacifists moderate their opposition to war?

CONCLUSION

The boundaries of community are continually in flux, always being challenged by new claims for membership. The First Amendment fulfills its classic role of facilitating peaceful social change in a democracy by keeping open the channels of communication and allowing new ideas to be heard. The examples from American history reviewed in this chapter illustrate the critical role of free speech in allowing powerless groups to be heard and to win a place in the American community.

We cannot know who or what group will make a claim for membership in the future. The animal rights movement, for example, makes a claim that the creatures conventionally defined as "animals" are entitled to many of the same rights as human beings.[81] In short, they should be admitted as members of the community. Similarly, pursuing a comment made by Justice William O. Douglas in an environmental law case, law professor Christopher Stone asked whether trees should have standing to sue in court.[82] This idea argues, implicitly, that objects in the natural environment have at least some limited "rights" in the sense that human beings do. These questions are closely related to the more urgent one discussed earlier about whether the fetus is a person with rights.

This is not the place for a full discussion of whether animals and redwood trees should have rights. (Having thought about it during the course of writing this book, I have concluded that they should not.) The point is simply that the boundaries of community are continually being tested, as new ideas arise and as people rethink their perspective on the world. The right of free speech fulfills an essential function in keeping open the channels of communication, facilitating social change, and making possible the continuing redefinition of the American community.

Chapter Five
THE CONFINED AND THE ACCUSED

KENNETH DONALDSON: HARMLESS BUT CONFINED

KENNETH DONALDSON spent fourteen years in the Florida state hospital. Originally diagnosed as a "paranoid schizophrenic" in 1957, he spent most of those years in a locked room with fifty-nine other patients. His "treatment" consisted of an average of about fourteen minutes per year with a psychiatrist. Although never diagnosed as dangerous to himself or to others, he was not allowed to participate in occupational therapy programs and was denied grounds privileges that would allow him to leave his room.

After suing the state of Florida for violating his constitutional rights, Donaldson was finally released in 1971. Three years later, the Fifth Circuit Court of Appeals upheld his release in a decision that considered "for the first time the far-reaching question of whether the Fourteenth Amendment guarantees a right to treatment to persons involuntarily civilly committed to state mental hospitals."[1]

The Confined and the Rights Revolution
Kenneth Donaldson's case is emblematic of one of the most important components of the rights revolution: the rights of institutionalized persons, notably the mentally retarded, the mentally ill, and prison inmates. At the same time, the courts also established new rights for public school students, their teachers, and military personnel.[2] Litigation in these areas not only sought to protect the rights of individual plaintiffs but also represented a new strategy of social reform: to change public institutions through constitutional litigation. Thus, much litigation looked beyond the immediate

interests of the plaintiffs in the case to broader questions of institutional practices and social policy.[3]

One result of this reform strategy was the intervention of the
federal courts into the details of prison and hospital administration. Federal judges assumed the task of prescribing minimum
standards such as the size of prison cells and the proper staff-
patient ratio for hospitals.[4] In some instances, judicially appointed
"special masters" or other oversight bodies assumed a key role in
running institutions.[5]

The intervention of the courts transformed the culture of these
institutions. Notions of rights penetrated deep into their daily life,
restructuring the balance of power and altering the consciousness of
everyone involved. As the discussion in Chapter 2 indicated, public
school officials are alert to potential lawsuits in every problem that
arises and every decision they make. Prison wardens are similarly
preoccupied with actual or potential prisoners' rights litigation. Prisoners have learned that the law gives them some potential leverage
over their keepers. When a new inmate enters prison, one of the first
steps is the presentation of a copy of the official rules and regulations—a brief summary of the prisoner's rights, and the avenues of
redress if he or she thinks some injustice has been done.[6]

Rights litigation has also changed the politics of public institutions. Many policy decisions are constrained by actual or potential
litigation. Governors and legislators have been confronted with radically escalating costs of public institutions, as they have been
forced to comply with court-ordered minimum standards. In some
instances, prison officials have covertly welcomed an ACLU prisoners' rights suit as a means of leveraging construction appropriations
from an otherwise reluctant legislature.[7]

In short, the impact of the rights revolution on public institutions sweeps far beyond specific holdings in court decisions related
to individual rights, encompassing everything from day-to-day
institutional life to broad external questions of politics and social
policy. Conservative critics argue that the net result has been social
chaos. They see the growth of the rights of prisoners and students,
in particular, as limiting the power of officials to control the unruly.[8]
Institutions become overwhelmed with disorder and violence. Critics cite the fact that in the Texas prisons, fifty-two inmates were
murdered and over seven hundred stabbed in 1984 and 1985 as a
consequence of the implementation of the prisoners' rights suit *Ruiz
v. Estelle.* The decision in *Ruiz* ordered a complete overhaul of the

management of Texas prisons, including an end to using inmates as guards. The violence that ensued was more than had occurred in the previous decade.[9] (The critics do not, however, point out that the number of murders subsequently fell to a rate comparable to those in other state prison systems.)[10] The critics argue that as a result of litigation, the horizons of administrators shrink and focus on day-to-day "crisis management" instead of addressing broad institutional goals. Paralyzed, institutions drift. Prisons neither rehabilitate criminals nor deter crime; public education declines, and with it America's future. Richard E. Morgan, one of the harshest critics of the rights revolution, argues, "The disappointing contemporary performance of American public education . . . has almost nothing to do with money and almost everything to do with the erosion of the moral authority of teachers, administrators, and parents."[11]

For their part, the rights advocates who led the attack on prisons and mental hospitals were profoundly chastened by the mid-1980s. The mid-1960s had been a period of boundless optimism about the possibilities for sweeping institutional reform. Aryeh Neier, who as executive director of the New York Civil Liberties Union (NYCLU) had played a major role in this movement, characterized the mood of the period as one of "the courts can-do-anything."[12] By the late 1980s, these goals had been, at best, only partially fulfilled. Instead of a court order and quick institutional reform, prisoners' rights activists have found themselves engaged in lengthy and often frustrating struggles to implement their nominal victory. Along with many of the original leaders of the movement to reform institutions through litigation, Aryeh Neier looked back and found that their efforts had been "only modestly successful."[13] Much had been accomplished, but much remained to be done to make prisons and hospitals decent and effective institutions.

Considerable scholarly energy has been devoted to assessing the full impact of the rights revolution on public institutions. There is a vigorous debate over prison conditions and whether a generation of prisoners' rights litigation has improved them or made them worse. The answers are not immediately clear because the subject has proved to be so enormously complex.[14]

This chapter examines the impact of rights-oriented litigation on public institutions, mental hospitals, prisons, and the police. One of the main points is that, even to the surprise of the activists who brought this litigation, the development of new legal rights for the confined had a powerful impact on society outside the institutions that were originally sued. To be sure, the institutions themselves were transformed, making them more humane and professionally managed. At the same time, by dissolving the boundaries between the confined and society at large, rights litigation transformed the nature of community in America.

THE "WILLOWBROOK WARS"

How Geraldo Got His Start

The neglect and deprivation of liberty that Kenneth Donaldson suffered during his fourteen years in the Florida State Hospital were relatively mild compared with the fate of Paula Silvers. In 1972, she was one of 5,400 patients in Willowbrook, the New York hospital for the retarded on Staten Island. On their visits to the hospital, Paula's parents often sensed that something was terribly wrong. They would find the daughter bruised and bitten, and no staff person seemed able or willing to explain the injuries. The waiting room where they picked her up for outings was filthy and smelled of urine. Profoundly brain damaged, Paula could not tell them about her situation, but her sobs and moans, which usually grew louder as they brought her back to Willowbrook, told them it was a fearful place.[15]

The situation at Willowbrook changed dramatically on January 6, 1972. Michael Wilkins, a staff member who had been fired the day before for protesting conditions in the hospital, made a surprise return with an investigative reporter and camera crew from a New York City television station. The reporter was a young and then-unknown Geraldo Rivera. His sensational report on conditions in Willowbrook, broadcast that night, catapulted him to national fame and set in motion a long legal battle over the rights of Willowbrook's patients.[16]

Rivera's tapes exposed the ghastly conditions in Willowbrook. The ten-minute segment caught glimpses of children with spindly, twisted arms and legs and swollen heads. Children crouched on the floor, naked and unattended. One room had no furniture except for a wooden bench and a chair. Toilets were broken, there was often no toilet paper, and the walls were covered with feces. Because of understaffing and absenteeism, one attendant often supervised as many as one hundred retarded children. Children like Paula Silvers were repeatedly attacked by others. And yet, in one of the most shocking aspects of the entire story, despite these conditions and the near-complete absence of medical treatment and programs, Willowbrook was fully accredited by the proper medical authorities.

The Willowbrook Litigation

Geraldo Rivera's revelations about conditions in Willowbrook led to a class action suit by the NYCLU on behalf of the clients. The case arrived at a propitious moment in American history. New ideas about the scope of constitutional rights were percolating through society, among civil liberties activists, and in the law schools. The civil rights movement had fostered a new and expansive thinking about human freedom and the role of the Bill of Rights. The Supreme Court, which was then at the high point of its activist, libertarian phase, encouraged rights activists to pursue new issues and new arguments. As Aryeh Neier put it, the prevailing mood among civil libertarians was that "the courts-can-do-anything."[17]

The ACLU, which had been drawn into the civil rights movement in the Deep South and in northern ghettos, was particularly receptive to new ideas about the rights of persons in large public bureaucracies. The leaders of the NYCLU conceptualized the problem in terms of what they called the "enclave" theory. As they saw it (and sketched out on a delicatessen napkin over lunch in midtown Manhattan), American society was filled with enclaves of despotism, in the form of public bureaucracies, where the Bill of Rights had no practical meaning.[18] The ACLU, as well as other public interest groups, found financial support for these new and expensive efforts in a number of private foundations, which were equally influenced by the new climate.

The NYCLU had taken on the issue of the rights of New York City public school students who had been expelled for exercising their right to protest, with no due process and in a pattern that reeked of race discrimination. In 1972 the ACLU was consolidating prisoners' rights efforts from Virginia, New York, and other states into a National Prison Project that over the next quarter century would sue virtually every state prison system.

The Willowbrook case became an important early chapter in an emerging concept of a "right to treatment" for medical patients. Morton Birnbaum, both a physician and a lawyer, had published a pioneering law review article on this idea in 1960.[19] The social, political, and legal climate of the United States was not ripe for this radical concept in 1960, but by the end of the decade all the necessary elements were in place: new ideas about the law; institutional support from the ACLU, other advocacy groups, and sympathetic foundations; and sympathetic federal judges.

Kenneth Donaldson presented an opportunity to put Birnbaum's theory to the test. Judge David Bazelon was the first judge to acknowledge it, in a 1966 decision involving St. Elizabeth's Hospital in Washington, D.C.[20] Another suit on behalf of patients in the Alabama state mental hospital system produced a favorable ruling in 1971.[21] The Willowbrook case brought together all the forces in this new area: a new theory of rights, the institutional support of the NYCLU, financial support from private foundations, and creative lawyers such as Bruce Ennis, the lead NYCLU attorney, and Charles Halpern, head of the Mental Health Law Project. Halpern's organization was one of the early and influential public interest law firms that played a major part in the rights revolution.[22]

In the spring of 1975, three years after filing their initial suit against Willowbrook, the NYCLU lawyers won what seemed at the time to be a momentous victory. The twenty-nine-page decision by the relatively conservative Judge Orrin Judd not only established minimum standards for Willowbrook but also committed the state to reducing the hospital's population from over 5,000 to 250 within six years. In a radical experiment in deinstitutionalization, the patients were to be placed in community facilities representing the "least restrictive alternative."

Deinstitutionalization was not a new idea by 1975. For nearly twenty years, reformers in several areas of social policy had been questioning the wisdom of segregating people in large institutions. Many argued that large hospitals and prisons did more harm than good to their clients. Advances in pharmacology had facilitated the treatment of the mentally ill in community-based facilities or through outpatient care.[23] In the area of correctional treatment, states greatly expanded community-based probation and parole systems. As a result, the national prison population actually declined in the 1960s, even as the crime rate began a dramatic rise.[24]

In the larger context of the deinstitutionalization movement, the Willowbrook patients represented a special class of persons. Many were severely handicapped and thought to be completely incapable of surviving outside of an institution. That, in fact, was one of the main reasons the ghastly conditions in Willowbrook had continued to exist. Society preferred to keep these problem cases out of sight and out of mind. Parents were co-opted into this arrangement because institutional confinement freed them of what in many cases would have been an impossible burden of caring for their severely disabled children. In certain respects, then, a conspiracy of silence surrounded the conditions in Willowbrook.

As it turned out, Judge Judd's 1975 decision was the beginning and not the end of the struggle. The history of the Willowbrook litigation is described in detail in the *Willowbrook Wars*, by David and Shelia Rothman. A professor of history at Columbia University and a committed civil libertarian, David Rothman had previously published a highly praised and extremely influential history of the origins of the American prison in the early nineteenth century. *The Discovery of the Asylum* was deeply skeptical about the capacity of prisons and other institutions to treat their clients, and equally skeptical about the motives of prison reformers.[25] Shelia Rothman, meanwhile, had abandoned the social work career for which she was trained and was studying the history of women in social reform. In short, their professional and personal commitments were ideally suited for a study of the Willowbrook case.[26]

The Rothmans describe in agonizing detail how the case dragged on for a decade, consuming far more time and money than anyone had ever expected. At the outset, the activist civil libertarians thought it would be a relatively simple matter of documenting the wrongs, litigating the case, winning the suit, and then watching the court enforce its decree to remedy the wrongs. It was not to be that easy. Cases involving institutional reform proved to be fundamentally different than the typical First Amendment case that ACLU attorneys were familiar with. In a free speech case, the court decision orders the parade permit or invalidates the law, and that is the end of the matter. As the ACLU's new National Prison Project also discovered, implementing a court order regarding a large public bureaucracy is enormously complicated. The original Willowbrook decision plunged the litigators into a long battle with neighborhood leaders, the legislature, the governor, and the human services bureaucracy.

Although it ultimately may have failed to achieve some of its objectives, the Willowbrook suit effected a revolution in the care of the mentally retarded in New York State. The official data on institutional populations tell part of the story. In 1976, the state of New York had 20,000 retarded persons in its care, all of them housed in large institutions like Willowbrook. By 1982, there were 25,000 clients, but 13,000 were in community placements—foster care, group homes—where the basic conditions were decent and where they were able to achieve a measure of normal human existence.[27]

National trends paralleled developments in New York. The number of residents in state facilities for the mentally retarded declined by nearly two-thirds between 1970 and 1993, from 189,956 to 73,856. At the same time, the number of facilities rose from 190 to 1,756. The decrease in the average population from about 1,000 to about 40 reflected the shift from giant institutions such as Willowbrook to small, community-based facilities. Meanwhile, the number of private facilities increased fivefold between 1977 and 1993, from 10,219 to 58,790 (unfortunately, the number of residents in these institutions is not published).[28] At the same time, the population of state psychiatric hospitals fell from 457,000 people in 1972 to 158,000 in 1990.[29]

These numbers, however, do not begin to tell the story of the impact of deinstitutionalization. Placing the mentally retarded had a billiard ball effect, setting in motion a host of changes: arousing opposition in several quarters, creating new constituencies for change in others, and introducing new, complex, and completely unanticipated issues related to the rights of the mentally retarded. These issues reach far beyond the specific legal points in the case and touch on the definition of community in America.

Community Placement/Community Hostility

The effort to place the Willowbrook patients in community settings introduced an entirely new and unanticipated chapter of the saga. The Metropolitan Placement Unit (MPU), a new agency created to develop community facilities, soon found that the fiercest opposition came from the residents of neighborhoods where it sought to establish group homes. According to the Rothmans, these angry property owners represented "the most prominent barrier to group homes."[30] Neighborhood leaders expressed great concern for the safety of the retarded children, but it was plainly evident that they were really worried about their property values. They were afraid that a group home would set in motion a downward spiral of neighborhood deterioration and wipe out the value of their homes. It was also clear that their opposition reflected traditional stereotypes of the retarded as people who are subhuman and probably dangerous.[31]

The MPU eventually succeeded in overcoming much of the neighborhood opposition and establishing group homes, in large part because it was blessed with extremely imaginative and tenacious leaders who developed skillful political tactics. This primarily involved cultivating sources of support for group homes within neighborhoods. The Catholic Church proved to be particularly supportive. The MPU found that economic self-interest could cut different ways. In some instances the Church owned property that could be converted into facilities for the retarded. Even more important, the MPU discovered that some real estate companies had extensive property holdings that were suited for group homes. These interest groups became converted into active supporters of group home placement. Meanwhile, newly activated parents' groups and other advocates for the retarded emerged as neighborhood-based supporters of community placement.

The Rothmans conclude that one of the unanticipated effects of the Willowbrook case was the creation of "constituencies for change *after* the fact."[32] Community placement aroused opposition in some quarters but called into being important new sources of support in others. As I will discuss in more detail shortly, one of the issues in cases such as Willowbrook is the question of who speaks for the powerless. The point here is that implementation of the court's decision created new advocates for those who cannot speak and act for themselves.

The Retarded and the "Community"

The fierce neighborhood opposition to community placement of the Willowbrook patients exposes another dimension of the relationship between rights and community. Neighborhood leaders fought to preserve the quality of life in their communities, as they understood it, which, to be blunt about it, was defined largely in terms of protecting property values. The idea of community placement, and the underlying concept of normalization, represented a different and more cosmopolitan definition of community. It is cosmopolitan in the sense that it defines community in broader geographic terms (New York State rather than a local neighborhood), uses general categories of people (the retarded, as opposed to our neighbors), and frames the issues in terms of broad social policy (the treatment of the retarded, as opposed to the condition of our neighborhood). Furthermore, it pursues its goals by relying on an agency of the national state (the federal courts) to enforce abstract legal principles.

The point, of course, is that there is no consensus over what different people mean by "community." Moreover, some definitions are not necessarily the most attractive to anyone outside the immediate group. The property values orientation of the neighborhood residents in the Willowbrook struggle defined community in the narrowest, crassest, and least humane terms. A similar dynamic lies at the heart of the entire history of housing discrimination in this country. The preservation of "community" usually means keeping out "others" who are perceived to be "different" and as such a threat to property values. In the end, the cosmopolitan, rights-based definition of community triumphed over the parochial, neighborhood-centered definition. The net result was a more inclusive, tolerant, and human-centered (as opposed to property value–centered) definition of community.

The conflict between different definitions of community poses a serious challenge to communitarianism, which posits a dichotomy between "rights" and "community." As I will argue at greater length in the next chapter, there are at least five different definitions of community; moreover, these conceptions of community often conflict. To invoke "community" as an alternative to "rights" is to gloss over the kind of problems that arose in the Willowbrook case.

Community placement of the Willowbrook patients had other far-reaching ramifications. In the most literal sense, patients entered the community. Instead of being segregated and set apart, they were now living in group homes or with foster parents. The Willowbrook settlement reflected the concept of normalization that had already won much support in the mental health field. Normalization holds that the mentally ill and the mentally retarded are far more capable of living normal lives than was previously thought, and that official policy should be directed toward that end.[33]

The concept of normalization challenges the traditional stereotypes of retarded persons as less than human and potentially dangerous to others. In this respect as well, rights-oriented litigation redefined the boundaries of community. David Rothman's history of the origins of the prison, published in 1971 and now widely regarded as a classic, argues that the prison, the insane asylum, and similar institutions defined their clients as "others," as threats to social stability, and segregated them from the community.[34] Community placement was a radical break with this historic tradition. The retarded now not only reside in the community in a literal sense but also, through their physical presence, impinge on our consciousness, forcing us to acknowledge their existence, their humanity, and their claims upon us.

Perhaps nothing better symbolizes the transformation of the status of the mentally retarded in the last quarter century than the behavior of one of the most prominent families in the country. One of the leading advocacy groups working for the mentally retarded is the Joseph P. Kennedy Foundation. The Kennedy family created the foundation because Rosemary Kennedy, sister of the late president and current senator, was mentally retarded. Yet, as is well known, the Kennedy family's public acknowledgment of her condition and their own interest in this issue were very late in coming. For many decades, they treated Rosemary's retardation as something too shameful to even mention. During the time of John F. Kennedy's presidency, the family lied, claiming that Rosemary was working with children in Wisconsin when in fact she was institutionalized there after having had a lobotomy.[35] The change in the behavior of the Kennedy family is emblematic of the change in societal values. A condition that was once too shameful to mention publicly is now one that can be acknowledged and accepted; members of the family who once had to be hidden from view are now a part of the living community.

Who Speaks for the Powerless?

The Willowbrook suit gave the retarded a meaningful voice in community affairs, albeit through surrogates in the form of their attorneys. In this respect they were no longer passive recipients of care who depended on the paternalistic benevolence of others. The judicially defined rights of institutionalized persons that emerged in the 1970s gave them a "voice" in the same way that the expansion of First Amendment rights gave other groups a voice.

The role of public interest lawyers raises difficult questions about who speaks for those who cannot speak for themselves, and who speaks for the public interest. The standard criticism of public interest lawyers is that they represent an elite who pursue their own agenda, defined by abstract legal principles, rather than the best interests of their clients. Robert H. Bork, for example, believes that the "cultural disaster" engulfing the United States is a result of a liberalism foisted on the country by the "cultural elite."[36] It is from this perspective that we should consider the failure of other voices in the larger community to effectively speak for the Willowbrook patients.

The parents of the Willowbrook patients represented one obviously important voice. They were organized through the New York State Association for Retarded Children (NYARC). Organized in

1948, this group had about thirty thousand members by the early 1970s. Its leader, Joseph Weingold, was a vigorous lobbyist with a creditable record of winning support for the retarded in the New York legislature.[37] But as the conditions in Willowbrook clearly indicated, there was much that he and NYARC had not been able to do to secure even minimally decent treatment for its members' children. In effect, Weingold and the parents made a painful compromise. Certainly, many knew that conditions were terrible at Willowbrook and other institutions. But they also could not imagine any alternative to institutional confinement for these severely retarded children. Thus, they accepted present conditions and found hope and self-respect in working to improve them, however, marginally. Accepting the compromise, however, severely limited their horizons. And it is in this context that the NYCLU activists and the new generation of mental retardation professionals represented such a radical break: not bound by the compromise, they could imagine a different world.

Whereas we can understand the compromise made by the parents, and the painful choice it represented, it is difficult to exculpate the medical profession, which was probably the most powerful group with respect to Willowbrook and its clients. Geraldo Rivera's exposé clearly indicated the extent to which it had failed. The most telling aspect of this failure was Willowbrook's continued accreditation. As the Rothmans point out, the accrediting body functioned "not as a scrupulous auditor but as a sympathetic fellow administrator."[38] The 1967 accreditation report, for example, noted the evident problems of "overcrowding and understaffing," high staff turnover, and the quality of some staff, but it nonetheless ended on a positive note. Willowbrook was "on the move" and "headed in the right direction" under a "very dynamic" superintendent.

The ghastly conditions in Willowbrook in January 1972 exposed the accreditation process as a sham that excused current conditions instead of pointing toward minimally decent conditions. To a certain extent, the medical profession made its own compromise. It was responsible for a large public bureaucracy that needed many millions of dollars but operated in an environment where many other social services competed for precious tax revenues. The medical profession's compromise, not unlike the parents', was to work for incremental improvements. This, of course, meant not thinking about radical alternatives and accepting conditions that in their hearts they must have known were unacceptable. Unfortunately, in this context of public budgeting, the mentally retarded children in Willowbrook were too easily forgotten. Aryeh Neier suggests that rights litigation may have had more impact with respect to the mentally retarded because they "had been even more hidden from public view than other institutional inmates" and as a result were "previously confined in the worst conditions of all."[39]

Voices and Empowerment

The question of who speaks for the powerless offers a valuable perspective on another frequent criticism of the rights revolution. Communitarian and conservative critics argue that the prominent role of the federal courts in social policy has "disempowered" local communities. Mary Ann Glendon, for example, argues that "gradually, the Courts removed a variety of issues from legislative and local control."[40] This loss of control has two dimensions. One refers to the day-to-day operations of public institutions. According to Glendon, the most notable aspect of this process, "from the average citizen's point of view, was the active role that lower federal court judges assumed . . . using their remedial powers to oversee the everyday operations of prisons, hospitals, and school systems." Political philosopher Michael J. Sandel, in a recent and highly praised book, *Democracy's Discontent*, sees a "loss of mastery" in the contemporary American society dominated by judicially enforced rights. "Despite the expansion of rights and entitlements," he writes, "Americans found to their frustration that they were losing control of the forces that governed their lives."[41]

At first glance, the Willowbrook case appears to be an excellent example of this judicial "usurpation." New York State authorities lost their previously unrestricted power to set policy for care of the retarded. Administrators of both the remaining large institutions and the new community-based facilities operated within the framework of court-imposed standards. Neighborhood residents, meanwhile, lost the power to control their communities. Power shifted to a mix of "outsiders": a federal judge, the ACLU lawyers, and the national-level professional experts retained by the plaintiffs.

Viewed from the perspective of the Willowbrook patients, however, the story acquires a very different meaning. When Sandel writes that "Americans" are "losing control," we are entitled to ask which Americans he is referring to. The Willowbrook patients certainly did not lose control of their lives. Nor did their parents. Both groups, in fact, gained enormous new powers, and the quality of their lives improved immeasurably as a result. To be sure, the patients and to a large extent their parents exercised this power only through their advocates, the public interest lawyers, but they gained power nonetheless. And with that power came a new degree of membership in the community. It is also proper to raise questions about the values and objectives of the groups that lost power in this process. The neighborhood residents' values were defined, literally, in terms of property values. State officials, and the voting public that elected them, mainly lost the power to keep the severely retarded children out of sight and out of mind, where they were subject to the horrendous conditions exposed that night in January 1972.

As the Rothmans noted, the court order created new constituencies for change; that is to say, it created new advocates for the powerless. The net result is not the "disempowerment" and "loss of control" that Glendon, Sandel, and other critics see but an expansion and broadening of participation. As the Rothmans put it, "Decisions made on behalf of a minority will not spur an endless chain of seemingly autocratic rulings, *but enhance political involvement, reducing the insularity of the minority that caused much of the problem in the first place.* [emphasis added]"[42] In short, the ironic result of the intervention of elitist and undemocratic courts is a more democratic and inclusive community.

It would seem that Sandel, Glendon, and the other communitarian critics of the rights revolution have ignored both the language and the spirit of the famous footnote 4 of *United States v. Carolene Products,* the 1938 decision that may be regarded as the founding statement of the rights revolution. Justice Harlan Fiske Stone wrote that "prejudice against discrete and insular minorities may be a special condition . . . which may call for a correspondingly more searching judicial inquiry."[43] The original Willowbook children are precisely the kind of "insular," and we might add powerless, minority the Court had in mind. Judicial intervention on their behalf has served to bring them into a greater measure of community membership.

The Expansive Dynamic of Rights

Another important dimension of the case is the extent to which, to the surprise of the original group of lawyers, implementation of the Willowbrook settlement generated a host of new problems, including new and unanticipated civil liberties issues. Rights litigation had an expansive dynamic: the establishment of one fairly limited right set in motion a chain of events that raised new and often more difficult ones.

As already noted, the effort of neighborhood residents to block group homes introduced the aspect of housing discrimination. Although a relatively new issue at the time, federal law now prohibits discrimination in the location of group homes for the retarded or other facilities for persons classified as disabled.

Even more significant was the impact of community placement on the public schools. New York school officials were simply not prepared to handle a group of students who, because of the severity of their retardation, had such special needs. Complicating the problem was the prevalence of hepatitis B among Willowbrook's former patients, and the health risk they posed for other public school students.[44] School officials refused to accept them, and the Rothmans argue that the opposition by the New York City Board of Education and the Department of Health was "the single most unanticipated conflict" in the entire Willowbrook story.[45]

As with housing, federal legislation ultimately addressed this issue. The 1975 Education for All Handicapped Children Act requires all school districts receiving federal aid to provide educational services for all handicapped students.[46] The result has been a revolution in special education across the country. In 1970, it was estimated that at least 2 million handicapped children were not enrolled in school at all. By the early 1990s, there were 4.5 million children enrolled in special education programs.[47]

The impact on public schools has been enormous. In addition to huge costs related to special education, the schools have been enveloped in elaborate legal procedures related to the classification of handicapped students, controversies over the quality of educational programs, and a thorny church-state problem with respect to public funds for handicapped students in parochial schools.[48] School administrators and local taxpayers, who regard the federal mandate as overly burdensome and frustrating, yearn nostalgically for the simpler days of the past. The costs are real, in terms of both dollars and the pains of litigation. But when we consider this issue from a community perspective, it is clear that the old days were simpler because we excluded an entire group from full participation.

National data on children enrolled in special education add a poignant perspective to the issue of stereotyping the mentally retarded. Between 1980 and 1993, the percentage of all the children in special education programs who were classified as "mentally retarded" fell from 21.7 to 11.3 percent. The percentage of those classified as "learning disabled," meanwhile, rose from 31.9 to 51.3 percent.[49] One of the main reasons for this shift has been the desire of parents to avoid having the stigmatizing label of "retarded" placed on their children, and their preference for the more precise label of "learning disabled." This dynamic suggests the extent to which normalization is not merely an abstract concept dreamed up by isolated professionals and enforced by remote federal judges. It indicates, instead, the powerful and fully understandable desire of parents to have the children they love treated as normal human beings as nearly as possible.

These aspects of the Willowbrook case offer a perspective on the allegation that the rights revolution involves an uncontrolled and destructive "rights inflation." According to Communitarian leader Amitai Etzioni and conservative columnist George Will, new rights are being "minted" every month, creating what they see as absurd categories, such as the rights of single people, and devaluing truly important values such as freedom of speech.[50]

The Willowbrook case illustrates the extent to which much of our national experience over the past quarter century has involved not the creation of new rights but the application of established rights in new contexts (as in the principle of fair housing related to group homes for the retarded) and the process of working out the full implications of a new principle. (To cite perhaps an even more complex and controversial example, when the Supreme Court enunciated a constitutional right to privacy in the 1965 *Griswold v. Connecticut* case, few people imagined the many issues that would eventually flow from it: a right to abortion, a teenager's right to abortion, the issue of "fetal abuse," and so on.)

Rights, as I argued in chapter 2, involve claims on others. In the typical free speech controversy—when someone burns the American flag, for example—the basic claim is one of tolerance for a speaker or idea that offends us. But the speech itself is easily avoided. The Jewish residents of Skokie could easily have stayed at home, with the shades pulled, to avoid the planned Nazi demonstration in 1976 (no "march" through town was even proposed).[51] Institutional reform cases such as Willowbrook, however, involve inescapable claims, such as the financial cost of special education programs. We should think of these costs not as some externally imposed "unfunded mandate" but as an inevitable part of a more inclusive community. The exclusion and consequent stereotyping of the severely retarded children that prevailed prior to the Willowbrook suit was terribly efficient. It was far cheaper than our current programs and relieved parents of a burden they could not bear alone. It is difficult to argue, however, that it represented a humane and inclusive form of community.

An International Perspective

As a final note on the "Willowbrook Wars," we should consider international developments with respect to the rights of the mentally retarded. Mary Ann Glendon and other critics of the rights revolution argue that the American approach to rights is uniquely harmful in its extreme pursuit of individual rights at the expense of the needs of the community.[52] Yet, as I argued in chapter 2, the international human rights movement of the past half century suggests that the United States is not so unique after all. The case of the mentally retarded supports this interpretation.

On December 20, 1971, the United Nations adopted the Declaration on the Rights of Mentally Retarded Persons, which affirms the principle that "the mentally retarded person has, to the maximum degree of feasibility, the same rights as other human beings."[53] In short, such persons are full members of the community. The declaration goes on to enumerate specific rights, including the right "to proper medical care and physical therapy and to such education, training, rehabilitation and guidance as will enable him to develop his ability and maximum potential." The declaration also expresses the same preference for community placement found in the Willowbrook settlement, asserting, "Whenever possible, the mentally retarded person should live with his own family . . . and participate in different forms of community life." Finally, the retarded are entitled to due process in the form of "proper legal safeguards" in any procedure restricting their rights.

In short, the basic principles of the UN Declaration on the Rights of Mentally Retarded Persons are indistinguishable from those that have guided the American movement for the rights of the mentally retarded. If policy in this country is different from that in other countries, that is more likely a consequence of our generally inadequate system of social services. In fact, we may be more litigious because those services are so often inadequate, as they were at Willowbrook in 1972, and because our legal framework of constitutional rights provides a viable avenue for attacking those problems.

An Imperfect Outcome

Deinstitutionalization, of both the mentally retarded and the mentally ill, has by no means had a completely happy ending. One of the alleged effects, in fact, has been cited as evidence of the disastrous consequences of the rights revolution.

According to some critics of current social policy, the related problems of homelessness, crime, and the deterioration in the quality of civic life are a direct result of the movement to secure the rights of the institutionalized. According to this argument, tens of thousands of people who are not able to completely care for themselves have been "dumped" on the city streets. We should note quickly, however, that this argument is generally made with reference to the mentally ill rather than the mentally retarded. According to the critics, these deinstitutionalized persons often become homeless, and either criminal offenders or crime victims. They degrade the quality of civic life in many ways: by sleeping on the street, in parks, or in subway or train stations; by aggressive panhandling; and often by urinating in public. Some critics blame much, if not most, of the homelessness problem on deinstitutionalization and the movement for the rights of the confined. This is seen as just one more way in which the rights revolution has destroyed the fabric of American life.

In a sober examination of the problem of the homeless, social critic Christopher Jencks takes a hard look at this argument.[54] This is not the place for a full review of his superb review of this social problem, but it is appropriate to examine his analysis of the relationship between the problem of homelessness and the rights of institutionalized persons. He begins by sorting his way through the controversy over the actual number of homeless people in America. He debunks the highly publicized estimate of "one million homeless" offered by activist Mitch Snyder as completely without foundation. The evidence suggests that there were slightly more than two hundred thousand homeless in 1984 and that the number nearly doubled by 1987–88 and then fell to about three hundred thousand by 1990.[55]

Jencks cites deinstitutionalization as one of several possible explanations for the increase in homelessness (among others are the crack epidemic, changing employment and marriage patterns, "the destruction of skid row," and budget cuts). He quickly points out two problems with the alleged connection between deinstitutionalization and homelessness. First, studies have consistently found that only about one-quarter of the homeless had spent time in a mental hospital; one study estimated that 33 percent had been diagnosed as currently mentally ill.[56] The surveys, of course, did not examine causality, and it is entirely possible that many of those 33 percent developed mental health problems *after* becoming homeless or as a result of their homelessness. In short, deinstitutionalization of the mentally ill could, at most, account for only a part of the homeless problem.

More serious is the fact that deinstitutionalization began in the late 1950s, long before homelessness became a political controversy in the early 1980s. In fact, the major decline occurred between 1960 and 1970, well before rights litigation could have had any impact. Kenneth Donaldson's case was not settled until 1974, and the initial Willowbrook decision occurred the following year.

Jencks persuasively argues that "deinstitutionalization was not a single policy but a series of different policies."[57] Moreover, the policies that were adopted before 1975 tended to work, while those that followed in later years tended to aggravate the problem of homelessness. The pre-1975 policies included an intellectual revolution in the medical field that questioned the effectiveness of long-term institutionalization; the arrival of Medicaid in 1965, which offered federal funds for outpatient care but not hospitalization; the development of new drugs that allowed people to function in society; and a 1972 change in Social Security policy that provided Supplemental Security Income (SSI) for people who could not hold a job because of mental illness. As of the mid-1970s, these changes had not produced a serious problem of homelessness.

The post-1975 policy changes did, however. Most important was the national tax revolt that led to major cutbacks in social services for the mentally ill at the state level. In the early 1980s, the Reagan administration cut back funding for Community Mental Health Centers and dropped nearly three hundred thousand people from the Social Security rolls, including Jencks's estimate of perhaps one hundred thousand with mental health problems. According to Jencks, "Almost everyone agrees that what happened to the mentally ill after 1975 was a disaster."[58]

Who, then, is to blame for this disaster? Jencks sensibly points out that "both liberals and conservatives blame this disaster on their opponents," adding quickly that "both are half right."[59] It is clear that the rights revolution, meaning specifically the rights of institutionalized persons, was at most only one of several factors in deinstitutionalization. This will come as something of a disappointment to many in the ACLU who would like the organization to take credit for the revolution in social policy. Moreover, the post-1975 disaster was primarily the result of economic changes and the deterioration of the safety net of social services. The 1996 welfare reform law represents a radical reversal in social policy and a much smaller safety net. In light of Jencks's analysis, one can only anticipate a worsened disaster beginning in the year 2000 when needy persons begin to exhaust their three year limit on benefits.

The problem of the homeless adds further perspective on Mary Ann Glendon's communitarian argument that our rights culture aggressively pursues individual rights and ignores social responsibilities.[60] Glendon's attack, however, is misdirected. Implicitly, she suggests that the ACLU, the NAACP, and the National Organization for Women are responsible for the problems of the needy, rather than the business community, the Republican Party, and conservative ideologues who have relentlessly fought the development of a comprehensive network of social services. Jencks's evidence suggests that a variety of economic and social welfare policies, and not judicially enforced rights, are responsible for the problems associated with the homeless.

THE PROCESS WE ARE DUE: INDIVIDUAL RIGHTS AND INSTITUTIONAL REFORM

In 1976, Burt Taylor, Jr., an inmate in the Nebraska penitentiary, sued the state to recover some hobby materials that prison officials had lost through negligence. The items in question were worth exactly $23.50. His case ultimately reached the U.S. Supreme Court, which ruled (*Parratt v. Taylor*) that Taylor had not been denied due process of law under the Fourteenth Amendment because the state tort claims law provided him with an adequate avenue of relief regarding the loss of his property.[61]

The *Parratt* case is a classic example of what many critics see as the utter madness of the rights revolution. As Justice William Rehnquist put it in his opinion in the case, "One might well inquire why respondent brought an action in federal court to recover damages of such a small amount." Critics of the rights revolution have a ready answer to his question. Inmate Taylor went to court, and eventually reached the Supreme Court itself, because we have developed a culture of rights that not only makes such action possible but even

encourages it. Not only was there a legal principle and a set of prece-
dents that gave Taylor the possibility of winning, but there is a civil
rights bar—what has been called the "rights industry"—willing and
able to assist him with his case.[62] The case was in fact handled by the
ACLU, whose National Prison Project has been the workhorse of
prisoners' rights litigation. The result was that a seemingly trivial
incident, involving only twenty-three dollars, occupied the federal
courts for five years and consumed a considerable amount of our
time, money, and energy, including that of the U.S. Supreme Court.

The nature and impact of due process rights related to criminal
suspects and prisoners is a particularly volatile aspect of the rights
revolution, in large part because of the pervasive public alarm about
crime. The idea that judicially enforced limitations on the police are
responsible for high crime rates first entered American politics in
1964.[63] Because the argument was made by conservative Republican
candidate Barry Goldwater and segregationist Alabama Governor
George Wallace, it was dismissed as a racist attack on the civil rights
movement.[64] Steadily over the next thirty years, however, more and
more Americans accepted this view and demanded "get-tough"
anticrime measures. In national politics, Republicans successfully
seized the crime issue as their own. Most political analysts argued
that a major part of President Bill Clinton's electoral and public
opinion success in 1996 was due to the fact that he recaptured the
crime issue by convincing the public that he was as tough on criminals as the Republicans.

In a nutshell, the conservative criticism is that judicially enforced
rights of suspects and prisoners have "disabled" institutions—the
police and prisons—and as a consequence harmed society by allowing crime to flourish.[65] As a number of critics put it, a society cannot
call itself free if its citizens live in daily fear of crime. Amitai Etzioni,
leader of the Communitarian Network, adds that if we don't take
reasonable measures to control crime, the public will demand
extreme policies that will represent genuine government tyranny.[66]

Because of the intense public concern about crime, this attack
has completely obscured the extent to which judicial protection of
the rights of suspects and prisoners has been a crucial instrument of
institutional reform, with broad benefits for the community as a
whole. The connection between the rights of the criminal suspect
and the larger community is difficult to see, even for many experts
in the criminal justice field, because the changes occur over the
course of years or even decades in a subtle and incremental manner.

The Courts and the Cops

According to a commander in the narcotics section of the Chicago Police Department, the exclusionary rule "is not a detriment to police work. In fact, the opposite is true. It makes the police department more professional. It enforces appropriate standards of behavior."[67] Many other Chicago narcotics detectives seconded his opinion. Such comments from a working police officer come as a surprise to most people. We are not accustomed to hearing police officers defend the constitutional rights of suspects, certainly not the highly controversial exclusionary rule which prohibits the use of evidence obtained through an illegal search.[68] The Chicago Police Department, it might be added, has not always had a reputation for high standards of professionalism.[69] And finally, narcotics detectives, who among all police officers are most often affected by the exclusionary rule, might be expected to be its most bitter opponents.

These comments were elicited in a fascinating study of the impact of the exclusionary rule by Myron Orfield in the 1980s.[70] Ignoring the rhetoric of ideological conservatives, he went directly to the source and asked working police officers what they thought about the rule. Instead of hostility, he found a high degree of support for this allegedly unreasonable constraint and a keen appreciation of its role in maintaining standards of professionalism.

The 1961 *Mapp* decision prompted a number of institutional reforms in the Chicago detective unit. In one of the most important changes, prosecutors began screening applications for search warrants to make sure they met the proper legal standard of probable cause. This practice apparently began on an informal basis in the 1960s and was formalized in a written policy directive sometime in the mid-1970s. (Orfield was able to locate one policy directive dated 1980 and a revision issued in 1984; veteran officers informed him of the earlier practices.)[71] From one perspective, this practice represented a new mode of supervision, filling a large and important void. From another perspective, it represented an in-service training program, as officers are repeatedly instructed in the current law of search and seizure. As a part of the general reform process, the state's attorneys office initiated a program of formal training in constitutional law issues for Chicago police officers. Coverage of Fourth Amendment issues in the Chicago Police Academy's recruit training also increased. Orfield talked to one officer who reported that there had been no training related to search-and-seizure issues when he joined the force in 1954.[72]

The changes stimulated by *Mapp* (and, by extension, other key decisions) represented a great leap forward in the direction of greater professionalism, by any definition of that term. Police reformers had been urging improvements in police training since early in the twentieth century, but with only limited success.[73] In passing, it might be noted that the closer cooperation between police and prosecutors helped to overcome the "fragmentation" of the criminal justice system. One of the standard criticisms of that system in the 1960s was directed at the lack of cooperation between police, courts, and correctional officials.[74] The exclusionary rule, by giving both sides an incentive to cooperate, addressed this problem in a largely hidden but nonetheless important way.

In addition to the supervision of warrants, the advent of the exclusionary rule produced a "dramatic" increase in the use of warrants by narcotics detectives.[75] The Fourth Amendment permits two kinds of searches and seizures, with or without a warrant, barring only "unreasonable" searches. Common sense suggests that searches with a warrant are likely to be more valid than on-the-street warrantless searches. The grounds for the search have been reviewed and approved by an independent authority, thereby curbing the tendency of the police officers to undertake an impulsive, spur-of-the-moment search. In the 1960s, according to Orfield, Chicago narcotics detectives hardly ever used warrants at all; by the 1970s, warrants were widely used, and evidence obtained through warrant-based searches was rarely, if ever, suppressed. One officer reported that, based on his own experience in court, "the vast majority of your on view [warrantless search] cases are losers."[76]

The police department instituted office performance rating systems that used instances where judges had excluded evidence as an indicator of poor performance (particularly in narcotics cases, suppression of evidence often results in the dismissal of the case). According to one supervisor, two or more suppressions in a year would directly translate into a lower rating. As one detective put it, "If it is something you did wrong, you are set down and talked to. . . . Two big ones and you're out."[77]

Finally, there is the matter of the officers' experience in court. Traditionally, cops have regarded this experience as a degradation ceremony, where the defense attorney tries to win the case by embarrassing and humiliating them on the stand. The Chicago detectives Orfield interviewed, however, said that while they were subjected to vigorous challenges when testifying, it was the best training they got. Instead of a classroom lecture about abstract legal principles, the courtroom experience provided very practical training in legally permissible search-and-seizure practices. One officer said, "You get evidence suppressed and you try to do it differently from that point on, and that's all there is to it."[78]

It might be added that one of the reasons that cross-examination was such a humiliating experience in the past was that the untrained and poorly educated officers (about 80 percent had only a high school education in the early 1960s) were totally outclassed by defense attorneys.[79] By stimulating higher recruitment standards and more extensive training, *Mapp* and the other Supreme Court decisions on police practices helped to put police officers on a more even footing for these on-the-stand confrontations.

Communicating Values

In ways that are subtle but nonetheless powerful, the organizational reforms resulting from the intervention of courts communicate a set of positive, community-centered values within the police subculture. This aspect of the rights revolution has been almost completely neglected in the midst of the relentless attacks on judicial protection of the rights of suspects. With respect to values, the critics of rights see judicial intervention producing only negative ones. Elaborate standards of due process, they argue, foster a legalistic culture that transforms the criminal process into an adversarial "sporting context" rather than a search for truth. (Actually, Roscoe Pound made the same argument in the 1920s.)[80]

As Orfield's research suggests, judicial intervention helped to create a culture of accountability. Even the officers have come to accept, however grudgingly, the idea that there are limits on their behavior and that they have to answer to someone for their actions. To fully appreciate the full impact of this development, it is necessary to take a brief excursion into the history of American policing, and the history of police misconduct in particular.

One of the central themes of American police history is the long tradition of utter police lawlessness. Until the due process revolution made its first tentative appearance in the mid-1950s, there were, for all practical purposes, no meaningful controls over on-the-street police behavior.[81] Officers were free to do what they wanted, and they knew it. It requires little imagination to guess how the famous New York City detective Alexander "Clubber" Williams got his nickname.[82] Everyone in the department, from sergeants to police chiefs, took no interest in the problem of police brutality. The police department "manuals" were tiny books that could fit in a shirt pocket and said nothing about the use of physical or deadly force, or treating citizens with courtesy and respect. The mayors and city council members who had formal authority to oversee the police were primarily interested in the opportunities for graft and jobs for their friends.[83] Nor was there a local NAACP or ACLU office ready and able to handle a police brutality case.[84] The victim of a brutal police beating had nowhere to turn. By contrast, the London police were subject to strict administrative controls from the very beginning and developed a reputation for restraint and professionalism that contrasted sharply with that of their American counterparts.[85]

Some idea of the quality of American policing can be gleaned from the 1931 Wickersham Commission Report entitled *Lawlessness in Law Enforcement*, the first comprehensive study of what was then called the "third degree" and what we call police brutality. The report found "the inflicting of pain, physical or mental, to extract confessions or statements" was "extensively practiced" across the country. Newark police used "protracted questioning, long starvation, several nights' loss of sleep," and beatings with rubber hoses. In San Francisco, reporters in the press room could regularly hear the cries of suspects being beaten across the hall. Detectives in Cleveland forced one suspect to strip naked and lie on the floor, then lifted him up by his genitals to force a confession. Detroit police put suspects "around the loop," moving them from station house to station house to isolate them from family, friends, and lawyers.[86] Orfield heard reports of a similar practice in Chicago, along with stories of hanging suspects out a ninth-floor window.[87] The chief of the Buffalo police summed it up by announcing, "If I have to violate the Constitution or my oath of office, I'll violate the Constitution."[88]

By the 1950s, the Los Angeles Police Department was almost universally regarded as the paragon of professionalism, with an allegedly strict system of internal discipline and a reputation for doing police work "by the book." Nevertheless, its value system was radically skewed. Officers could expect severe punishment for damaging a patrol car but did not have to worry about even a serious inquiry if they shot or killed a citizen.[89]

The values embedded in the principle of accountability have a broad community orientation. They include respect for all citizens and equality. Even the vilest criminal is due a minimum level of respect, and there can be no systematic mistreatment of groups, whether they be racial minorities, the homeless, homosexuals, or any others. The very idea of accountability itself embodies the notion that others, and the community as a whole, have a claim on you, and can properly ask you (the police officer in this instance) to explain your behavior.

The communication of values through legalistic rules is perhaps best illustrated by the recent developments in the area of police use of deadly force. Through the early 1970s, most police departments operated under the old "fleeing felon" rule, which permitted them to shoot to kill any fleeing suspect. This wholesale delegation of discretion transformed the cop on the street into judge, jury, and executioner. With this broad license, the police shot and killed unarmed fourteen-year-old boys suspected of burglary (as was the case with Edward Garner, whose case ultimately reached the Supreme Court). Not surprisingly, most of the victims in these outrageous shootings were African American. In some years during the 1960s, the ratio of blacks to whites shot and killed by the police was as high as eight to one.[90]

Beginning in the early 1970s, and as a result of sustained protests and litigation by civil rights groups, police departments replaced the fleeing felon rule with the "defense of life" rule, limiting the use of deadly force to the protection of the life of the officer or some other person. The rule is now accompanied by elaborate reporting and review mechanisms to ensure compliance. As a result, the number of people shot and killed by the police dropped nearly 40 percent between the 1970s and the 1980s. The number of police officers feloniously killed in the line of duty dropped even more during the same period—despite the proliferation of violent drug gangs, automatic weapons, and drive-by shootings of citizens.[91]

The defense of life rule dramatically altered the values of the police department. The old fleeing felon rule valued arrests, communicating in unmistakable terms that if it was necessary to shoot someone to make an arrest, so be it. The defense of life rule reverses the order of priority, placing the highest value on the protection of life. Where there is no such threat, arrest is a secondary priority; if an unarmed suspect escapes, so be it.

In a similar fashion, recent police policies mandating arrest in domestic violence incidents communicate the value of equal protection. They advise officers that they may not devalue an assault on a woman either because she is a woman or because she is married (and thus the "property" of her husband).[92] Recent restrictions on high-speed pursuits by police officers communicate a scale of values similar to the deadly force rules. The new rules typically limit chases of persons suspected of minor crimes and/or chases where road conditions or pedestrian traffic might endanger the lives of the officer or others. The basic values are clear: protection of life takes precedence over arresting suspects.[93]

The new scale of values is communicated to officers not in a one-time classroom lecture that is quickly dismissed or forgotten but in a formal written policy that governs day-to-day work. These written rules are part of the notorious "paperwork" that is alleged to be one of the worst aspects of modern bureaucracies. The standard criticism of bureaucracies is that their obsession with formal written rules and reporting requirements is a dead hand that stifles flexibility, creativity, and organizational change. The case of police use of deadly force suggests, to the contrary, that written rules are the vehicle for communicating values and controlling behavior in the direction of greater fairness and equal treatment.

Institutional Reform

A similar process of institutional reform arising from the intervention of the court has occurred in the area of corrections. Prisoners' rights litigation spurred three important professional associations to develop minimum standards for prisons and other correctional facilities.

The case of the American Bar Association Standards entitled *The Legal Status of Prisoners* is instructive. The ABA began working on the comprehensive *Standards for Criminal Justice* in 1963. The issue of the rights of prisoners was not included in the original project. As the ABA later explained, "The virtual absence of prisoner-rights litigation and dearth of publications about problems in corrections at that time generated no need for bar leadership to provide guidelines in the area."[94] It took the prisoners' rights movement to provoke the ABA to even think about this issue. The resulting standards reflected most of the issues that the prisoners' rights movement had litigated: First Amendment rights, such as mail privileges and reasonable visitation rights; minimum standards of medical care (it says something about the previous state of the prisons when the ABA has to declare that "prisoners should receive routine and emergency medical care";[95] due process rights in disciplinary hearings, and so on.

As has been the case with police organizations, the ABA standards on the rights of prisoners reach deep into prisons and transform the organizational climate in important respects. Perhaps most important in this regard are the standards stating that "correctional authorities should promulgate clear written rules for prisoner conduct" and that "a personal copy of the rules should be provided to each prisoner upon entry to the institution."[96] This is supplemented by the recommendation that each prison facility have a "formal procedure to resolve specific prisoner grievances."[97] Both of these recommendations, which have been largely implemented across the country, have established the rule of law in prisons (at least with respect to staff-inmate relations) and curbed the arbitrary exercise of total power that characterized the history of prisons prior to the 1960s.

The prisoners' rights movement also prodded the National Council on Crime and Delinquency (NCCD), a correctional reform organization with roots in the Progressive Era, to promulgate its own Model Act for the Protection of Rights of Prisoners in 1972.[98] Finally, and perhaps most important for the long term, the American Correctional Association (ACA), representing prison officials, established a formal accreditation process for correctional facilities in 1970 and published its first set of standards in 1977.[99] The accreditation movement essentially institutionalized a process of professional self-regulation that had been completely missing prior to the advent of the prisoners' rights movement. (A similar accreditation movement in law enforcement emerged a few years later and continues today, although with significantly less impact than the movement in corrections.)

In short, the argument that the rights revolution has "crippled" public institutions such as prisons and reduced them to chaos overlooks both the immediate improvements in institutions and the long-term process of institutional reform that it provoked.

CONCLUSION

This chapter began with the story of Kenneth Donaldson, who sat for fourteen years in a state mental hospital, confined and untreated. Our brief excursion through the history of the Willowbrook case and police reform has argued that the rights revolution's focus on the rights of the confined and criminal suspects has had a sweeping impact on society. Rights litigation on behalf of the mentally retarded brought these individuals out of the shadows of confinement and neglect and gave them a voice in community affairs.

In the terms defined by Michael Walzer, it conferred community membership upon them.[100] In the process, such litigation redefined the boundaries of community and forced society to come to terms with its obligations to those who are dependent on others. In a similar fashion, judicial protection of the rights of criminal suspects has stimulated long-overdue reforms within police organizations and has altered the values of those institutions and the people working in them. The critics of the rights revolution, focusing only on certain negative consequences, have failed to appreciate the broad social benefits that have resulted from the introduction of a rights culture in our public bureaucracies.

Chapter Six

THE LIMITS OF COMMUNITARIANISM

THE COMMUNITARIAN ALTERNATIVE

THE MOST IMPORTANT alternative to the idea that rights should serve as the organizing principle for law and public policy is the philosophy known as *communitarianism*. The basic principle of communitarianism is that individual rights should be balanced by responsibilities: responsibility to the needs of the larger community and responsibility for one's personal behavior. The Communitarian Network Platform declares that no community can "long survive unless its members dedicate some of their attention, energy, and resources to shared projects. The exclusive pursuit of private interest erodes the network of social environments on which we all depend."[1]

The communitarians agree with social conservatives such as William J. Bennett and Robert H. Bork that the question of rights and responsibilities is fundamentally a cultural problem. It is not a matter of a particular set of Supreme Court decisions, or even of the Court itself, but a deep and fundamental set of values. The value of individual freedom has degenerated into a cult of irresponsible self-indulgence. As communitarian leader Etzioni puts it, our society needs to move "back to we."[2]

This chapter examines the communitarian alternative, focusing on the specific policy proposals offered by the leading communitarians. The first section examines the official Communitarian Network Platform, which translates general principles into a concrete program of action.[3] The second section returns to the subject of the international human rights movement, examining the communitarian argument that other countries offer a model for the proper balance of rights and responsibilities. The third section discusses the communitarian argument that corporations should be more responsible to the communities in which they are located. The final section explores the basic question of what communitarians mean by "community."

The Origins of Communitarianism

Communitarianism originated in academic circles in the 1970s, developing somewhat independently among political philosophers, legal scholars, sociologists, and others. The most important center of intellectual activity was in the field of philosophy, where communitarianism emerged as a response to John Rawls's enormously influential book, *A Theory of Justice*. Building on a philosophical tradition that reaches back to Locke and Kant, Rawls argues that "each person possesses an inviolability founded on justice that even the welfare of society as a whole cannot override."[4] This conception of justice, with the individual and the rights of individuals as the foundation, provides a philosophical basis for the contemporary rights culture.

Communitarian critics of Rawls, notably Harvard political philosopher Michael J. Sandel, argue that he posits an atomistic view of individuals that completely ignores the social dimensions of human existence. Rawlsian notions of justice assume that society should be governed by principles of equity and fair play that "do not themselves presuppose any particular conception of the good."[5] This is simply an elaborate way of stating contemporary law with respect to free speech: society's rules (in this case the First Amendment) should guarantee everyone the right to speak without presuming that any particular speech or idea is preferable ("the good"). Communitarians are deeply troubled by this purely. procedural approach that does not define any substantive values: the emphasis on *rights* but not on *rightness*; on the right of free speech but not on the right thing to say; on the right to sexual freedom but not on the right kind of conduct.[6]

Along similar lines, a group of legal scholars, while deeply committed to principles of individual liberty, began to argue that the law of rights had been carried to an unwarranted extreme, claiming that

excessive concern with individual rights had undermined important and necessary aspects of constitutional democracy. This school
of thought came to be known as *civic republicanism*. Cass Sunstein of
the University of Chicago Law School argues that the central purpose of the Constitution is not to protect individual rights for the
sake of rights but to promote democratic self-government. Thus, for
example, the First Amendment does not (or at least should not) protect racial epithets. Such insults express no ideas and contribute
nothing to the process of "deliberative democracy."[7]

Communitarianism entered the political arena in 1990 when
sociologist Amitai Etzioni organized the Communitarian Network,
a nonprofit public interest group. Etzioni is a widely published
scholar, with a long-standing interest in public policy and a more
recent concern with the moral dimensions of public policy.[8] In
1995, he was elected president of the American Sociological Association. The Communitarian Network adopted an official platform,
established a journal, *The Responsive Community*, and published
position papers on a number of public policy questions.[9]

The appeal of communitarianism to self-professed liberals and
conservatives lies in its comprehensive explanation of current social
problems—everything from crime and drugs, to the alleged deterioration of national politics—and an alternative political philosophy
based on noble, altruistic principles. Who, after all, could disagree
with the idea that we should take an active interest in public affairs
and, in doing so, place the common good above our own narrow
self-interests?

For a brief period, it appeared that the Network might have some
significant impact on public policy. It had the support of both a
number of politicians, such as then-Senator Bill Bradley, and prominent intellectuals. President Bill Clinton and Hillary Rodham Clinton both indicated that communitarianism represented their values,
and the president appointed Communitarian Network cofounder
William A. Galston to his staff as deputy assistant for domestic
affairs. Galston was a faculty member of the Institute for Philosophy
and Public Affairs at the University of Maryland, as well as the
author of *Liberal Purposes*, a highly regarded critique of the philosophical underpinnings of modern liberalism.[10] By 1996, however,
Galston had resigned his White House position, and it was difficult
to identify anything distinctively communitarian in the administration's policies. If anything, the 1996 welfare reform law was a complete violation of communitarian principles.[11]

The Varieties of Communitarianism

Communitarianism is not a monolithic school of thought or a cohesive movement. It is a broad intellectual current, with adherents in the fields of law, sociology, philosophy, and political science. No single version has any claim to orthodoxy. The leading thinkers differ in terms of their points of emphasis, their specific proposals, and the quality of their arguments.[12] Etzioni's two most recent books are little more than political tracts, with some often embarrassingly simpleminded thoughts. At one point he seriously suggests that we can change society by joining community folk dancing groups or holding neighborhood potluck dinners.[13] Mary Ann Glendon's work, on the other hand, is a richly informed analysis of our new culture of rights.[14] William Galston and Michael Sandel have written serious intellectual books, but at an abstract theoretical level that never quite comes to grips with the day-to-day problems of ordinary Americans.[15]

THE COMMUNITARIAN NETWORK PLATFORM

The Communitarian Network merits special attention because it has attempted to translate general communitarian principles into a concrete program of action, which is found in the Network's official Platform. Our inquiry is animated by a simple question: Does that Platform represent a meaningful program for changing American law and policy in a more positive direction?[16]

The Platform opens with a declaration of the basic communitarian themes. We need a new "moral voice" in American politics; our current "language of rights" is "morally incomplete," particularly with its neglect of individual responsibility; there has been an erosion of "the network of social environments on which we all depend." The specific proposals include strengthening the family, restoring moral education to the public schools, reforming the political process, responding to the problem of hate speech, and enhancing public safety. Let us examine each of these items.

Strengthening the Family

To build a healthy society on communitarian principles, the Communitarian Network Platform says we must "start with the family."[17] In this respect it captures the widespread concern about the alleged collapse of the family in contemporary America. The Platform sees the family as the primary locus of "moral education and character formation," and therefore the development of morally responsible citizens requires healthy families. The Platform argues, however, that in our success-oriented society, parents have become preoccupied with "making it" at the expense of attention to the needs of their children. From the communitarian perspective, this is a classic example of individuals placing their self-interests ahead of their responsibilities to others, even their own children.

The Platform offers two specific proposals for shoring up the family: workplace reforms to allow parents more time for their families and discouraging divorce. The workplace reforms include parental leave, flextime, shared jobs, opportunities for work at home, and greater opportunities for parents to work in child care centers. These ideas are all worthy and long overdue. There is little doubt that a comprehensive parental leave program would make life much easier for most Americans and would greatly ease the burdens of raising a family. The United States is the only industrialized country without such a program of paid leave. The 1993 Family and Medical Leave Law is pathetically inadequate by international standards and was enacted only with major compromises forced by the fierce opposition to it.[18]

The problem with these proposed workplace reforms, however, is that they have little connection with the standard communitarian criticisms of rights. A program of paid parental leave, for example, is fully compatible with a rights-based society. It could represent an extension of individual rights into the economic sphere and could be justified under the rubric of childrens' rights. Many international human rights declarations incorporate economic rights along with political and civil rights, and several have specific provisions related to the economic needs of families and children. The Universal Declaration of Human Rights, for example, affirms a "right to work," "just and favorable remuneration," sufficient for "an existence worthy of human dignity," "the right to rest and leisure," and "special care and assistance" for mothers and children."[19] The 1989 Convention on the Rights of the Child states that children have a right to a "standard of living adequate to the child's physical, mental, spiritual, moral, and social development." To that end, each country has an obligation to "provide material assistance and support programmes, particularly with regard to nutrition, clothing and housing."[20]

Communitarian leader Mary Ann Glendon argues that Americans could benefit from borrowing international concepts of rights and responsibilities,[21] an idea that will be examined in more detail later. On this particular issue, however, it does not necessarily follow that the expansion of economic rights would require weakening political and civil rights. Glendon, Etzioni, and other communitarians have created a false dichotomy between civil liberties and desirable social welfare policies.

The question of economic rights has, in fact, been the subject of a long-running debate within the ACLU. For over thirty years, a minority faction in the organization has sought to expand the official ACLU agenda to include constitutional guarantees of food, jobs, and shelter. The majority in the ACLU has consistently rejected this proposal and maintained the organization's focus on traditional political and civil rights, addressing the problems of poor people through established principles of equal protection, freedom of association, and due process (as in the right of welfare recipients to due process in eligibility proceedings.)[22] It would seem that if communitarians were interested in developing a program of economic rights, they should align themselves with the ACLU minority. Instead of endlessly bashing the ACLU for its "radical individualism," they should support its more radical wing.

The fact that the leading communitarians choose to attack the ACLU rather than support a broader agenda of rights is symptomatic of a larger problem within the Communitarian Network: a refusal to attack the powerful economic and political groups that are responsible for our inadequate social welfare policies.[23] The lack of a comprehensive system of social services, including paid family leave, in this country is hardly the fault of the ACLU, the NAACP, NOW, or any of the other rights groups. It is wholly due to the fierce opposition of the business community, its conservative allies in the Republican and Democratic Parties, and the conservative intellectual community.[24] These forces have been extraordinarily successful in labeling proposals for expanded social services as "big government" or "socialism," if not "communism." Etzioni and Glendon are discretely silent about these powerful interest groups, however. Instead, their relentless attacks on rights imply that the ACLU and other rights groups are to blame for our inadequate network of social services. Their choice of villains not only ignores the realities of American politics but also represents a cynical political cop-out.

The second family-oriented proposal in the Communitarian Network Platform calls for discouraging divorce. This, too, addresses a subject of widespread concern. About half of all first marriages today end in divorce, and there is special concern about the economic consequences of divorce for both recently divorced women and their children. This is one of the factors that contributes the fact that the United States has a higher rate of children living in poverty (22 percent of all children and 46 percent of African American children) than any other industrialized country.[25] There is also a widely recognized connection between single-parent families and poor school performance, delinquency, drug abuse, and other social problems. The trend in the law over the past thirty years has been to ease the restrictions on obtaining a divorce. The underlying principle of no-fault divorce is consistent with the general thrust of the rights revolution: that marriage should be a matter of free choice and that the state should not impose any undue restrictions on that choice. Although reform of the divorce laws was originally seen as a step in the direction of women's liberation, some feminists now argue that no-fault divorce laws have had a disastrous effect on the economic status of newly divorced women.[26] There is much debate over the impact of no-fault divorce and on the causes of childhood poverty in this country. But even if we assume for the purposes of discussion that divorce has harmful social consequences, the Communitarian Network Platform offers little more than vacuous rhetoric as a response. In fact, it explicitly disavows any desire to make divorce more difficult to obtain. Instead, it recommends that "divorce laws should be modified, not to prevent divorce, but to signal society's concern" that divorce is bad.

In practical terms this "signaling" of concern means nothing. The Platform does not even propose any statutory language that would express the desired "signal." The entire discussion manages to ignore the fact that as a matter of long-standing custom (as opposed to law) we have always signaled this concern and communicated the high value we place on marriage. Marriages are accompanied by large, happy ceremonies that bring families together, while divorces are shameful, embarrassing, and painful events. Apart from the occasional cynic who throws a "divorce party," no one celebrates divorce.

Yet, in the face of this deeply ingrained custom, American divorce rates are high. Neither the Communitarian Platform nor the manifestos by Etzioni or Glendon offer any serious discussion of the factors contributing to this problem. In particular, there is no reference to the changing American economy, the decline in real earnings since the mid-1970s, the erosion of health care benefits, and the consequent economic pressures placed on families. In the end, the Communitarian Network Platform offers nothing more than moral exhortation about divorce, very much like the "Just say no" campaign against drugs. The sentiment is laudable, but it is not backed up with any realistic program of action.

The Communitarian Platform also expresses great concern about nonpayment of child support, which is indeed a serious problem that causes untold hardship for children and their custodial parents. Only 51 percent of court-ordered child support payments are fully paid; 24 percent are paid only in part, while the remaining quarter are not paid at all.[27] These figures, moreover, do not take into account the neglect of children by fathers who are never taken to court in the first place.[28]

Enforcement of child support payments is another important and long-overdue reform. As is the case with family leave policy, however, this proposal by the Communitarians is unrelated to their criticisms of individual rights. Increased enforcement of child support payments could be defined as advancing childrens' rights, without requiring any limitations on political or civil rights. In fact, the movement toward stricter enforcement in recent years can be seen as closely related to the rights revolution. The first important step was the creation of the Office of Child Support Enforcement (OCSE) in 1975, just as interest in the rights of children was beginning to blossom; this advance was reinforced by the 1984 Child Support Enforcement amendments and the 1988 Family Support Act.[29] Concern about child support enforcement, and the broader issue of childrens' welfare, in short, is fully consistent with the general thrust of the rights revolution.

The real problem with child support enforcement is not with the law and general principles of rights but with law *enforcement*. A good argument can be made that nonsupport is one manifestation of a deep-seated sexism in the legal system, in which a male-dominated enforcement machinery overlooks a predominantly male crime. This is, of course, the essential feminist critique of the American legal system (and, we should note, a view shared by feminists with very different perspectives).[30] A heightened rights consciousness, far from conflicting with the goal of proper support for children, offers a rationale for more vigorous enforcement in the name of the rights of children.[31] As with family leave policy, the Communitarians have identified a serious social problem but are very selective about assigning blame for it.

Schools: The Second Line of Defense

The Communitarian Network Platform regards the public schools as "the second line of defense" in building a morally healthy society and proposes a curriculum of "moral education." This stance reflects the basic communitarian argument that a moral voice has vanished from the dialogue over public affairs in this country. It is also fully consistent with conservative arguments about the need to reestablish "values."

Heading off the anticipated criticism from civil libertarians, the Platform quickly assures readers that it is not calling for "religious indoctrination." In fact, it does not recommend officially sponsored school prayer as is demanded by the Religious Right. Etzioni goes to great lengths to dissociate his position from the Religious Right, arguing that the Right has captured the issue of values precisely because liberals and moderates have not emphasized moral instruction.[32]

As an alternative to the Religious Right's program, the Communitarian Network Platform proposes that the schools *"teach those values Americans share."* These values include the idea "that the dignity of all persons ought to be respected, that tolerance is a virtue and discrimination abhorrent, that peaceful resolution of conflicts is superior to violence, that generally truth telling is morally superior to lying, that democratic government is morally superior to totalitarianism and authoritarianism."

This seemingly innocuous proposal is disingenuous in light of Communitarian rhetoric and ignores a number of basic practical problems. The values of equality, respect for all persons, and tolerance for different groups and ideas, as I have argued in the three previous chapters, are the essential elements of the rights revolution. If the Communitarians are really serious about teaching these values, we might expect them to propose a model curriculum on the First Amendment, the equal protection clause (including a history of the civil rights movement and other struggles for equality), due process rights, and privacy.

The Communitarian Network Platform offers no such model curriculum. Nor is one to be found in the books by Etzioni or Glendon. The reason for this silence is simple. Any curriculum of this sort would be an explicit endorsement of the very rights revolution that is the favorite Communitarian whipping boy. On this point as on others, the Communitarians are playing a cynical game. On the one hand, their call for moral education in the schools appeals to people who interpret that to mean religious training. At the same time, however, they explicitly dissociate themselves from the Religious Right as a way of reassuring liberals and moderates who object to religion in the schools. By avoiding any specific discussion of a model values-oriented curriculum, the Communitarians are trying to appeal to both sides at once.

The Platform also ducks the practical problems that inevitably arise from its own proposal. There has in fact been a vast national effort to teach respect for all people. It has primarily involved incorporating more material on minority groups in public school curricula and textbooks.[33] Generally known as *multiculturalism*, this effort has touched off a political firestorm. Conservatives savagely attack it as undermining American education by removing (or at least devaluing) the classic works of Western civilization (Aristotle, Shakespeare, the Declaration of Independence, and so on) and replacing them with lesser works designed to offer "representation" for other cultures. This attack is one of the central points of Allan Bloom's best-selling and hugely influential book, *The Closing of the American Mind,* along with other conservative tracts that have followed in its wake.[34] Others, meanwhile, argue that multiculturalism has contributed to the growth of a divisive form of "identity politics." This is the point of Todd Gitlin's description of the fight over textbooks in Oakland, which was discussed in chapter 2.[35] Liberals such as Arthur M. Schlesinger, Jr., worry that an emphasis on discrete groups is undermining the sense of a common national identity.[36] In short, the principal effort to teach equality and tolerance for all groups has aroused opposition from conservatives, leftists, and liberals alike.

One example illustrates the political problems associated with attempting to teach equality and respect for others. Bitter controversies have erupted in school districts where the schools have attempted to use materials that treat same-sex relationships in a nonjudgmental fashion. The book *Heather Has Two Mommies* has become a national cause célèbre in this regard.[37] It would also be interesting to know whether the Communitarian Network Platform envisions including specific reference to lesbians and gays when it addresses equality and whether it regards privacy as one of the "values Americans share." There are similar conflicts over the teaching of issues related to women's equality, since conservatives regard some of those issues as part of a "radical feminist" agenda. The point, of course, is that once we move beyond slogans, the values Americans share quickly become extremely problematic.

The political problems involved in a values-oriented curriculum are brilliantly illuminated in Toni Massaro's book *Constitutional Literacy*.[38] Addressing the question of a national educational curriculum, she suggests that constitutional values such as free speech and equality represent a core set of principles around which a curriculum could be built. Yet she quickly notes that these constitutional principles are bitterly contested ground. Free speech is a wonderful thing that everyone can agree on in the abstract. Whether it includes the right to burn the American flag, however, is a bitterly divisive issue. Whether it includes the right of a public school student to wear a T-shirt with the slogan "Shit Happens," or even "Question Authority," is quite another matter in the context of a public school curriculum.

Following the lead of Gerald Graff and some others in the debate over multiculturalism, Massaro's recommended solution is to "teach the conflict."[39] Addressing free speech and other constitutional law controversies is a way of introducing students to both the underlying issues and the fact of the diversity of American life. This admirable solution, however, is not likely to satisfy social conservatives, who object to acknowledging such things as the rights of homosexuals or the principle of separation of church and state. Nor is it likely to win much favor with public school administrators who have to deal with the very real political conflict that results from "teaching the conflict."

The important point here is that Massaro does what the Communitarian Platform fails to do: offer a concrete proposal for a values-laden curriculum involving "those values Americans share." Suffice it to say that her proposal illuminates the enormous difficulties with implementing the idea and exposes the utter vacuousness of the Communitarian Network rhetoric.

Reforming American Politics

The third major plank in the Communitarian Network Platform is a call for reforming the political process. The communitarians believe that American politics has degenerated to the point where the process no longer addresses social problems effectively, and as a result large numbers of people have withdrawn from active participation. Several factors are responsible for this development: politics has been corrupted by the influence of special interest money, and the media have reduced political dialogue to empty "sound bites." Underlying these factors, however, is the larger problem of an absorption in self-interest on the part of so many people, as a consequence of the new culture of excessive individualism and group thinking.

The Communitarian Platform asserts that every citizen has certain "duties to the polity." These include being "informed about public affairs," voting, paying one's taxes, and serving on juries. The communitarian call for greater civic activism parallels the civic republican call for a rebirth of "civic virtue."[40]

The civic duties mentioned in the Platform are all worthy activities, but it is hard to see how they would transform either the political process or American society. More seriously, the call for greater civic activism exposes one of the less attractive aspects of communitarianism.

Millions of Americans *do* make a great effort to inform themselves, to vote, and to otherwise be involved in civic affairs. They do it through public interest groups related to the environment, women's issues, child welfare, abortion (pro and con), racial equality, free speech (yes, the ACLU), international human rights, and many other issues. The innumerable civil rights, civil liberties, and human rights groups that exist today represent a massive upsurge in civic activism over the past forty years. One reference book lists 477 women's organizations in the United States, and it undoubtedly overlooked many local and ad hoc organizations. Another book estimated that there are 3,400 international women's organizations.[41] The *Encyclopedia of Associations* lists 294 civil rights and civil liberties groups, 45 groups devoted to human rights, and another 31 under the heading "Constitution."[42] And these figures do not include the many organizations devoted to African Americans, Hispanics, and other groups.

The Communitarians, however, condemn most of this activity as being too narrowly *self*-interested and too little concerned with the common good. Their basic criticism of our new rights culture is that we are too absorbed in the pursuit of self-interest, which in the political sphere means group self-interest: women's rights, lesbian and gay rights, and so on. Unfortunately, the implicit Communitarian message with respect to civic activism is: do it, but do it our way. The Communitarians (and civic republicans) want more civic activism but don't like the way millions of people have chosen to be active.[43] Their position is both elitist and authoritarian.

A revealing example of this kind of elitism is a widely discussed article entitled "Bowling Alone" by Robert Puttnam, a Harvard professor of government.[44] As evidence of the withering of civic activism, Puttnam cites the decline in membership in such groups as the PTA and the League of Women Voters. Instead of acting together to better our communities, he argues, we now pursue our private interests—that is, we bowl alone. By focusing on only a handful of older organizations, Puttnam ignores the millions of activists involved in environmental, civil rights, women's rights, gay rights, and other issues. Nor does he seem to be aware of how the organizations he cites have traditionally been tied to certain social and economic arrangements. The PTA and the League of Women Voters were always the bastions of women who did not work outside the home. If membership in these organizations has declined, it is because the rise in working wives has drained off much of their traditional membership base, while the many other new areas of social activism—abortion, women's rights, the environment—have offered more attractive challenges for the politically minded. In a direct reply to Puttnam, Andrew Greeley, a Catholic priest, sociologist, and novelist, cites international poll data which indicate that volunteering is not only not in decline in the United States but is substantially higher than in Western European countries.[45]

Turning to another issue, the Communitarian call for revitalizing American politics exhibits a romanticized view of American history. The Platform seeks *"a major social movement, akin to the Progressive movement of the beginning of the century,"* to pursue the public interest. This is an idealized image of Progressivism that takes at face value the reformers' rhetoric about their goals and ignores a vast body of historical research. Many historians view Progressivism as a mosaic of distinct special interest movements, many of which had conflicting goals, and some of which hardly served the best interests of "the people."[46] A number of important Progressive reforms served the interests of the business community.[47] Racism and disdain for immigrants was another theme in Progressivism. The period of Progressive "reform" marked the triumph of de jure segregation in the South and racist theories about the superiority of Western European peoples.[48] Prohibition, one of the less attractive chapters in the history of social reform, was a product of the Progressive spirit.[49] In short, Progressivism was not the unified, altruistic movement the Communitarians imagine it was; if anything, it illustrates the long history of self-interested politics.

Communitarian discontent with the quality of contemporary political discourse represents an equally romanticized view of American history. Etzioni and Glendon both argue that election campaigns have been reduced to "sound bites" devoid of any real substance.[50] They argue that this development has produced cynicism and apathy among voters, and has contributed to the decline in voter participation.

A cursory review of American history, however, suggests that sound bites are hardly new in politics. The old campaign slogans of "54, 40, or Fight" (1848) and "Free Silver" (1896) were little more than emotionally charged catchphrases for their audiences. Nor have political campaigns been free of mudslinging and "negative" attacks on the moral character of candidates. Thomas Jefferson's opponents raised the issue of his alleged relations with his slaves, while Grover Cleveland's opponent accused him of fathering a child out of wedlock.

The second and more substantive Communitarian Platform proposal for improving the political process is a call for campaign finance reform. Sharing the concerns (indeed, the disgust) of many other Americans, it condemns the influence of big money on the political process and recommends public funding of political campaigns, along with "some access to radio and TV." The problem, in fact, appears to be getting worse. Spending in the 1996 presidential election campaign set an all-time record, and fund-raising for the year 2000 campaign began almost immediately.

The Communitarian Network proposal to curb the influence of big money in American politics, while well-intentioned, ignores all the difficult and now familiar questions that reformers have been wrestling with for decades.[51] Assuming for the sake of argument that we could craft a law severely limiting *contributions to* and *spending by* both candidates and parties, the question becomes how to control spending by independent organizations related to abortion, guns, the environment, and other issues. In virtually every political race it is clear which candidate is pro-choice and which is pro-life, which is for gun control and which is not. To limit the influence of money on elections it would be necessary to control these independent organizations. It is not clear where such controls would end, and the Communitarian Platform offers no guidance.

Other problems also arise. It is not clear when a "campaign" begins. Is it only after a candidate has announced? Or are there to be limits on spending by any and all individuals who might run for office? Who, exactly, is a "candidate" and who is not? In short, how do we effectively limit campaign spending without massive limitations on all forms of expression and without creating a huge government bureaucracy to enforce the new limits?[52]

These are not new questions. Nor are they easy ones. Perhaps we will find some way to resolve them. The Communitarian Platform, however, makes no substantive contribution to this issue and instead offers only vague platitudes.

The Communitarian proposals for public funding of election campaigns and access to free television time also involve familiar and very difficult questions. Do the Communitarians propose public funding for *all* parties, including the Communist Labor Party, the Temperance Party, white supremacist parties, and every other fringe party? If not, they need to explain how they would distinguish between "legitimate" and "illegitimate" parties, and how they would reconcile their criteria with both the First Amendment and the equal protection clause. They avoid discussing these difficult questions, and once again the reader detects an implicit elitism that distinguishes between "deserving" and "undeserving" political parties.[53]

There are indeed many problems with the American political process, and the solutions are by no means self-evident. Our twenty-five-year experiment with campaign finance reform suggests, if nothing else, that both contributors and political party operatives can be enormously creative in finding loopholes in the law. The Communitarian Platform ignores these well-known problems and instead simply repeats the vague mantra of campaign finance reform.

The Problem of Hate Speech

The Communitarian Network Platform addresses the question of how to respond to hate speech. The issue arose in the 1980s as a result of an apparent upsurge in overt expressions of racism, including many appalling incidents on some of our best college campuses. The Platform reaffirms the value of freedom of speech and counsels against any restrictions on First Amendment rights. It states forthrightly that "the First Amendment is as dear to Communitarians as it is to libertarians and many other Americans." Instead of restricting hate speech through law, the Platform recommends responding with nonlegalistic measures. A college, for example, might conduct a teach-in on racism in response to a campus incident. Etzioni points out that hate speech is only the symptom of a deeper disease, and he advises us to "seek deeper and more educational remedies."[54]

The Communitarian position on this issue is somewhat surprising, given all their rhetoric about the evils of "rights absolutism." The prevailing law on free speech is precisely the kind of "absolutist" approach to rights and "radical individualism" the communitarians incessantly attack. The Communitarian position on hate speech is in fact identical to the official policy of the ACLU.[55] On every other issue, the Communitarians use the ACLU as their favorite whipping boy, repeatedly denouncing its "radical individualism" and destructive "absolutist" approach to rights. The Communitarian Platform does not acknowledge this contradiction.

Perhaps the Communitarians believe that the First Amendment occupies a special place in a hierarchy of rights because of its central role in the political process of a democracy, which is a long-standing and respected position in First Amendment theory. If so, however, they have an obligation to explain it in detail and reconcile it with their attacks on "radical individualism" on other issues.

Enhancing Public Safety
On the issues of public safety and public health, the Communitarian Platform offers the most specific proposals for scaling back on individual rights. The proposals are presented as a challenge to "the ACLU and other radical libertarians." To promote public safety it recommends expanding police powers of search and seizure, particularly with reference to sobriety checkpoints, the screening of passengers at airports, and substance abuse tests for pilots, train engineers, and employees in similar occupations. It also recommends requiring people with AIDS and other communicable diseases "to disclose their illness to previous sexual contacts or to help health authorities to inform them."

The proposal for expanding police powers of search and seizure is identical to the long-standing conservative crime control agenda. "Law-and-order" advocates have demanded this expansion for over thirty-five years, ever since the 1961 Supreme Court decision in *Mapp v. Ohio* established the "exclusionary rule" forbidding the use of evidence obtained through an unreasonable search.[56] The main problem with this proposal is that it fails to acknowledge the substantial body of research on the subject.[57] Studies of the exclusionary rule have consistently found that it does not significantly limit the crime-fighting powers of the police. Relatively few cases are "lost" because of excluded evidence. Search-and-seizure issues are raised in only a small percentage of cases, and motions to suppress evidence are remarkably unsuccessful. Rather than consider this extensive body of evidence, the Communitarians embrace the public hysteria about crime and uncritically accept the conservative rhetoric about how thousands of dangerous criminals allegedly "beat the system" because of "technicalities."[58]

The issue of sobriety checkpoints issue also illustrates the Communitarian failure to examine the relevant evidence. The authors of the Platform do not seem to be aware that the Supreme Court upheld the constitutionality of such checkpoints in the 1990 *Sitz* decision.[59] In short, they are loudly demanding something that already exists. The Michigan Supreme Court later found the same checkpoints unconstitutional under the state constitution, but in most jurisdictions police have sufficient legal authority to do what the Communitarians want. Law enforcement agencies do not conduct checkpoints on a massive scale, however, for very practical reasons. They are extremely expensive in terms of personnel and quite unproductive in terms of catching or deterring drunk drivers. Again, the Communitarians embrace conservative rhetoric about the need for expanded law enforcement powers without considering the readily available evidence about the efficacy of the policy.

In his books and other writings, Etzioni has argued for limiting the scope of the *Miranda* warning. He would allow confessions or other evidence where there was only a "technical" violation of the *Miranda* requirement but no bad faith on the part of the police officer.[60] As with the exclusionary rule, he blithely ignores substantial evidence that the *Miranda* warning does not prevent the police from interrogating suspects and obtaining confessions in a high percentage of cases.[61] In short, the Communitarian proposals for limiting the protections of individual rights are not going to reduce crime and promote public safety. The Communitarians also seem unaware of the extent to which *Mapp, Miranda,* and other Supreme Court decisions protecting the rights of individuals have been an important stimulus to police reform, prodding the police to improve recruitment, training, and supervision standards.[62] They have contributed to a new sense of professionalism that includes standards of fairness and equal treatment in dealing with citizens—standards that are an essential element of a truly inclusive community.

The Platform also calls for gun control, arguing that "domestic disarmament" is necessary for reducing violent crime and promoting public safety. It explicitly rejects the argument that the Second Amendment guarantees the right of individual gun ownership.

The gun control proposal is a worthy idea, but like so many others it lacks specificity. The Platform offers no details about how the availability and use of firearms are to be limited. This involves a number of practical problems that gun control advocates have wrestled with for decades.[63] If the Communitarians want to ban ownership of all guns, how do they plan to eliminate the estimated 70 million handguns already in private hands? As a practical matter, it could only be accomplished through massive government intrusion into the homes of about half the households in America. Such an effort would arouse militant resistance and only inflame the already conspiratorially minded far right. If, on the other hand, the Communitarians only want greater restrictions on the sale and ownership of handguns, other well-known problems arise. For many decades we have had innumerable laws designed to keep guns out of the hands of "bad" people (mainly people with criminal records or histories of mental illness), yet large number of these people manage to obtain guns and use them to commit crimes. What do the Communitarians propose to do about the black market in handguns, which is a major source of guns for criminals?[64]

These are only a few of the many practical questions related to gun control. The point is simply that a vague call for "domestic disarmament," however admirable, offers little in the way of practical guidance for public policy.

The Communitarian Cop-Out

In the end, the Communitarian Network Platform offers little in the way of specific proposals that would achieve its own goal of healthier communities. Several problems pervade the proposals in the Platform. On some issues, such as divorce, the proposals offer little more than feel-good rhetoric. On others, such as family leave, they refuse to confront the conservative political forces that have in fact blocked the development of a strong national network of social services. On the issue of crime policy, the Platform uncritically adopts conservative rhetoric without examining the evidence. These problems will reappear as we examine other aspects of communitarianism in the remainder of this chapter. All of these failures, it should be noted, seem particularly serious in a group led by academics— people who devote their professional lives to thinking deeply about issues and examining scholarly evidence.

BALANCING RIGHTS AND RESPONSIBILITIES: LESSONS FROM ABROAD?

With respect to the basic communitarian argument that we need to balance rights with responsibilities, Mary Ann Glendon suggests that we look overseas for guidance. She believes that other countries have achieved a better balance than we have.[65] She has the most cosmopolitan perspective of all the Communitarians, and is extremely knowledgeable about international developments with respect to rights.[66] The subtitle of her comparative study of abortion and divorce law, *Abortion and Divorce in Western Law: American Failures, European Challenges,* summarizes her basic view that the United States has failed because of its extreme individualism, while European countries have embraced a healthier respect for community.[67]

Glendon illustrates her argument about the imbalance between individual rights and social responsibilities in the United States with the poignant example of a poor pregnant woman, who has her "constitutional right to privacy and little else."[68] Her right to an abortion is secured by law, and there is an array of well-organized interest groups defending that right (Planned Parenthood, the ACLU, National Abortion Rights Action League, NOW, the Center for Reproductive Law and Policy, and others). Yet the network of social services for that woman, both during her pregnancy and after the child is born, is the weakest in the entire industrial world. These services include prenatal health care, medical services for her and the child after the child is born, public assistance, day care services, and so on. Moreover, all of the political rhetoric about "family values" in the 1990s has produced only further erosions of those services for the poor, most notably in the 1996 welfare reform law.

Glendon's point about the inadequacies of American social services is beyond dispute. The relevant policy question is, What should we do to correct this problem? As I argued in my discussion of the Communitarian Network Platform, communitarians have created a false dichotomy, and the development of a more comprehensive network of social services does not require limiting existing political and civil rights. Let us now turn our attention to the international examples recommended by Glendon as a guide to achieving a better balance between rights and responsibilities.

Balancing Principles

The basic question is a simple one: What principles should we use to balance rights with responsibilities? Although the question is simple, the answers are extremely difficult, and far more problematic than Glendon or other communitarians suggest.

The place to begin is the 1948 Universal Declaration of Human Rights, which established the framework for virtually all subsequent human rights declarations (see Table 2.1). With respect to rights and responsibilities, it asserts that "everyone has duties to the community in which alone the free and full development of his personality is possible" (Article 29). Article 19 of the 1966 International Covenant on Civil and Political Rights affirms a broad array of rights, including freedom of speech, equality, and due process, but then asserts that rights carry "special duties and responsibilities" and "may therefore be subject to certain restrictions." Similar language appears in virtually every international human rights document.[69]

What exactly are these "duties" and "responsibilities"? The International Covenant on Civil and Political Rights provides that individual rights may be limited if necessary "(1) for respect of the rights or reputations of others, (2) for the protection of national security or of public order (*ordre public*), or of public health or morals." This language is borrowed from the Universal Declaration of Human Rights and has been incorporated into virtually all other human rights documents. The 1981 Declaration on the Elimination of All Forms of Intolerance and of Discrimination Based on Religion or Belief, for example, states that religious freedom may be restricted when "necessary to protect public safety, order, health or morals, or the fundamental rights and freedoms of others."[70]

One hardly needs to be a card-carrying member of the ACLU to see the problems raised by these standards. Such phrases as "public order" and "national security" are open invitations to all sorts of denials of individual rights. In fact, we can view the entire history of the growth of First Amendment rights and other civil liberties in this century as the story of struggles against precisely those rationales for restricting individual rights.[71]

The "national security" rationale offers an obvious case in point. The suppression of dissent during World War I, the internment of Japanese Americans during World War II, the attack on political beliefs in the cold war, and the attempt to suppress dissent during the Vietnam War were all justified in terms of national security, in the sense of national needs in a time of war. As we saw in the discussion of the Japanese Americans in chapter 3, a wartime emergency (read: threat to national security) led to one of the grossest violations of civil liberties in our history—a violation that hardly anyone defends today. Modern First Amendment law begins with Justice Oliver Wendell Holmes's dissent in the 1919 *Abrams* case, which defined for the first time the limits of such claims over the individual.[72] The growth of free speech law in the ensuing decades represents an elaboration and extension of Holmes's basic point.

If Glendon seriously believes that the international human rights documents offer a model for balancing rights and responsibilities, she has an intellectual obligation to address the national security rationale and to explain how it would not be used to justify violations of individual rights in the face of, for example, real or alleged threats by international terrorists.

The idea that rights can and should be limited to protect the "rights and reputations of others" also raises a number of familiar problems. Among other things, it has direct implications for the current American controversies over hate speech and pornography. The advocates of restrictive hate speech codes argue that racist and sexist speech harms the "rights and reputations" of minorities and women. Catharine MacKinnon and Andrea Dworkin, meanwhile, argue that pornography does real harm to women.[73]

If Glendon believes that the balancing principles in the various international human rights documents offer a useful guide, she has an obligation to tell us whether she supports restrictive hate-speech codes and the MacKinnon-Dworkin proposal for restricting pornography. If she does, we can then consider her general argument in that light. If not, she needs to explain what alternative balancing principle she prefers. Unfortunately, we get no such detail, only a vague blanket endorsement of "balancing." We might note in passing that the leading communitarians appear to be quite divided on this issue. It is precisely out of a recognition of the importance of unrestricted free speech in a democratic society that the Communitarian Network Platform itself opposes any balancing-oriented restrictions on freedom of expression.[74]

The idea that rights can and should be limited in the name of protecting "public health and morals" presents another set of problems. This was precisely the rationale used in a broad range of censorship efforts directed at sexually oriented expression and behavior. As I argued in chapter 4, it was the rationale for Mayor Curley's ban on Margaret Sanger and for the federal Comstock Law banning birth control information and devices from the mail. The prohibition of same-sex relationships, along with literature discussing the subject, has always been based on protecting public morals.

Adjudicating Rights

Even when she does offer a specific example of how the European approach is superior to the American, Glendon selectively interprets the case to her own advantage. In *Rights Talk,* she describes the *Dudgeon v. United Kingdom* case, in which the European Commission on Human Rights, and later the European Court of Human Rights, overturned a conviction for homosexual acts, using international human rights concepts.[75] She contrasts this with the U.S. Supreme Court decision in *Bowers v. Hardwick* (1986), where the Court rejected the argument that consensual homosexual acts are protected by a constitutional right to privacy. She applauds the more tolerant result in the European case; although a critic of our current style of rights, she is definitely not an antihomosexual bigot. Her point is that European precepts are more "flexible" than the rigid American definitions of rights and in this case produced a result more tolerant of diversity.

There are two serious problems with Glendon's analysis. First, even she concedes that the different outcomes in the two cases owed much to the more tolerant attitude toward homosexuality in Europe, compared with the strong religious moralism in the United States (and, we might add, in Georgia, where the *Hardwick* case arose).[76] A far more serious problem, which Glendon completely ignores, is the process by which the *Dudgeon* case was resolved. The case arose in Ireland, and the law in question expressed the religious values of the Irish community (just as the law in the *Hardwick* case expressed the values of the majority of the people in Georgia). It was overturned by higher courts reflecting cosmopolitan values, in exactly the same way that the U.S. Supreme Court overturns state and local laws that reflect community norms.

In short, we could easily read Glendon's account of the *Dudgeon* case as the story of the destruction of Irish "community" values in the name of abstract legalistic principles reflecting the cosmopolitan values of the European community. This is precisely the process that she and other communitarians and civic republicans deplore.

Glendon does not seem to appreciate the ambiguous meaning of this case and the problems is raises for her own argument.

The problem raised by the *Dudgeon* case is a fundamental one. Put simply, what do we mean by "community"? Which set of "community" values are trying to preserve? Are they the particularistic values of Ireland and Georgia, or the more cosmopolitan values of larger national and international communities? I will explore this issue in more detail at the end of this chapter when I take up the Communitarian policy on organ donation.

In the end, then, the international approach to balancing rights and responsibilities does not offer the solutions that Glendon believes it does. The criteria for limiting rights it offers are precisely the ones that have been bitterly contested in our own constitutional history.

CORPORATE RESPONSIBILITIES TO COMMUNITIES

Although it is not mentioned in the Communitarian Network Platform, leading communitarians have raised the issue of the responsibilities of private corporations to the communities in which they are located. Etzioni urges corporations "to become not only more family-friendly, but also more community-friendly."[77]

The problem is both a familiar and a serious one. Across the country, entire communities have been devastated by factory closings and the transfer of jobs overseas. Industrial cities such as Cleveland and Detroit have been particularly hard hit by the changes in the steel and automobile industries. The problem is no less serious in small towns where, for example, a meatpacking plant is (or was) the primary employer. The destructive consequences of factory closings ripple through the community: jobs are lost; small businesses, such as the family-owned drugstore on the corner, close; property values deteriorate, wiping out many peoples' investments; an atmosphere of decline and hopelessness about the future descends; crime and drug abuse increase; children, especially the talented and ambitious, leave for opportunities elsewhere.[78] From a community perspective, this is a critical issue. It is pointless to talk about building and maintaining healthy communities without reference to the economic base that makes it possible for people to work, to raise families, to create healthy neighborhoods, and to have some reason to believe in the future.

The Case of Poletown

Pursuing her basic argument regarding the imbalance between rights and responsibilities in American law, Mary Ann Glendon points out that the law offers no effective remedy for communities faced with plant closings. She cites the case of "Poletown," a Detroit, Michigan, community that was scheduled to be destroyed to make room for a new Cadillac assembly plant. Enticed by the promise of six thousand jobs, the city of Detroit had agreed to use its power of eminent domain to clear about five hundred acres, demolish nearly fourteen hundred homes, and relocate thousands of people. This would effectively destroy a community with a rich history and a strong sense of identity tied to traditions of work and ethnicity.

Challenging the threat to their community in court, attorneys for the residents relied on the Michigan Environmental Protection Act, arguing that it included the protection of "cultural, social, and historical institutions." They tried this creative use of the state environmental protection law for the simple reason that no other law offered any hope. The Michigan courts rejected the plaintiffs' novel interpretation of the state environmental protection law, and the suit failed.[79]

Remedies for Corporate Irresponsibility?

Glendon's critique of current law is well taken. Communities, as such, are not defined as entities with rights in the same sense that individuals have them. In their book *The Deindustrialization of America*, Barry Bluestone and Bennett Harrison document the virtual uselessness of existing laws related to plant closings.[80] In 1981, the Supreme Court ruled that employers do not have to negotiate with unions about closing plants. The 1988 Worker Adjustment and Retraining Notification (WARN) Act requires only a written notification prior to a plant closing or "mass layoff," along with retraining opportunities for situations that meet certain criteria. In short, the law is only a buffer designed to ease the pain of the disaster, but not to prevent the disaster itself.

Glendon cites this problem as another example of the imbalance between rights and responsibilities in American law. We have no laws that effectively curb corporate irresponsibility because our individualistic ethos does not provide the language for even talking about community-wide harms. Glendon believes that we need a framework of rights that takes into account social, collective, and communal interests. Having defined the problem, however, she offers nothing in the way of a concrete solution. She proposes no language for a model Social Environmental Protection Act designed to protect a community such as Poletown.[81]

Other Communitarians are equally evasive. The Communitarian Network Platform is silent on the issue of corporate responsibility to communities. Etzioni addresses the issue in his book but merely advises corporations to become more "community-friendly." He suggests they rethink their policy of moving executives every three years, in order to allow these individuals to develop longer-term involvement in community affairs. With respect to plant closings, however, he suggests only that they "should not be undertaken capriciously or abruptly." In the vaguest terms, he hints at possible "laws that slow plant closings by corporations that are grossly insensitive to community needs." The comment is limited to one sentence, and there is no discussion of what such laws might look like.[82]

There is an obvious reason why Glendon and Etzioni provide no specifics on this issue. Any meaningful program would involve some kind of legislation limiting the power of corporations such as General Motors to close a factory. This would be a genuinely radical departure for American economic and social policy, placing formal restrictions on the investment and disinvestment of capital. It would introduce the principle that corporations have legal obligations not just to their stockholders but to the communities where they operate. We can already hear the attacks from the business community, denouncing such a policy as "socialism" or "communism." Even political moderates would oppose it as "big government," "regulation," and an impediment to economic growth and the value of their stock portfolios. The political climate of the past two decades, moreover, has become steadily more hostile to all forms of government regulation.

Bluestone and Harrison frame the issue of plant closings in terms of a clash between "capital and community."[83] Their point is that the values of community, and community preservation, are in direct conflict with the values of modern capitalism, with its emphasis on profit maximization. The Communitarians, although they invoke "community" as a mantra, cannot bring themselves to face the political realities of this issue. Even to mention some restrictions on big business would expose them to attack as "radicals" and frighten off much of their present membership. Their refusal to outline a meaningful program of action, after they have introduced the issue, represents a serious intellectual and political failure of nerve.

THE MANTRA OF "COMMUNITY"

We now come to an even more fundamental problem with communitarianism. Its leaders invoke the word "community" as a mantra, a principle that offers the solution to all our problems. A commitment to the common good is presented as a healthy alternative to the excessive individualism that is at the root of our current social crisis.

The communitarians, however, rarely define what they mean by "community," leaving it a vague concept. One sociologist, in fact, cited ninety-four different definitions.[84] Etzioni rises to the challenge and declares that "community can be defined with reasonable precision." It consists of two essential characteristics: "first, a web of affect-laden relationships among a group of individuals . . . and second, a measure of commitment to a shared set of values, norms, and meanings, and a shared history and identity."[85]

When we try to apply this definition to the realities of American history and culture, we find that it solves none of the basic problems. The term has several meanings, and there are several different communities that involve "a shared history and identity." These different conceptions of community often conflict with each other, with profound ramifications for law and policy. Complicating the picture even further is the fact that we all belong to several communities that lay claims upon us, or that we can choose as our primary source of identity. The Communitarian Network Platform, in fact, recognizes this fact. Its preamble opens with the declaration that "American men, women, and children are members of many communities— families; neighborhoods; innumerable social, religious, ethnic, workplace, and professional associations; and the body politic itself."[86]

Because it illuminates this problem in the context of a concrete issue, the official Communitarian position paper on organ donations serves as a useful introduction to this problem.

The Communitarians and Organ Donations

In addition to the official Platform, the Communitarian Network has published a series of official position papers on important issues. The Communitarian position paper entitled "The Rights and Responsibilities of Potential Organ Donors" calls for "a major revision of the moral basis of public policy concerning the retrieval of transplantable human organs from the newly dead."[87] Current policy in the United States relies on voluntary donations, which is consistent with the individualistic, free-choice ethos of our rights culture. Communitarians regard this as morally objectionable because a system based on private individual choice does not take into account public need. The result, according to the position paper, is that "thousands of organs are wasted" every year, while an equal number of people needing organs suffer or even die.

Communitarian principles dictate that organ donation should be "a social duty—that is, everyone would be expected to donate their organs after dying." The position paper points out that public policy—in all areas of life—is a statement about "the kind of community we take ourselves to be."[88] Obligatory donation expresses the value of responsibility to others, as opposed to the self-centered individualism of current law and policy.

The idea of mandatory organ donations immediately raises the specter of body parts being harvested from the dead without their consent. For many people this conjures up images of a totalitarian society where the individual is subordinated to the needs of the state, and where cultural and religious minorities are forced to conform to national needs. The Communitarian position paper hastens to assure us that they "are not authoritarians." Their proposal allows for conscientious objection to mandatory donation with "ample opportunity" for individuals to opt out of the system. Individuals could have their objection noted on a driver's license or some other piece of identification, or by designating family members to block the taking of organs.[89]

The right of conscientious objection, however, is withdrawn almost as soon as it is offered. The position paper immediately declares that the procedures for opting out do "not necessarily signal that citizens of the community have an established 'right' to withhold their organs."[90] Unfortunately, it does not then spell out the exact scope of one's rights. The net result is complete ambiguity; it is not clear whether there is an absolute right of conscientious objection, or what kind of circumstances would sustain a successful claim.

The Communitarians are unwilling to concede an unqualified right of conscientious objection to organ donation for an obvious reason. To do so would be to acknowledge the validity of an absolute claim of individual rights vis-à-vis the government. To concede the priority of an individual right over "responsibility," "duty," and "obligation" in the area of organ donations would undermine the core principle of communitarianism.

In its attempt to justify mandatory organ donation, the Communitarian position paper only makes matters worse. With a wave of the hand it declares that "the possible value of organs to those who are dead is, at best, obscure."[91] It adds that "it is far from clear that any serious, direct interest of the dead or their families could be violated by organ transplantation." Dismissing the value of the dead as "obscure" expresses a shocking insensitivity to cultural and religious diversity throughout human history. Japanese culture, for example, has traditionally not made a distinction between body and soul, regarding body parts not as parts of a machine but as reservoirs of character.[92] If the authors of the position paper had done even the most cursory research, they would have found enormous variations in traditions regarding care for the dead, not just between different religions and cultures but within groups that are usually considered homogeneous. There are, for example, very different beliefs about the nature of the dead body between Native American tribes and between Orthodox and non-Orthodox Jews.[93]

The issue of conscientious objection to organ donation illuminates the conflict between different conceptions of community. The Communitarian position paper clearly defines community in national terms: the individual's obligation to meet national needs for transplantable organs. To this end, it dismisses the unique claims of religious and ethnic communities. This brings us to the larger issue of the definition of community.

Five Aspects of Community in America

The concept of community has at least five different meanings in the context of American society. (We will for the moment not explore the ninety-four meanings identified by one sociologist)[94] In fact, some commentators suggest that a recent Supreme Court decision has raised the possibility of a sixth definition. These are not abstract theoretical definitions but are the source of some of the most important political and legal controversies issues in modern American history. Let's consider each of these definitions.

1. *Community as the Neighborhood.* When most people speak of their community, they are thinking about where they live: a residential neighborhood involving a small but distinct geographic area. This is what people usually mean when they say "my community." It is what most political activists mean when they talk about "community organizing," and, to cite a specific example, what the recent movement toward community policing movement means.

2. *Community as the Region.* Some people define community in terms of a larger geographic region, such as New England, the South,

the Southwest, and so on. This also refers to a distinct geographic area, and one with an identifiable set of values or culture. The most famous (or infamous) version of this definition was the old pre–civil rights era South. When people referred to the "southern way of life," they meant a distinct set of values and social customs that were different from those in the rest of the country.

3. *Community as the Nation.* A third definition of community refers to the nation-state, or what the Communitarian Platform refers to as "the body politic itself." Although the word "community" is not often used in this context, the meaning is the same. It refers to the idea that all citizens of the United States (or any other country) have a community of interest, with certain common values and obligations. One of the major crises identified by some of the New Jeremiahs is the alleged loss of a unifying sense of American identity.

4. *Community as the Group.* We also routinely refer to various ethnic, racial, religious, cultural, and other groups as communities. The Communitarian Platform includes "workplace" and "professional association" communities. Our daily discourse is filled with casual references to the black community, the Catholic community, the Hispanic community, and so on. These communities involve associations and identities that are national in scope and transcend local, state, and regional boundaries.

5. *Community as the International Human Community.* Some people believe that we are all members of a larger international human community. This idea is the mainspring behind the international human rights statements mentioned in several chapters of this book. The underlying principle is that there is a set of universal standards shared by all people and all nations. That is to say, we are all members of the same community.

A Cyberspace Community? Recently, a major Supreme Court decision raised the possibility of yet another dimension of community: a community in cyberspace. In June 1997, the Supreme Court struck down the Communications Decency Act, which restricted expression on the Internet. As many observers have noted, if courts or legislatures attempt to justify censorship in terms of "community standards," the question becomes, Exactly what and where is the cyberspace community? The answer would seem to be that it is everywhere and nowhere at once. It is not confined to any identifiable geographic space, as is the case with three of the definitions discussed earlier. It is far more transgeographic than any of the group definitions and far more elusive than anything imagined in all the discussions of international human rights, which assume a set of nation-states responsible for what happens within their geographic boundaries.

Communities in Conflict: Lessons from Recent American History

Given these conflicting definitions, invoking the term "community" as a solution to our problems is meaningless. The term becomes a mantra, a slogan, and a cliché. Most important, it evades all the difficult questions about how to resolve the many conflicts that pervade American society. And, as I have already indicated, these conflicts are not abstract theoretical matters. Nor are they the kind of hypothetical problems that a law professor might conjure up for purposes of classroom discussion. Let us consider briefly the basic problems that arise with each of these definitions of community.

Whose Neighborhood? We can begin with the neighborhood definition of community. It should be obvious that this has been the source of virtually every form of housing discrimination in our history. The opposition to community placement of the Willowbrook children, described in chapter 5, is only one of innumerable examples that could be cited. Race discrimination has probably the longest history, but the attempt to exclude "others" has also involved religion, social class, disability, and other categories of people.

The point here is that the neighborhood definition of community has always been exclusionary rather than inclusive, designed to preserve "our" neighborhood by keeping "those" people out. Clearly, this is hardly consistent with the healthy and positive definition of community implicitly advanced by communitarians. And as the discussion in chapter 5 indicated, the exclusionary efforts of neighborhood residents have been challenged by, and with some limited success overcome by, abstract universalistic standards of rights representing a very different notion of community.

What Regional Values? The idea of a regional definition of community offers an even more embarrassing historical example. The infamous "southern way of life," of course, represented the racial caste system of the era of segregation, which prevailed roughly from the 1890s to the civil rights era of the 1960s. The defenders of segregated public schools and other forms of Jim Crow saw the caste system expressing a distinct set of community values. Of course, it was an exclusionary definition of community, based on the core principle of keeping a large segment of the population out of the mainstream of social, economic, and political life.

As was the case with housing discrimination, the exclusionary aspects of the regional definition of community were attacked and, in de jure terms at least, demolished through a concerted attack that we refer to as the civil rights movement. One of the principal weapons of that movement was the invocation of abstract and universalistic notions of rights.

What Do We Owe the National Community? The definition of community as the nation touches on one of the transcendent issues of modern politics in the twentieth century: What are the obligations of individual citizens to the state? Totalitarian regimes are based on the principle that the individual is subordinate to the state. The Anglo-American legal tradition is based on the contrary principle that each citizen has certain inviolable rights vis-à-vis the state. These rights include freedom of speech, protection against unreasonable searches and seizures, and so on.

The Communitarian Network position paper on organ donation exposes the conflict between obligations to the national community and religious and cultural community traditions—and blithely resolves it in favor of the nation-state. This conflict is the basis for our long and bitter political and legal conflict over the right of conscientious objection to compulsory military service. The idea of compulsory national or community service, which communitarians endorse, raises the issue in a slightly different context.

Communitarians will undoubtedly shout "Foul!" at being associated with totalitarianism. But there is no avoiding the fact that if we resolve the conflict in favor of the nation-state we are stepping onto a very slippery slope that can easily lead to totalitarianism. To take the contrary view—that people retain certain rights vis-à-vis the nation-state, based on religious community traditions—is to affirm the kind of absolutist notion of rights that communitarians endlessly disparage.

Which Group's Values? The group definition of community introduces a more subtle and complex set of issues. At first glance it seems difficult to object to the idea that each group should be allowed to live according to its own values, whether those values are rooted in religion or ethnic or racial tradition. That principle is the essence of the cultural pluralism that has become, in many respects, one of the operating principles of American democracy. The minute we consider religious values, however, we plunge headlong into some of the most bitterly divisive controversies in American history and contemporary politics. Let us consider an obvious contemporary one: abortion.

Abortion is a bitterly divisive issue precisely because it involves a conflict over fundamental religious values. The official position of the Roman Catholic Church and some Protestant denominations is that human life begins at conception and, consequently, abortion is murder. Other religious groups have different views about when life begins and, consequently, no absolute objection to abortion per se. Invoking the idea of "community" in this context is meaningless. The basic pro-choice position is a pluralist approach that tolerates different religious values. The right-to-life position, however, regards this stance as an abomination. Since abortion is murder, it should not be tolerated, any more than other forms of homicide. Thus, we are faced with a question of whose community values shall prevail as national law and policy. The mantra of "community" only begs the question and offers no practical answers.

The ongoing controversy over religion in public schools is a variation on the same problem. The point of the discussion in chapter 3 was that state-imposed religious practices adopted in the name of the majority community are disrespectful of minority religious community values.

Which Nation's Cultural Values? The idea of an international human community, with certain transcendent rights, introduces similar problems on a larger scale. The many international human rights documents, of which there are more than forty, share three basic elements. All are written documents, all define human rights in terms of individual (as opposed to communal) rights, and all borrow the basic categories of rights from the American Bill of Rights: freedom of speech, press, and assembly; religious freedom; due process of law; and equality. (On the issue of economic rights they differ considerably, however.)

This universalistic concept of rights, which derives from the modern American approach to rights, has been attacked, however, by leaders in some non-European countries as a distinctly "Western" concept that is alien to non-European cultures. One survey of international human rights observed that "Opposition to the measuring of rights and classifying countries . . . centers on the perception that the purpose has a Western liberal bias. This is undeniably true." All of the international human rights declarations, along with the United Nations itself, embody the western liberal tradition of individual freedom taking precedent over religious and communal traditions.[95]

This controversy has received the most attention recently over the issue of clitorectomy, which is widely practiced in many African countries. By the standards of American and most Western European countries, clitorectomy is a barbaric practice that primarily serves to subjugate women. The United States has had to confront the question of whether to grant asylum to women who do not want to return to their native countries for fear of being forcibly subjected to clitorectomy. The question in these cases is whether clitorectomy is a human rights violation. African nations that continue the practice regard the American position as an arrogant attack on their culture, a form of human rights imperialism. The point here is that the notion of an international human rights community is as problematic as all the other definitions.[96]

In a fascinating sidelight on cultural differences within other countries with respect to rights, a study of the introduction of the UN Convention of the Rights of the Child in Japan found that there were three separate Japanese translations of the document, prepared by the government, the UN, and a private childrens' advocacy group. All three groups translated key passages in different ways to conform to their own views of the role of children.[97] In short, consensus over this issue has proved difficult to achieve even in the highly homogenous society of Japan.

With the end of the cold war and the demise of the old "free world" versus "Communism" dichotomy, the world is increasingly fragmented along cultural lines. On the one side stands the Western culture of individualism, secularism, rationality, and internationalism, while on the other stands a culture of communalism, religion, tradition, and localism. One commentator defined this fragmentation in terms of *Jihad v. McWorld*.[98] Another asks, "Can we have an international discussion of human rights in a world of cultural difference?"[99] Although the question was asked with reference to women's rights, it has a far broader applicability: simply substitute the word "community" for "culture."

A unique variation of this problem exists with respect to Native

Americans in the United States. Under the law, Native American tribes are sovereign nations, with broad powers of self-government and autonomy from federal and state laws. In this respect, tribes represent distinct communities that are defined by law in a way that is not true of the other forms of community we have just considered. A routine criminal case can raise many complex legal considerations depending on who did what to whom (Native American versus non–Native American) and on what piece of land (reservation or nonreservation). An authoritative guide to the subject simply declared that "criminal jurisdiction in Indian country . . . is complex and difficult to explain."[100]

In 1968, Congress enacted the Indian Civil Rights Act, conferring certain rights on individual Native Americans and authorizing the federal courts to enforce them. The law remains highly controversial and exposes the fundamental problem of defining community. Are Native Americans fully members of their tribal communities, and therefore exclusively subject to tribal law and custom, or are they members of the larger American community, and therefore subject to at least some of the laws of the United States? More specifically, are individual Native Americans protected by the Bill of Rights even when some of its provisions conflict with tribal custom? Which community prevails in such situations?[101]

The Problem with Community

The claims of community are many and complex. Merely to invoke the word, without specifying what it means in a given context, evades rather than solves difficult questions. Search the writings of the leading communitarians and you will find not only no answer to these questions but no acknowledgment that the problem even exists. Instead, we find a ritualistic invocation of "community" as the solution to our social, moral, and political problems. As two sociologists observed more than twenty years ago, "Community tends to be a God word. . . . when it is mentioned, we are expected to abase ourselves before it rather than attempt to define it."[102] Our primary task here is not to define it; but anyone who uses the term as an organizing principle for social policy does have an obligation to do so.

In the absence of a clear definition, the problem becomes one in which everyone substitutes his or her own definition—much as people have their own definitions of "the good life," or "the American way of life." Burt Neuborne, New York University professor of law and former ACLU legal director, warns of the latent authoritarianism in theories that claim to represent *the* shared values of the community. He points out that there have been many attempts throughout history to forge "true communities of shared values." These have included shared values of race (as with Nazi Germany), economic theory (as with the Soviet Union), religion (present-day Islamic states, not to mention the Puritan colonies in America), and so on. Neuborne observes somberly, "Not one has avoided descent into tyranny and abuse."[103] This is a warning the Communitarians have, to their peril and ours, not reflected upon sufficiently.

CONCLUSION: THE COMMUNITARIAN FAILURE

Communitarianism represents the most coherent alternative to the idea that a system of rights should be given as the organizing principle for our society. It is an appealing philosophy that addresses many, if not most, of our current social problems and offers a comprehensive principle for responding to them. Unlike other criticisms of rights, communitarianism is not merely negative in tone and not confined to a single issue. Most important, it appeals to our nobler aspirations, asking us to put the needs of the community above narrow self-interest.

On closer inspection, however, we find that communitarianism does not offer a viable alternative to the principle of rights. Many of its specific proposals are little more than empty rhetoric that evades difficult and well-known problems. Communitarian spokespersons have a bad tendency to avoid any direct challenge to powerful economic interests and instead attack the far less powerful groups. International principles of human rights, which some communitarians recommend as a model, fail to address the problems of balancing rights and responsibilities that we have wrestled with in our own history of constitutional law. There is also a disturbing elitism and latent authoritarianism in communitarian thinking. Too often the discussions of the common good assume that its conception of that good is the true one and that alternative definitions are invalid. Finally, and perhaps most seriously, the communitarians have not defined what they mean by community, and they ignore the conflicts that arise between competing definitions.

The values underlying the rights revolution, on the other hand, do embody a coherent definition of community. These are the values of individual liberty, inclusion, and tolerance for different ideas, values, and lifestyles. As various sections of this book have indicated, there is no getting around the fact that this definition of community conflicts with, and in my view is preferable to, alternative definitions. Many communities may claim that homosexuality offends their community values; many neighborhood residents will argue that group homes for the mentally retarded will destroy their community; some will argue that allowing certain kinds of speech (books, posters, demonstrations, etc.) offends their community values. All of these claims, however, represent exclusionary definitions of community, with the goal of keeping people *out*. The open, tolerant, and inclusive definition of community embodied in the rights revolution represents a preferable vision of a good society.

Chapter Seven
CONCLUSION:
NEW RULES FOR AMERICAN SOCIETY

HOW DO WE WISH TO LIVE?

WHAT KIND OF society do we wish to live in? What values do we want to guide us in the making of law and policy? What rules do we want to govern how we relate to each other, as individuals and as groups? These are fundamental questions of political philosophy. They are also the questions at the heart of the debate over the place of rights in American society.

I began this book with a fable about a hypothetical Reitz van Winkle who fell asleep in the 1950s and awoke forty years later, astonished at how much American society had changed. The point of the story was that the really significant changes did not involve technology or styles of dress but were reflected in the new rules about how people live and the new opportunities available to them.

In chapter 1 I reviewed a series of harsh critics of contemporary American society who, although they represented very different political persuasions, essentially agreed that some or all of our most serious problems were the result of this tremendous expansion in individual rights. Even those liberals and leftists who celebrate the civil rights movement as one of the great achievements in American history worry that it unleashed a destructive "identity politics" that threatens our political system.

Can it be that the pursuit of individual liberty—the highest ideal of American constitutional democracy—is indeed responsible for the many social ills attributed to it? Has it really led us into a moral abyss? Has it unleashed a poisonous balkanization that divides rather than unites us? Has it undermined the foundations of community in America?

In the context of contemporary world politics, the criticisms of our rights culture are especially ironic. Individual rights, in the sense of formal limits on the power of government over its citizens, are the hallmark of the Anglo-American system of constitutional democracy. With the collapse of the Soviet Union and the Communist states of Eastern Europe, the principal alternative to constitutional democracy has all but disappeared. It is curious that at the moment of its apparent triumph our system is racked by pervasive doubts from within.

This book has argued that the critics are wrong, that despite the many problems created by our new rights culture, the gains far outweigh the costs. The critics fail to appreciate what has happened in American society for several reasons, which can be summarized as follows.

First, and most important, the critics lack a proper historical perspective. Their "decline and fall" view of recent American history rests on an invented view of our society in the 1950s. They imagine it to have been a time of peace and harmony. As I have attempted to argue, the critics simply ignore the many forms of discrimination and exclusion that were taken for granted at that time: from the blatant race discrimination of de jure segregation to the more hidden exclusion of helpless mentally retarded children.

Second, the critics fail to appreciate the extent to which the rights revolution has produced a more inclusive and tolerant community. They focus on the liberating side of the rights revolution—the expressive individualism—and do not see that every new right embodies a consequent set of constraints. For the most part, those constraints prohibit those in power from limiting the full participation of other groups in American society.

Third, many critics fail to appreciate the dilemmas of difference in a society with a powerful legacy of discrimination and equality. They attack "identity politics" but fail to offer any reasonable solution to the question of how those who are excluded because they are "different" can overcome that exclusion without heightening awareness of that difference in the process. There is no easy resolution to this dilemma, but it does not help us to move in the direction of full equality by asking the historic victims of discrimination to pretend that they have not been treated differently.

Fourth, some of the most prominent critics believe that European countries, and the standards of the international human rights movement in particular, offer a better balance of rights and responsibilities than we currently have in the United States. Yet, on closer inspection, it turns out that the balancing principles used elsewhere are couched in vague terms ("national security," "public health and morals") that we have wrestled with in our struggles over constitutional law and have rejected.

Fifth, many of the critics of rights improperly assess the blame for the problems that do afflict American society. If there is an inadequate network of social services—leaving the single pregnant woman and the homeless man without needed support—that is hardly the fault of our rights advocates. The critics of our rights culture consistently refuse to blame the conservative opponents of a wider and stronger social safety net. On the issue of the responsibility of corporations to the communities where they operate, the critics refuse to even suggest any laws or policies that might arouse the wrath of the truly powerful.

Sixth, the most comprehensive alternative to a rights-oriented society is the philosophy of communitarianism. Yet those who posit a conflict between "rights" and "community" rarely, if ever, define what they mean by community. As various chapters in this book have attempted to illustrate, there are many different forms of community in America. Moreover, there are often fundamental conflicts between these notions of community: between neighborhood residents and groups they do not like; between the national government and religious community traditions; between the majority (be it national, regional, or local) and minority groups. Simply invoking the word "community" as some kind of mantra does not help us address the very real conflicts we face.

Seventh, the critics attack the new rights culture as lacking a moral voice and encouraging an excessive and amoral individualism. They fail to see the values inherent in a society organized around a system of rights: the values of tolerance, equality, fair play, and privacy. These values constrain as much as they liberate, and they constitute the new rules for American society.

The American experiment in constitutional democracy is now in its third century. The United States is the oldest such constitutional democracy in the world. The experiment continues. The last forty years have witnessed a crucial new era in that experiment. We are still coming to terms with the full ramifications of some of the new ideas that have arisen, just as we are still attempting to come to terms with the implications of the promise of freedom set forth in the Declaration of Independence, the Constitution, and the Bill of Rights.

NOTES

Introduction

1. The idea of using a modern day Rip van Winkle to illustrate the changes that have occurred in American society with respect to rights was inspired by Lawrence M. Friedman, *The Republic of Choice: Law, Authority, and Culture* (Cambridge, Mass.: Harvard University Press, 1990), p. 1. Kenneth L. Karst uses a 1952 "snapshot" to make the same point, *Law's Promise, Law's Expression* (New Haven, Conn.: Yale University Press, 1993), pp. 3–4.

2. Ronald Dworkin, *Life's Dominion: An Argument About Abortion, Euthanasia, and Individual Freedom* (New York: Knopf, 1993), pp. 28–29.

3. Mary Ann Glendon, *Rights Talk* (New York: Free Press, 1991).

4. Friedman, *The Republic of Choice*, p. 1. He develops many of the same themes in a subsequent book, *Total Justice* (New York: Russell Sage Foundation, 1985).

5. Amitai Etzioni, *The New Golden Rule: Community and Morality in a Democratic Society* (New York: Basic Books, 1996), p. xv.

6. Amitai Etzioni, the founder of the Communitarian Network, sets forth his views in *The Spirit of Community: Rights, Responsibilities, and the Communitarian Agenda* (New York: Crown, 1993). The book also contains the official Communitarian Network Platform (pp. 251–267). The Communitarian Network has also published the journal *The Responsive Community*, from 1990–91 to the present.

7. In Etzioni, *The Spirit of Community*, p. 253.

8. Samuel Walker, "The Communitarian Cop-Out," *National Civic Review* 82 (Summer 1993): 246–254.

9. Samuel Walker, *Sense and Nonsense About Crime and Drugs*, 4th ed. (Belmont, Calif.: Wadsworth, 1998).

10. Peter Edelman, "The Worst Thing Bill Clinton Has Done," *Atlantic Monthly*, March 1997, pp. 43ff.

11. Glendon, *Rights Talk*.

12. Arthur M. Schlesinger, Jr., *The Disuniting of America: Reflections on a Multicultural Society* (New York: Norton, 1992); Todd Gitlin, *The Twilight of Common Dreams* (New York: Henry Holt, 1995); Michael Tomasky, *Left*

for Dead (New York: Free Press, 1996); This issue is discussed at length in chapter 1.

13. Etzioni, *The New Golden Rule,* p. 62.

14. There is a large literature on this problem. For a particularly fascinating debunking of an invented tradition, see Stephen Nissenbaum, *The Battle for Christmas* (New York: Knopf, 1996). For one more directly relevant to the subject of this book, see Stephanie Koontz, *The Way We Never Were: American Families and the Nostalgia Trap* (New York: Basic Books, 1992).

15. For a view similar to mine, see Ira Glasser, "Those Weren't the Days, My Friend," *Visions of Liberty,* #2 June 9, 1996 (New York: ACLU, 1996); Evan Thomas, "The Tricks of Memory," *Newsweek,* December 26, 1994, p. 40.

16. The argument that basic civil liberties values—about free speech, equality, due process, and privacy—are widely shared by people of all persuasions requires elaboration and defense in a separate book. I have previously developed the argument in Samuel Walker, *In Defense of American Liberties: A History of the ACLU* (New York: Oxford University Press, 1990), and in *Hate Speech: The History of an American Controversy* (Lincoln: University of Nebraska Press, 1994).

Chapter One: The Problem of Rights

1. "Justice Thomas Calls for Responsibility," *New York Times,* May 17, 1994. The published version of the speech, which does not include the attacks on judicial activism that were reported in the *Times,* is a more thoughtful discussion of moral authority and criminal responsibility. See Clarence Thomas, "The Rights Revolution and America's Urban Poor," *Vital Speeches of the Day* 60 (June 15, 1994): 514–517.

2. Proceedings are to be published by the Madison Society.

3. Robert H. Bork, *Slouching Towards Gomorrah: Modern Liberalism and American Decline* (New York: Regan Books, 1996), p. 2.

4. William J. Bennett, *The Index of Leading Cultural Indicators* (New York: Touchstone Books, 1994), p. 8.

5. Alan Dershowitz, *The Abuse Excuse* (Boston: Little, Brown, 1994).

6. Arthur M. Schlesinger, Jr., *The Disuniting of America: Reflections of a Multicultural Society* (New York: Norton, 1992).

7. Bork, *Slouching Towards Gomorrah.*

8. Perry Miller, *The New England Mind: The Seventeenth Century* (Boston: Beacon Press, 1939), pp. 471–472.

9. Samuel Walker, *Hate Speech: The History of an American Controversy* (Lincoln: University of Nebraska Press, 1994).

10. Mark V. Tushnet, *Making Civil Rights Law: Thurgood Marshall and the Supreme Court, 1936–1961* (New York: Oxford University Press, 1994).

11. Samuel Walker, *In Defense of American Liberties: A History of the ACLU* (New York: Oxford University Press, 1990).

12. The extent to which our sense of our legal tradition is the result of

"narrative" and "storytelling," in which certain values are embedded in the story (as opposed to rigorous analysis of legal texts), is one of the main points of Critical Race Theory. See the collection by Richard Delgado, ed., *Critical Race Theory: The Cutting Edge* (Philadelphia: Temple University Press, 1995).

13. See especially Mari J. Matsuda, "Public Response to Racist Speech: Considering the Victim's Story," in *Words That Wound: Critical Race Theory, Assaultive Speech, and the First Amendment,* ed. Mari J. Matsuda, Charles R. Lawrence, IV, Richard Delgado, Kimberle Williams Crenshaw (Boulder, Colo.: Westview Press, 1993), pp. 17–51.

14. Michael Pertschuk and Wendy Schaetel, *The People Rising: The Campaign Against the Bork Nomination* (New York: Thunder's Mouth Press, 1989). Bork's version of the struggle, with a defense of his own views, is found in Robert H. Bork, *The Tempting of America: The Political Seduction of the Law* (New York: Free Press, 1990), pp. 267–349.

15. William Safire, *Safire's New Political Dictionary* (New York: Random House, 1993), p. 76.

16. Bork, *The Tempting of America.*

17. Edwin Meese III, "The Law of the Constitution," *Major Policy Statements of the Attorney General* (Washington: U.S. Department of Justice, 1988) pp. 45–51. Bork's views on the subject are found in *The Tempting of America,* pp. 143–160. For the views of two historians, see Leonard W. Levy, *Original Intent and the Framers' Constitution* (New York: Macmillan, 1988); and Jack N. Rakove, *Original Meanings: Politics and Ideas in the Making of the Constitution* (New York: Knopf, 1996).

18. Bork, *The Tempting of America,* p. 75.

19. On the role of professional historians in the *Brown* case, see Peter Novick, *That Noble Dream: The "Objectivity Question" and the American Historical Profession* (New York: Cambridge University Press, 1988).

20. Bork, *The Tempting of America,* p. 77. A similar though less critical view appears in G. Edward White, *The American Judicial Tradition* (New York: Oxford University Press, 1976), chap. 14.

21. Bork, *The Tempting of America,* p. 84.

22. Ibid., pp. 75, 76.

23. Ibid., p. 352.

24. Michael J. Sandel, *Democracy's Discontent* (Cambridge, Mass.: Harvard University Press, 1996); Cass Sunstein, *Democracy and the Problem of Free Speech* (New York: Free Press, 1993).

25. Bork, *Slouching Towards Gomorrah.*

26. Bork's defense of his own views is found in *The Tempting of America,* pp. 323–336.

27. William J. Bennett, ed., *The Book of Virtues: A Treasury of Great Moral Stories* (New York: Simon and Schuster, 1993).

28. Bennett, *Index of Leading Cultural Indicators.* He develops many of the same ideas in *The De-Valuing of America: The Fight for Our Culture and Our Children* (New York: Summit Books, 1992).

29. Bennett, *Index of Leading Cultural Indicators,* p. 8.

30. Ibid., p. 9.

31. For a more balanced view of the rise of freedom of choice as a cultural value in America, see Lawrence M. Friedman, *The Republic of Choice: Law, Authority, and Culture* (Cambridge, Mass.: Harvard University Press, 1990).

32. This is the central point of the highly influential conservative analysis by Charles Murray, *Losing Ground: American Social Policy, 1950–1980* (New York: Basic Books, 1984).

33. For a historical survey that puts current thinkers in perspective, see William M. Banks, *Black Intellectuals: Race and Responsibility in American Life* (New York: Norton, 1996). For an important criticism, see Cornell West, "Demystifying the New Black Conservatism," in his *Race Matters* (Boston: Beacon Press, 1993), pp. 47–60.

34. Thomas Sowell, *Race and Economics* (New York: David McKay, 1975).

35. In addition to *Race and Economics*, see the following books by Thomas Sowell: *Civil Rights: Rhetoric or Reality?* (New York: Morrow, 1984); *A Conflict of Visions* (New York: Morrow, 1987); *The Economics and Politics of Race: An International Perspective* (New York: Morrow, 1983); *Markets and Minorities* (New York: Basic Books, 1981); *Preferential Policies: An International Perspective* (New York: Morrow, 1990); *Race and Culture: A World View* (New York: Basic Books, 1994).

36. Thomas Sowell, *Ethnic America: A History* (New York: Basic Books, 1981), p. 292. For an extended discussion, see Sowell, *Preferential Policies*.

37. Sowell, *Ethnic America*.

38. Ibid., p. 14.

39. Ibid., p. 5.

40. Ibid., p. 127.

41. Ibid., p. 294.

42. Shelby Steele, *The Content of Our Character: A New Vision of Race in America* (New York: HarperCollins, 1991), p. 113.

43. Martin Luther King, Jr., "I Have a Dream," in *A Testament of Hope: The Essential Writings of Martin Luther King, Jr.*, James Melvin Washington, ed., (San Francisco: Harper and Row, 1986), p. 219.

44. Steele, *The Content of Our Character*, p. 121.

45. Steele, *The Content of Our Character*, p. 132.

46. National Research Council, *A Common Destiny: Blacks and American Society* (Washington, D.C.: National Academy Press, 1989).

47. A valuable anthology is Delgado, *Critical Race Theory*.

48. Walker, *Hate Speech;* Matsuda et al., *Words That Wound;* Richard Delgado and Jean Stefancic, *Must We Defend Nazis? Hate Speech, Pornography, and the New First Amendment* (New York: New York University Press, 1997).

49. *Doe v. University of Michigan*, 721 F. Supp. 852 (E.D. Mich. 1989); *UWM Post v. Board of Regents of the University of Wisconsin*, 774 F. Supp. 1163 (E.D. Wisc. 1991); Walker, *Hate Speech*, chap. 7.

50. The most influential articles by these scholars are collected in Matsuda et al., *Words That Wound*. The most sophisticated criticism from an African American perspective is that of Henry Louis Gates, "War of Words:

Critical Race Theory and the First Amendment," in *Speaking of Race, Speaking of Sex*, ed. Henry Louis Gates (New York: New York University Press, 1994), pp. 17–58.

51. Mari J. Matsuda, "Public Response to Racist Speech: Considering the Victim's Story," in Matsuda et al., eds., *Words That Wound*, pp. 17–51; Mari J. Matsuda, *Where Is Your Body? And Other Essays on Race, Gender, and the Law* (Boston: Beacon Press, 1996).

52. Richard Delgado, "Words That Wound: A Tort Action for Racial Insults, Epithets, and Name Calling," in Matsuda et al., *Words That Wound*, pp. 89–110.

53. Charles Lawrence, "If He Hollers Let Him Go," in Matsuda et al., *Words That Wound*.

54. Catharine A. MacKinnon, *The Sexual Harassment of Working Women* (New Haven, Conn.: Yale University Press, 1979); *Meritor v. Vinson*, 477 U.S. 57 (1986).

55. Martha Minow, *Making All the Difference: Inclusion, Exclusion, and American Law* (Ithaca, N.Y.: Cornell University Press, 1990).

56. Aspects of this tangled history are found in Walker, *In Defense of American Liberties*.

57. Catharine MacKinnon, *Only Words* (Cambridge, Mass.: Harvard University Press, 1993).

58. Equality feminists would include, among others, ACLU president, Nadine Strossen, *Defending Pornography: Free Speech, Sex, and the Fight for Women's Rights* (New York: Scribner, 1995). A subtle and complex discussion of the problem of "difference" is found in Minow, *Making All the Difference*.

59. MacKinnon, *The Sexual Harassment of Working Women*; Catharine A. MacKinnon, *Feminism Unmodified: Discourses on Life and Law* (Cambridge, Mass.: Harvard University Press, 1987).

60. *Meritor v. Vinson*, 477 U.S. 57 (1986).

61. *American Booksellers Association v. Hudnut*, 771 F. 2d 323 (7th Cir. 1985). An excellent account is found in Donald Alexander Downs, *The New Politics of Pornography* (Chicago: University of Chicago Press, 1989).

62. Strossen, *Defending Pornography*.

63. Todd Gitlin, *The Twilight of Common Dreams: Why America is Wracked by Culture Wars* (New York: Henry Holt, 1995); Michael Tomasky, *Left for Dead: The Life, Death, and Possible Resurrection of Progressive Politics in America* (New York: Free Press, 1996).

64. The most sympathetic account of the early SDS is Jim Miller, *Democracy Is in the Streets* (New York: Simon and Schuster, 1987).

65. Todd Gitlin, *The Whole World Is Watching* (Berkeley: University of California Press, 1980).

66. Gitlin, *The Twilight of Common Dreams*, pp. 7–36.

67. Erving Goffman, *Stigma* (Englewood Cliffs, N.J.: Prentice-Hall, 1963), p. 114.

68. Minow, *Making All the Difference*, p. 20.

69. Tomasky, *Left for Dead*, chap. 3.

70. Ibid., p. 78.

71. Ibid.

72. Arthur M. Schlesinger, Jr., *The Disuniting of America: Reflections on a Multicultural Society* (New York: Norton, 1992).

73. Arthur M. Schlesinger, Jr., *The Vital Center* (Boston: Houghton Mifflin, 1949).

74. Robert Hughes, *The Culture of Complaint* (New York: Oxford University Press, 1993), p. 17.

75. Ibid.

76. Katie Roiphe, *The Morning After* (Boston: Little Brown, 1993); Christina Hoff Sommers, *Who Stole Feminism?* (New York: Simon and Schuster, 1994).

77. Charles J. Sykes, *A Nation of Victims* (New York: St. Martin's Press, 1992); Walter K. Olson, *The Excuse Factory: How Employment Law Is Paralyzing the American Workplace* (New York: Free Press, 1997).

78. Alan Dershowitz, *The Abuse Excuse* (Boston: Little, Brown, 1994).

79. Sommers, *Who Stole Feminism?*

80. Alan Dershowitz, *The Vanishing American Jew* (Boston: Little, Brown, 1997).

81. Michael J. Sandel, *Liberalism and the Limits of Justice* (Cambridge: Cambridge University Press, 1982); Frank Michaelman, "Law's Republic," *Yale Law Journal* 97 (1988), pp. 1493–1537.

82. The Platform is found in both Amitai Etzioni, *The Spirit of Community: Rights, Responsibilities, and the Communitarian Agenda* (New York: Crown, 1993), pp. 251–267, and *The Responsive Community* 2 (Winter 1991/92): 4–20.

83. Etzioni, *The Spirit of Community: Rights, Responsibilities, and the Communitarian Agenda* (New York: Crown Publishers, 1993), pp. 253–267; Amitai Etzioni, *The New Golden Rule: Community and Morality in a Democratic Society* (New York: Basic Books, 1996).

84. Etzioni, *The Spirit of Community*, p. 249.

85. Etzioni, *The New Golden Rule*, p. 5.

86. Robert N. Bellah, Richard Madsen, William M. Sullivan, Ann Swidler, and Steven M. Tipton, *Habits of the Heart: Individualism and Commitment in American Life* (Berkeley: University of California Press, 1985).

87. Mary Ann Glendon, *Rights Talk* (New York: Free Press, 1991), p. xi.

88. Walker, *In Defense of American Liberties*, pp. 299–320.

89. Mitchell Bernard, Ellen Levine, Stefan Presser, and Marianne Stecich, *The Rights of Single People* (New York: Bantam Books, 1985).

90. Glendon, *Rights Talk*, p. xii.

91. Etzioni, *The Spirit of Community*, p. 5.

92. Glendon, *Rights Talk*.

93. This point derives heavily from the highly influential sociological study by Robert Bellah et al., *Habits of the Heart: Individualism and Commitment in American Life*, and its follow-up, Robert Bellah, Richard Madsen, William M. Sullivan, Ann Swidler, Steven M. Tipton, *The Good Society* (New York: Vintage Books, 1992).

94. Glendon, *Rights Talk*, p. x.

95. Ibid., pp. x–xi.

96. Michaelman, "Law's Republic," 1493.

97. Sunstein, *Democracy and the Problem of Free Speech.*

98. Ibid., p. 198.

99. Matsuda et al., *Words That Wound;* MacKinnon, *Only Words.*

100. Mary Ann Glendon and David Blankenhorn, eds., *Seedbeds of Virtue: Source of Competence, Character, and Citizenship in American Society* (Lanham, Md.: Madison Books, 1995).

101. Sandel, *Democracy's Discontent,* p. 294.

102. Etzioni, *The New Golden Rule,* p. xv.

Chapter Two: The Transformation of American Life

1. Austin Sarat and Thomas R. Kearns, "Editorial Introduction," in *Law in Everyday Life,* ed. Austin Sarat and Thomas R. Kearns (Ann Arbor: University of Michigan Press, 1993), pp. 1, 8.

2. William E. Leuchtenburg, *The Supreme Court Reborn: The Constitutional Revolution in the Age of Roosevelt* (New York: Oxford University Press, 1995).

3. Martin Duberman, *Stonewall* (New York: Summit Books, 1993).

4. Nan D. Hunter, Sherrl E. Michaelson, and Thomas B. Stoddard, *The Rights of Lesbian and Gay Men* (Carbondale: Southern Illinois University Press, 1992).

5. Vincent Blasi, ed., *The Burger Court: The Counter-Revolution That Wasn't* (New Haven, Conn.: Yale University Press, 1983).

6. Robert H. Bork, *Slouching Towards Gomorrah: Modern Liberalism and American Decline* (New York: Regan Books, 1996).

7. I have argued this point in Samuel Walker, *Hate Speech: The History of an American Controversy* (Lincoln: University of Nebraska Press, 1994).

8. The best and most dispassionate analysis of this phenomenon is Lawrence M. Friedman, *The Republic of Choice: Law, Authority, and Culture* (Cambridge, Mass.: Harvard University Press, 1990).

9. Even Friedman, who is a sympathetic historian of the rise of expressive individualism, devotes little attention to the constraining side, see ibid.

10. Amitai Etzioni, *The Spirit of Community* (New York: Crown Books, 1993), p. 6.

11. Lawrence M. Friedman, "Limited Monarchy: The Rise and Fall of Student Rights," in *School Days, Rule Days: The Legalization and Regulation of Education,* ed. David L. Kirp and Donald N. Jensen (Philadelphia: Palmer Press, 1986), p. 245.

12. The issues are covered in *West Education Law Reporter* (St. Paul, Minn.: West Publishing, annual); and Arval Morris, *The Constitution and American Public Education* (Durham, N.C.: Carolina Academic Press, 1989).

13. David L. Kirp, "Introduction," in Kirp and Jensen, *School Days, Rule Days,* p. 1.

14. Richard E. Morgan, *Disabling America: The "Rights Industry" in Our Time* (New York: Basic Books, 1984), chap. 3, "Destabilizing the Schools," pp.

46–73. William A. Donohue, *Twilight of Liberty: The Legacy of the ACLU* (New Brunswick, N.J.: Transaction Books, 1994), chap. 2, "The Schools," pp. 63–91.

15. See Lawrence M. Friedman, *Total Justice* (New York: Russell Sage Foundation, 1985).

16. See the critique of the "law-first" approach to the study of law and society in Austin Sarat and Thomas R. Kearns, "Beyond the Great Divide: Forms of Legal Scholarship and Everyday Life," in Sarat and Kearnes, *Law in Everyday Life*, pp. 21–61.

17. *Meritor v. Vinson*, 477 U.S. 57 (1986).

18. The best ongoing monitor of these events is Nat Hentoff, *Free Speech for Me—But Not for Thee* (New York: HarperCollins, 1992), which is a collection of his newspaper columns.

19. Walker, *Hate Speech.*

20. Walter K. Olson, *The Excuse Factory: How Employment Law Is Paralyzing the American Workplace* (New York: Free Press, 1997).

21. University of Omaha, Request for Non-Instructional Personnel, May 6, 1952; copy in author's possession.

22. Samuel Walker, *In Defense of American Liberties: A History of the ACLU* (New York: Oxford University Press, 1990).

23. Samuel Walker, *The American Civil Liberties Union: An Annotated Bibliography* (New York: Garland, 1992), pp. 8–13. A current list is available from the ACLU.

24. Joel M. Gora, David Goldberger, Gary M. Stern, and Morton H. Halperin, *The Right to Protest* (Carbondale: Southern Illinois University Press, 1991).

25. For a particularly valuable benchmark in the development of the ACLU's thinking about rights, which covers many issues that did not develop as much as others, see Norman Dorsen, ed., *The Rights of Americans: What They Are—What They Should Be* (New York: Vintage Books, 1972).

26. For an international perspective on the troubling aspects of the idea of childrens' rights, see Michael Freeman, ed., *Childrens' Rights: A Comparative Perspective* (Brookfield, Vt.: Dartmouth Press, 1996).

27. Etzioni, *The Spirit of Community*, p. 5.

28. George Will, "Too Much of a Good Thing?" *Newsweek*, September 23, 1991 and "Our Expanding Menu of Rights," *Newsweek*, December 14, 1992, 90.

29. Etzioni, *The Spirit of Community*, p. 5.

30. Christopher D. Stone, *Should Trees Have Standing? Toward Legal Rights For Natural Objects* (New York: Avon Books, 1975).

31. *Bowers v. Hardwick*, 478 U.S. 186 (1986).

32. *Romer v. Evans*, 116 S. Ct. 162 (1996).

33. *Meritor v. Vinson*, 477 U.S. 57 (1986).

34. Mitchell Bernard, Ellen Levine, Stefan Presser, and Marianne Stecich, *The Rights of Single People* (New York: Bantam Books, 1985).

35. Jerry Falwell, forward, *Judgment Without Justice: The Dred Scott and Roe vs. Wade Decisions* (Lynchburg, Va.: Old-Time Gospel Hour, 1982).

36. "Who Owes What to Whom?" *Harper's,* February 1991, pp. 43ff.

37. Bork, *Slouching Towards Gomorrah,* p. 96.

38. For a criticism of childrens' rights that rejects the rights framework, see Laura M. Purdy, *In Their Best Interest? The Case Against Equal Rights for Children* (Ithaca, N.Y.: Cornell University Press, 1992).

39. Mary Ann Glendon, *Rights Talk* (New York: Free Press, 1991).

40. Ibid., chap. 6, "Rights Insularity." Her argument is rooted in her earlier book, *Abortion and Divorce in Western Law: American Failures, European Challenges* (Cambridge, Mass.: Harvard University Press, 1987).

41. Alexis de Tocqueville, *Democracy in America* (Garden City, N.Y.: Anchor Books, 1969); Seymour Martin Lipset, *American Exceptionalism* (New York: Norton, 1996).

42. Arthur M. Schlesinger, Jr., *The Disuniting of America: Reflections on a Multicultural Society* (New York: Norton, 1992).

43. Ian Brownlie, ed., *Basic Documents on Human Rights,* 3d ed. (New York: Oxford University Press, 1992). This collection contains forty-two separate documents.

44. Anthony Lester, "The Overseas Trade in the American Bill of Rights," *Columbia Law Review* 88 (1988): 537–561. The argument about an American "flavor" is developed in Walker, *Hate Speech,* chap. 5.

45. Glendon, *Rights Talk.*

46. Brownlie, *Basic Documents on Human Rights,* pp. 109–112.

47. Ibid.

48. For a reasoned criticism, see Purdy, *In Their Best Interests?*

49. Brownlie, *Basic Documents on Human Rights,* pp. 182–202.

50. Freeman, *Childrens' Rights.*

51. James Davison Hunter, *Culture Wars: The Struggle to Define America* (New York: Basic Books, 1991).

52. Walker, *In Defense of American Liberties,* pp. 313–314, 376–377, 378.

53. Brownlie, *Basic Documents,* p. 497.

54. For a general discussion of these limitations, see Charles Kiss, "Permissible Limitations on Rights," in *The International Bill of Rights: The Covenant on Civil and Political Rights,* ed. Louis Henkin (New York: Columbia University Press, 1981), pp. 290–310.

55. Glendon, *Rights Talk.*

56. Thomas Sowell, *Preferential Policies: An International Perspective* (New York: Morrow, 1990), p. 13.

57. Ibid., p. 13.

Chapter Three: Belonging to America: Rights and Membership

1. "Rejected as Clerk, Chosen as Justice," *New York Times,* June 15, 1993.

2. On the state of anti-Semitism in post–World War II America, see the

program of the Anti-Defamation League in Arnold Forster, *A Measure of Freedom* (New York: Doubleday, 1950).

3. David G. Savage, *Turning Right: The Making of the Rehnquist Supreme Court* (New York: Wiley, 1992), p. 21.

4. *Shelley v. Kraemer*, 334 U.S. 1 (1948).

5. "Rejected as Clerk, Chosen as Justice"; Deborah L. Markowitz, "In Pursuit of Equality: One Woman's Work to Change the Law," *Women's Rights Law Reporter* 2 (Summer 1989): 73–97.

6. Michael Walzer, *Spheres of Justice: A Defense of Pluralism and Equality* (New York: Basic Books, 1983), p. 31.

7. Ibid., p. 63.

8. William H. Chafe, *Civilities and Civil Rights: Greensboro, North Carolina, and the Black Struggle for Freedom* (New York: Oxford University Press, 1980).

9. These issues are discussed in William B. Rubenstein, "Since When Is the Fourteenth Amendment Our Route to Equality? Some Reflections on the Construction of the 'Hate Speech' Debate from a Lesbian/Gay Perspective," in *Speaking of Race, Speaking of Sex*, ed. Henry Louis Gates, Anthony P. Griffin, Donald E. Lively, Robert C. Post, William B. Rubenstein, and Nadine Strossen (New York: New York University Press, 1994), pp. 280–299.

10. Robert A. Burt, Esq., "Retardation, Legal Rights and the Communal Ideal," in *The Legal Rights of Citizens with Mental Retardation*, ed. Lawrence A. Kane, Phyllis Brown, and Julius S. Cohen (New York: University Press of America, 1988), pp. 33–49.

11. An exception is Kent Greenawalt, *Fighting Words: Individuals, Communities, and Liberties of Speech* (Princeton, N.J.: Princeton University Press, 1995), chap. 7.

12. *Cantwell v. Connecticut*, 310 U.S. 296 (1940).

13. James M. Penton, *Apocalypse Delayed: The Story of the Jehovah's Witnesses* (Toronto: University of Toronto Press, 1985); James A. Beckford, *The Trumpet of Prophecy: A Sociological Study of Jehovah's Witnesses* (Oxford: Basil Blackwell, 1975).

14. Joseph F. Rutherford, Enemies (Brooklyn, N.Y.: Watchtower Bible and Tract Society, 1937).

15. Samuel Walker, *Hate Speech: The History of an American Controversy* (Lincoln: University of Nebraska Press, 1994), chap. 3.

16. On the different hate groups in the 1920s and 1930s, see Walker, *Hate Speech*, chaps. 2 and 3; the Witnesses are covered in chap. 4.

17. A number of these confrontations resulted in Supreme Court cases that fashioned the first impressive body of free speech law. See, for example, *Lovell v. Griffin*, 303 U.S. 444 (1938), which struck down an ordinance on littering, and the Witness cases that followed.

18. Walker, *Hate Speech*, chap. 4.

19. David Manwaring, *Render unto Caesar: The Flag-Salute Controversy* (Chicago: University of Chicago Press, 1962).

20. Henry J. Abraham, *Freedom and the Court*, 5th ed. (New York: Oxford

University Press, 1988), pp. 297–298. On the NAACP, see Harry Kalven, Jr., *The Negro and the First Amendment* (Chicago: University of Chicago Press, 1966).

21. *Cantwell v. Connecticut*, 310 U.S. 296 (1940).

22. Ibid.

23. Abraham, *Freedom and the Court.*

24. *Cantwell v. Connecticut*, 310 U.S. 296 (1940).

25. *West Virginia State Board of Education v. Barnette*, 319 U.S. 624 (1943); Manwaring, *Render unto Caesar.*

26. Carla Gardina Pestana, "The Quaker Executions as Myth and History," *Journal of American History* 80 (September 1993): 441–469. On the history of violence arising from religious conflict, see Richard Hofstadter and Michael Wallace, eds., *American Violence: A Documentary History* (New York: Vintage Books, 1971).

27. Leonard J. Arrington and Davis Bitton, *The Mormon Experience: A History of the Latter-day Saints* (New York: Knopf, 1979), chap. 3.

28. William E. Leuchtenberg, *The Supreme Court Reborn: The Constitutional Revolution in the Age of Roosevelt* (New York: Oxford University Press, 1995).

29. *United States v. Carolene Products*, 304 U.S. 144, 152 n. 4 (1938). It is extraordinary that this important principle, which has guided the Court ever since, was enunciated in a footnote in an otherwise obscure case.

30. *Olmstead v. United States*, 277 U.S. 438 (1928).

31. "Studio Chief's Star Rises at Fox," *New York Times*, March 2, 1992.

32. Leo Pfeffer, *Church, State, and Freedom* (Boston: Beacon Press, 1953).

33. *Engel v. Vitale*, 370 U.S. 421 (1962).

34. *School District v. Schempp*, 374 U.S. 203 (1963).

35. *Engel v. Vitale*, 370 U.S. 421 (1962). The handful of most controversial decisions would include *Brown v. Board of Education*, 347 U.S. 483 (1954); *Baker v. Carr*, 369 U.S. 186 (1962); and *Miranda v. Arizona*, 384 U.S. 436 (1966).

36. Newt Gingrich and Richard Armey, *Contract with America* (New York: Times Books, 1994).

37. My own argument is that over time many conservatives have come to accept a number of basic civil liberties principles. See Samuel Walker, *In Defense of American Liberties: A History of the ACLU* (New York: Oxford University Press, 1990), and Walker, *Hate Speech.*

38. For a neoconservative interpretation, see Richard E. Morgan, *Disabling America* (New York: Basic Books, 1984). For the Communitarian view on teaching morality in the schools, see Amitai Etzioni, *The Spirit of Community: Rights, Responsibilities, and the Communitarian Agenda* (New York: Crown Books, 1993), pp. 89–115; the official Communitarian Platform is on pp. 258–259.

39. William J. Bennett, *The De-Valuing of American Society* (New York: Summit Books, 1992).

40. Robert H. Bork, *Slouching Towards Gomorrah* (New York: HarperCollins, 1996).

41. Richard John Neuhaus, *America Against Itself: Moral Vision and the Public Order* (Notre Dame, Ind.: University of Notre Dame Press, 1992); Richard

John Neuhaus, *The Naked Public Square: Religion and Democracy in America* (Grand Rapids, Mich.: W. B. Eerdmans, 1984).

42. Stephen Carter, *The Culture of Disbelief* (New York: Basic Books, 1993).

43. Mary Ann Glendon, *Rights Talk* (New York: Free Press, 1991).

44. Vashti Cromwell McCollum, *One Woman's Fight* (Boston: Beacon Press, 1952). The program was declared unconstitutional in *McCollum v. Board of Education*, 333 U.S. 203 (1948).

45. Leo Pfeffer, *Church, State, and Freedom* (Boston: Beacon Press, 1953), pp. 356–367. The New York program was upheld in *Zorach v. Clauson*, 343 U.S. 306 (1952).

46. Jesse H. Choper, *Securing Religious Liberty: Principles for Judicial Interpretation of the Religion Clauses* (Chicago: University of Chicago Press, 1995), p. xi.

47. David Hackett Fischer, *Albion's Seed: Four British Folkways in America* (New York: Oxford University Press, 1989).

48. Arthur M. Schlesinger, Jr., *The Disuniting of America: Reflections on a Multicultural Society* (New York: Norton, 1992), p. 53.

49. James Davison Hunter, *Culture Wars: The Struggle to Define America* (New York: Basic Books, 1991).

50. Charles Loring Brace, *The Dangerous Classes* (New York: Wynkoop and Hallenback, 1872).

51. James H. Timberlake, *Prohibition and the Progressive Movement* (Cambridge, Mass.: Harvard University Press, 1963).

52. Schlesinger, *The Disuniting of America*, p. 53.

53. Pfeffer, *Church, State, and Freedom*, pp. 281–286,

54. Until the World War II era, American Catholics generally opposed official support for religion in the public schools, mainly because they saw such programs as promoting Protestantism. In a historic reversal in the 1940s, they endorsed government support for religious activities, in large part because they now sought public financial support for parochial schools.

55. *Meyer v. Nebraska*, 262 U.S. 390 (1923).

56. *Pierce v. Society of Sisters*, 268 U.S. 510 (1925).

57. Ray Ginger, *Six Days or Forever?* (Chicago: Quadrangle Books, 1969); Edward J. Larson, *Trial and Error* (New York: Oxford University Press, 1985).

58. Pfeffer, *Church, State, and Freedom*, pp. 447–464.

59. *Lynch v. Donnelly*, 465 U.S. 668, 687–688 (1984). See the discussion in Kenneth L. Karst, "The First Amendment, the Politics of Religion and the Symbols of Government," *Harvard Civil Rights–Civil Liberties Law Review* 27 (Summer 1992): 503–530.

60. Choper, *Securing Religious Liberty*, p. 13.

61. Kay Mills, *This Little Light of Mine: The Life of Fannie Lou Hamer* (New York: Dutton, 1993).

62. John Dittmer, *Local People: The Struggle for Civil Rights in Mississippi* (Urbana: University of Illinois Press, 1994).

63. *Shaw v. Reno*, 509 U.S. 6301 (1993).

64. See the discussion in chapter 1.

65. These incidents are cited by the advocates of restrictive campus speech codes. See Mari Matsuda et al., *Words That Wound: Critical Race Theory, Assaultive Speech, and the First Amendment* (Boulder, Colo.: Westview Press, 1993).

66. National Advisory Commission on Civil Disorders, *Report* (New York: Bantam Books, 1968), p. 1.

67. The literature on African American culture is vast and growing. Two places to start might be the essays by the African American literary critic Henry Louis Gates, *Loose Canons: Notes on the Culture Wars* (New York: Oxford University Press, 1992), and the scholarship of the white historian Lawrence W. Levine, *Black Culture and Black Consciousness* (New York: Oxford University Press, 1977).

68. Erving Goffman, *Stigma* (Englewood Cliffs, N.J.: Prentice-Hall, 1963), p. 114.

69. Nan D. Hunter, "Life After *Hardwick*," *Harvard Civil Rights–Civil Liberties Law Review* 27 (Summer 1992): 546.

70. The literature on this chapter in American history is extensive. The best treatment of the Supreme Court decisions and an excellent introduction is Peter Irons, *Justice at War* (New York: Oxford University Press, 1983). Earlier works include Morton Grodzins, *Americans Betrayed* (Chicago: University of Chicago Press, 1949); and Jacobus ten Broek, Edward N. Barnhart, and Floyd Matson, *Prejudice, War, and the Constitution* (Berkeley: University of California Press, 1954). On the relocation centers see Richard Drinnon, *Keeper of Concentration Camps: Dillon S. Myer and American Racism* (Berkeley: University of California Press, 1987).

71. This observation is made by Irons, *Justice at War.*

72. Roger Daniels, Sandra C. Taylor, and Harry L. Kitano, eds., *Japanese Americans: From Relocation to Redress*, rev. ed. (Seattle: University of Washington Press, 1991).

73. Although Warren was obviously deeply embarrassed about it in later years, his public comments about his role in the affair were very guarded, and he never explicitly acknowledged that he was wrong. See G. Edward White, *Warren* (New York: Oxford University Press, 1982).

74. Sandra C. Taylor, "'Fellow-Feelers with the Afflicted': The Christian Churches and the Relocation of the Japanese During World War II," in Daniels, Taylor, and Kitano, *Japanese Americans*, pp. 123–129.

75. Irons, *Justice at War;* Walker, *In Defense of American Liberties.*

76. *Korematsu v. United States*, 232 U.S. 214 (1944).

77. *Hirabayashi v. United States*, 320 U.S. 81 (1943).

78. *Korematsu v. United States*, 232 U.S. 214 (1944).

79. Irons, *Justice at War*, p. 371.

80. Howard Ball, "Judicial Parsimony and Military Necessity Disinterred: A Reexamination of the Japanese Exclusion Cases," in Daniels, Taylor, and Kitano, *Japanese Americans*, pp. 176–185.

81. Glendon, *Rights Talk*, chap. 6, "Rights Insularity."

82. Universal Declaration of Human Rights, Article 29(2), in *Basic Docu-*

ments on *Human Rights,* 3d ed., ed. Ian Brownlie (Oxford: Clarendon Press, 1992), p. 27.

83. International Covenant on Civil and Political Rights, Article 21, in Brownlie, *Basic Documents on Human Rights,* pp. 132–133.

Chapter Four: Speaking and Belonging: Free Speech and Community

1. The controversy is covered in Samuel Walker, *In Defense of American Liberties: A History of the ACLU* (New York: Oxford University Press, 1990), pp. 661–62. On Curley, see Jack Beatty, *The Rascal King: The Life and Times of James Michael Curley* (Reading, Mass.: Addison Wesley, 1992).

2. Kenneth L. Karst, "Equality as a Central Principle in the First Amendment," *University of Chicago Law Review* 43 (1975): 21. For a fuller treatment, see Kenneth L. Karst, *Law's Promise, Law's Expression* (New Haven, Conn.: Yale University Press, 1993). On the "central meaning" of the First Amendment, see the landmark case *New York Times v. Sullivan,* 376 U.S. 254 (1964), and the discussion in Harry Kalven, Jr., "The *New York Times* Case: A Note on the Central Meaning of the First Amendment," *Supreme Court Review* (1964), pp. 191–221.

3. Michael Walzer, *Spheres of Justice: A Defense of Pluralism and Equality* (New York: Basic Books, 1983), p. 31.

4. Gara LaMarche and William Rubenstein, "The Love That Dare Not Speak: Censoring Gay Expression," *The Nation,* November 5, 1990, p. 524.

5. William B. Rubenstein, "Since When Is the Fourteenth Amendment Our Route to Equality? Some Reflections on the Construction of the Hate Speech Debate from a Lesbian/Gay Perspective," *Law and Sexuality: A Review of Lesbian and Gay Legal Issues* 2 (Summer 1992): 19–27; also published in *Speaking of Race, Speaking of Sex,* ed. Henry Louis Gates, Anthony P. Griffin, Donald E. Lively, Robert C. Post, William B. Rubenstein, and Nadine Strossen (New York: New York University Press, 1994), pp. 280–299.

6. Ibid., pp. 19–27.

7. Cass Sunstein, *Democracy and the Problem of Free Speech* (New York: Free Press, 1993); Kent Greenawalt, *Speech, Crime, and the Uses of Language* (New York: Oxford University Press, 1989); Kent Greenawalt, *Fighting Words: Individuals, Communities, and Liberties of Speech* (Princeton, N.J.: Princeton University Press, 1995); Harry Kalven, Jr., *A Worthy Tradition: Freedom of Speech in America* (New York: Harper and Row, 1988); Franklyn Haiman, *Speech and Law in a Free Society* (Chicago: University of Chicago Press, 1981); and Franklyn Haiman, *"Speech Acts" and the First Amendment* (Carbondale: Southern Illinois University Press, 1993); Rodney Smolla, *Free Speech in an Open Society* (New York: Alfred A. Knopf, 1992).

8. Catharine MacKinnon, *Only Words* (Cambridge, Mass.: Harvard University Press, 1993); reply by Nadine Strossen, *Defending Pornography: Free Speech, Sex, and the Fight for Women's Rights* (New York: Scribner's, 1995).

9. The most important articles are collected in Mari J. Matsuda, Charles R. Lawrence, III, Richard Delgado, and Kimberle Williams Crenshaw, eds., *Words That Wound: Critical Race Theory, Assaultive Speech, and the First Amendment* (Boulder, Colo.: Westview Press, 1993). See also Samuel Walker, *Hate Speech: The History of an American Controversy* (Lincoln: University of Nebraska Press, 1994).

10. Donald Alexander Downs, *Nazis in Skokie: Freedom, Community, and the First Amendment* (Notre Dame, Ind.: Notre Dame University Press, 1985), argues for a specific exception to the First Amendment for advocating genocide. See also Sunstein, *Democracy and the Problem of Free Speech.*

11. Mary Ann Glendon, *Rights Talk* (New York: Free Press, 1991).

12. Michael J. Sandel, *Liberalism and the Limits of Justice* (New York: Cambridge University Press, 1982).

13. Walker, *In Defense of American Liberties,* pp. 61–62.

14. This point is developed in Walker, *Hate Speech,* although originally suggested by Harry Kalven, Jr., *The Negro and the First Amendment* (Chicago: University of Chicago Press, 1966).

15. Ellen Chesler, *Woman of Valor: Margaret Sanger and the Birth Control Movement in America* (New York: Simon and Schuster, 1992), pp. 218–221.

16. Edward de Grazia and Roger K. Newman, *Banned Films: Movies, Censors, and the First Amendment* (New York: Bowker, 1982), pp. 16–17, 186–188.

17. Chesler, *Woman of Valor,* pp. 282–283; David J. Garrow, *Liberty and Sexuality: The Right to Privacy and the Making of* Roe v. Wade (New York: Macmillan, 1994), pp. 23–24.

18. Alice Wexler, *Emma Goldman in America* (Boston: Beacon Press, 1984), pp. 213–214.

19. Quoted in Linda Gordon, *Woman's Body, Woman's Right: Birth Control in America* (New York: Penguin Books, 1977), p. 231

20. Garrow, *Liberty and Sexuality;* Walker, *In Defense of American Liberties.*

21. Heywood Broun and Margaret Leech, *Anthony Comstock: Roundsman of the Lord* (New York: Literary Guild, 1927). A useful account is presented in Morris L. Ernst and Alan U. Schwartz, *Censorship: The Search for the Obscene* (New York: Macmillan, 1964).

22. The history of the case is reported in Mary Ware Dennett, *Who's Obscene?* (New York: Vanguard Press, 1930); and in Walker, *In Defense of American Liberties,* pp. 84–86. Constance M. Chen, *"The Sex Side of Life:" Mary Ware Dennett's Battle for Birth Control and Sex Education* (New York: The New Press, 1996).

23. Walker, *In Defense of American Liberties,* pp. 84–86. Chen, *"The Sex Side of Life."*

24. Morris L. Ernst and William Seagle, *To the Pure . . . A Study of Obscenity and the Censor* (New York: Viking, 1928); Morris L. Ernst and Alexander Lindey, *Hold Your Tongue!* (New York: Abelard Press, 1932); Morris L. Ernst and Alan U. Schwartz, *Censorship.* Harriet Pilpel joined his law firm in the late 1930s and eventually succeeded him as general counsel of both the ACLU and Planned Parenthood. She recalled that in the 1930s "there was

no one else doing reproductive rights litigation" (interview with author).

25. Ernst and Schwartz, *Censorship*, pp. 162–166.

26. June Rose, *Marie Stopes and the Sexual Revolution* (London: Faber and Faber, 1992).

27. Garrow, *Liberty and Sexuality*.

28. *Griswold v. Connecticut*, 381 U.S. 479 (1965). The background is developed in great detail in David Garow's aptly titled *Liberty and Sexuality*.

29. Strossen, *Defending Pornography*.

30. MacKinnon, *Only Words*, p. 71. A contrary view is developed in Strossen, *Defending Pornography*.

31. Brief *Amicus Curiae* of Feminist Anti-Censorship Task Force, *American Booksellers Association v. Hudnut*, 771 F. 2d 323 (7th Cir. 1985); F.A.C.T. Book Committee, *Caught Looking* (New York: Caught Looking, 1986).

32. Norton, interview with author; Walker, *In Defense of American Liberties*.

33. Algernon Black, *The People and the Police* (New York: McGraw-Hill, 1968).

34. *Rosenfeld v. New Jersey*, 408 U.S. 901 (1972); *Lewis v. New Orleans*, 408 U.S. 913 (1972); *Brown v. Oklahoma*, 408 U.S. 914 (1972).

35. Strossen, *Defending Pornography*, pp. 223–224. This point is discussed in Henry Louis Gates, "War of Words: Critical Race Theory and the First Amendment," in Gates et al., *Speaking of Race, Speaking of Sex*, pp. 45–46.

36. The best discussion is Harry Kalven, Jr., *The Negro and the First Amendment* (Chicago: University of Chicago Press, 1966).

37. Numan V. Bartley, *The Rise of Massive Resistance: Race and Politics in the South During the 1950s* (Baton Rouge: Louisiana State University Press, 1969).

38. Richard Kluger, *Simple Justice* (New York: Vintage Books, 1977), p. 752.

39. David M. Chalmers, *Hooded Americanism: The History of the Ku Klux Klan* (Chicago: Quadrangle Books, 1968).

40. Kalven, *The Negro and the First Amendment*.

41. *NAACP v. Alabama*, 357 U.S. 449 (1958); Kalven, *The Negro and the First Amendment*, pp. 91–99.

42. *NAACP v. Alabama*, 357 U.S. 449 (1958).

43. Ibid.

44. *Shelton v. Tucker*, 364 U.S. 479 (1960); Kalven, *The Negro and the First Amendment*, pp. 99–105.

45. *Gibson v. Florida Legislative Investigating Committee*, 372 U.S. 539 (1963).

46. Kalven, *The Negro and the First Amendment*, p. 66; Walker, *In Defense of American Liberties*.

47. "A Klansman's Black Lawyer, and a Principle," *New York Times*, September 10, 1993; Griffin, interview with author.

48. Griffin treats the case in Anthony P. Griffin, "The First Amendment and the Art of Storytelling," in Gates, et al., *Speaking of Race, Speaking of Sex*, pp. 257–279.

49. *Bryant v. Zimmerman*, 278 U.S. 63 (1928). The relationship of the two cases is discussed in Walker, *Hate Speech*, pp. 25–27, 116, 118.

50. Richard Delgado, ed., *Critical Race Theory: The Cutting Edge* (Philadelphia: Temple University Press, 1995).

51. *Gay Students Organization of the University of New Hampshire v. Bonner,* 509 F. 2d 652 (1st Cir. 1974).

52. Ibid.

53. Rubenstein, "Since When Is the Fourteenth Amendment Our Route to Equality?" p. 290.

54. This point is made by Kalven, *The Negro and the First Amendment.*

55. Rubenstein, "Since When is the Fourteenth Amendment Our Route to Equality?," 288.

56. *Bowers v. Hardwick,* 478 U.S. 186 (1986).

57. *Romer v. Evans,* 116 S. CT. 162 (1996).

58. *Gay Activists Alliance v. Lomenzo,* 31 N.Y. 2d 965, 341, N.Y.S. 2d 198 (1973).

59. Delgado, *Critical Race Theory.*

60. The campus speech code controversy is covered in Walker, *Hate Speech,* chap. 7.

61. Rubenstein, "Since When Is the Fourteenth Amendment Our Route to Equality?" p. 290.

62. Matsuda et al., eds., *Words That Wound: Critical Race Theory, Assaultive Speech, and the First Amendment.*

63. Sunstein, *Democracy and the Problem of Free Speech.*

64. Glendon, *Rights Talk.*

65. The Communitarian Network Platform is found in Etzioni, *The Spirit of Community,* pp. 251–267. This issue is discussed in detail in chapter 6.

66. On distinguishing between constitutionally protected and not protected behavior, see ACLU Reproductive Freedom Project, *Preserving the Right to Choose: How to Cope with Violence and Disruptions at Abortion Clinics* (New York: ACLU, 1986).

67. The position of different religious groups is examined in Frederick S. Jaffe, Barbara L. Lindheim, and Philip R. Lee, *Abortion Politics: Private Morality and Public Policy* (New York: McGraw-Hill, 1981).

68. *Planned Parenthood of Southeastern Pennsylvania v. Casey,* 505 U.S. 833 (1992).

69. *Terminiello v. Chicago,* 337 U.S. 1 (1949).

70. Sunstein, *Democracy and the Problem of Free Speech.*

71. Ibid., p. 198. Kent Greenawalt adopts a closely similar position but also makes no reference to antiabortion rhetoric in his *Fighting Words.*

72. *Cohen v. California,* 403 U.S. 15 (1971).

73. Glendon, *Rights Talk;* Amitai Etzioni, *The Spirit of Community: Rights, Responsibilities, and the Communitarian Agenda* (New York: Crown Books, 1993).

74. Etzioni, *The Spirit of Community,* pp. 251–267.

75. Cynthia Stokes Brown, ed., *Alexander Meiklejohn: Teacher of Freedom* (Berkeley, Calif.: Meiklejohn Institute, 1981).

76. Alexander Meiklejohn, *Free Speech and Its Relation to Self-Government* (New York: Harper and Brothers, 1948), p. 25.

77. Karst, "Equality as a Central Principle in the First Amendment," pp. 39–40.

78. Amitai Etzioni, *The New Golden Rule: Community and Morality in a Democratic Society* (New York: Basic Books, 1996), pp. 104–105.

79. Sunstein, *Democracy and the Problem of Free Speech.*

80. Greenawalt, *Fighting Words,* pp. 53, 55.

81. There are in fact a number of ideological positions within the animal rights movement. See James M. Jasper and Dorothy Nelkin, *The Animal Rights Crusade: The Growth of a Moral Protest* (New York: Free Press, 1992).

82. Christopher D. Stone, *Should Trees Have Standing? Toward Legal Rights for Natural Objects* (New York: Avon Books, 1975).

Chapter Five: The Confined and the Accused

1. *Donaldson v. O'Connor,* 493 F.2d 507 (1974).

2. See the list of ACLU handbooks in chapter 1.

3. For some important second thoughts by one of the leading figures in this effort, see Aryeh Neier, *Only Judgment: The Limits of Litigation in Social Change* (Middletown, Conn.: Wesleyan University Press, 1982). On the central role of the ACLU in this development, see Samuel Walker, *In Defense of American Liberties: A History of the ACLU* (New York: Oxford University Press, 1990), chap. 14, "The New Civil Liberties."

4. John J. DiIulio, Jr., ed., *Courts, Corrections, and the Constitution: The Impact of Judicial Intervention on Prisons and Jails* (New York: Oxford University Press, 1990). See, especially, Malcolm M. Feeley and Roger A. Hanson, "The Impact of Judicial Intervention on Prisons and Jails: A Framework for Analysis and a Review of the Literature," pp. 12–46.

5. Vincent Nathan, "The Use of Masters in Institutional Reform Litigation," *University of Toledo Law Review* 10 (1979): 419.

6 .The most detailed and most thoughtful analyses of these developments are presented in two books by James B. Jacobs: *Stateville: The Penitentiary in Mass Society* (Chicago: University of Chicago Press, 1977), and *New Perspectives on Prisons and Imprisonment* (Ithaca, N.Y.: Cornell University Press, 1983).

7. Author's conversation with Al Bronstein, former director of the ACLU National Prison Project.

8. John J. DiIulio, Jr., *Governing Prisons: A Comparative Study of Prison Management* (New York: Free Press, 1987); Richard E. Morgan, *Disabling America: The "Rights Industry" in Our Time* (New York: Basic Books, 1984).

9. John J. DiIulio, Jr., *No Escape: The Future of American Corrections* (New York: Basic Books, 1991), p. 157.

10. The data are in Bureau of Justice Statistics, *Sourcebook of Criminal Justice Statistics, 1994* (Washington, D.C.: Government Printing Office, 1995), p. 585. Interestingly, Texas now reports only total inmate deaths, without providing a breakdown by cause (e.g., natural causes, killed by other inmate), and would not release such figures to me.

11. Morgan, *Disabling America,* p. 73.

12. Neier, *Only Judgment,* p. 229.

13. Ibid., p. 192.

14. With respect to prisons, see DiIulio, *Courts, Corrections, and the Constitution;* and Jacobs, *New Perspectives on Prisons and Imprisonment.* On hospitals for the mentally retarded, see David J. Rothman and Shelia M. Rothman, *The Willowbrook Wars* (New York: Harper and Row, 1984).

15. Rothman and Rothman, *The Willowbrook Wars,* pp. 17–18.

16. Ibid., pp. 15–16.

17. Neier, *Only Judgment,* p. 229.

18. Walker, *In Defense of American Liberties,* p. 299.

19. Morton Birnbaum, "The Right to Treatment," *American Bar Association Journal* 46 (1960): 499–505.

20. *Rouse v. Cameron,* 373 F. 2d 451 (D.C. Cir. 1966).

21. *Wyatt v. Stickney,* 325 F. Supp. 781 (M.D. Ala. 1971).

22. On Ennis and Halpern, see Rothman and Rothman, *Willowbrook Wars,* pp. 54–63; Neier, *Only Judgment,* pp. 170–193. Halpern's own assessment of the contributions of public interest law firms is found in Charles R. Halpern, "The Public Interest Bar: An Audit," in *Verdicts on Lawyers,* ed. Ralph Nader and Mark Green (New York: Thomas Y. Crowell, 1976), pp. 158–171. See also Burton A. Weisbrod, ed., *Public Interest Law: An Economic and Institutional Analysis* (Berkeley: University of California Press, 1978).

23. For an incisive discussion of the impact of these changes on the problem of homelessness, see Christopher Jencks, *The Homeless* (Cambridge, Mass.: Harvard University Press, 1994).

24. The data are in Bureau of Justice Statistics, *Sourcebook of Criminal Justice Statistics, 1994.* On criminal justice policy, see Samuel Walker, *Popular Justice: A History of American Criminal Justice,* 2d ed. (New York: Oxford University Press, 1998).

25. David J. Rothman, *The Discovery of the Asylum* (Boston: Little, Brown, 1971).

26. Rothman and Rothman, *The Willowbrook Wars,* pp. 1–11.

27. Ibid., pp. 353, 358. The Rothmans themselves characterize the overall change in social policy as a "revolution" (p. 358).

28. Bureau of the Census, *Statistical Abstract of the United States, 1995* (Washington, D.C.: Government Printing Office, 1995), Table 202.

29. Bureau of the Census, *Statistical Abstract of the United States, 1992* (Washington, D.C.: Government Printing Office, 1992), Table 167.

30. Rothman and Rothman, *The Willowbrook Wars,* p. 180.

31. Ibid., p. 180.

32. Ibid., p. 356.

33. Robert J. Flynn and Kathleen Nitsch, eds., *Normalization, Integration, and Community Services* (Baltimore, Md.: University Park Press, 1980).

34. Rothman, *The Discovery of the Asylum.*

35. Doris Kearns Goodwin, *The Fitzgeralds and the Kennedys: An American Saga* (New York: St. Martin's Press, 1988), pp. 740–746.

36. Robert H. Bork, *Slouching Towards Gomorrah: Modern Liberalism and American Decline* (New York: Regan Books, 1996), especially the introduction and chaps. 5 and 6.

37. Rothman and Rothman, *The Willowbrook Wars*, pp. 60–62.

38. Ibid., p. 30.

39. Neier, *Only Judgment*, p. 191.

40. Mary Ann Glendon, *Rights Talk* (New York: Free Press, 1991), pp. 6–7.

41. Michael J. Sandel, *Democracy's Discontent* (Cambridge, Mass.: Harvard University Press, 1996), p. 294.

42. Rothman and Rothman, *The Willowbrook Wars*, p. 356.

43. *United States v. Carolene Products*, 304 U.S. 144, 152 n. 4.

44. Rothman and Rothman, *The Willowbrook Wars*, pp. 257–295.

45. Ibid., p. 257.

46. Several illuminating articles on this law and the larger issue of litigation and the public schools are found in David L. Kirp and Donald N. Jensen, eds., *School Days, Rule Days: The Legalization and Regulation of Education* (Philadelphia: Falmer Press, 1986).

47. Bureau of the Census, *Statistical Abstract of the United States, 1995,* Table 262, p. 171.

48. An excellent discussion of the implementation issues related to the 1975 federal law, which is highly skeptical of litigation as an instrument of social reform, is found in David Neal and David L. Kirp, "The Allure of Legalization Reconsidered: The Case of Special Education," in Kirp and Jensen, *School Days, Rule Days*, pp. 343–365.

49. Ibid.

50. Amitai Etzioni, *The Spirit of Community: Rights, Responsibilities, and the Communitarian Agenda* (New York: Crown Books, 1993), p. 5. The principal theme of Glendon's *Rights Talk* is the "absolutist" quality of the way we think about rights and the unrealistic expectations that have resulted.

51. Walker, *In Defense of American Liberties*, pp. 323–327; Donald Alexander Downs, *Nazis in Skokie: Freedom, Community, and the First Amendment* (Notre Dame, Ind.: University of Notre Dame, 1985).

52. Glendon, *Rights Talk*.

53. United Nations General Assembly, Declaration on the Rights of Mentally Retarded Persons, December 20, 1971; cited in Paul R. Friedman, *The Rights of Mentally Retarded Persons* (New York: Avon Books, 1976).

54. Christopher Jencks, *The Homeless* (Cambridge, Mass.: Harvard University Press, 1994).

55. Ibid., p. 17.

56. Ibid., p. 22.

57. Ibid., p. 24.

58. Ibid., p. 39.

59. Ibid.

60. Glendon, *Rights Talk*, p. 65.

61. *Parratt v. Taylor*, 451 U.S. 527 (1981).

62. Morgan, *Disabling America*.

63. A good contemporary account is found in Fred P. Graham, *The Self-Inflicted Wound* (New York: Macmillan, 1970). A historical overview is presented in Walker, *Popular Justice.*

64. Walker, *Popular Justice.* For a conservative criticism of the failure of liberals to take the crime issue seriously, see James Q. Wilson, *Thinking About Crime* (New York: Basic Books, 1975), especially chap. 4

65. Morgan, *Disabling America.*

66. Etzioni, *The Spirit of Community*, p. 166.

67. Quoted in Myron Orfield, "The Exclusionary Rule and Deterrence: An Empirical Study of Chicago Narcotics Officers," *University of Chicago Law Review* 54 (1987): 1016.

68. *Mapp v. Ohio*, 367 U.S. 643 (1961).

69. A 1920s investigation is described in Illinois Association for Criminal Justice, *Illinois Crime Survey* (Chicago: Illinois Association for Criminal Justice, 1929). One view of the situation as of the 1960s is found in Mike Royko, *Boss: Mayor Richard J. Daley of Chicago* (New York: New American Library, 1971). On reforms in the 1960s, see William J. Bopp, *O.W.: O. W. Wilson and the Search for a Police Profession* (Port Washington, N.Y.: Kennikat Press, 1977), chaps. 9 and 10.

70. Orfield, "The Exclusionary Rule and Deterrence."

71. Ibid., pp. 1026–1027; see especially n. 51.

72. Ibid., p. 1028.

73. Samuel Walker, *A Critical History of Police Reform: The Emergence of Professionalism* (Lexington, Mass.: Lexington Books, 1977).

74. Daniel L. Skoler, *Organizing the Non-System* (Lexington, Mass.: Lexington Books, 1977).

75. Orfield, "The Exclusionary Rule and Deterrence," p. 1029.

76. Ibid., p. 1038.

77. Ibid., p. 1046.

78. Ibid., p. 1037.

79. Ibid., p. 1042.

80. Roscoe Pound, *Criminal Justice in America* (1924; New York: Da Capo, 1975).

81. Samuel Walker, "Historical Roots of the Legal Control of Police Behavior," in *Police Innovation and Control of the Police*, ed. David Weisburd and Craig Uchida (New York: Springer-Verlag, 1993), pp. 32–55.

82. James F. Richardson, *The New York Police: Colonial Times to 1901* (New York: Oxford University Press, 1970), pp. 204–207.

83. Mark Haller, "Historical Roots of Police Behavior: Chicago, 1890–1925," *Law and Society Review* 10 (Winter 1976): 303–324.

84. This point is made by Lawrence M. Friedman and Robert V. Percival, *The Roots of Justice: Crime and Punishment in Alameda County, California, 1870–1910* (Chapel Hill: University of North Carolina Press, 1981).

85. Wilbur R. Miller, *Cops and Bobbies* (Chicago: University of Chicago Press, 1977).

86. National Commission on Law Observance and Enforcement, *Lawless-*

ness in Law Enforcement (Washington, D.C.: Government Printing Office, 1931), pp. 103, 121, 153.

87. Orfield, "The Exclusionary Rule and Deterrence," p. 1030 n. 63.

88. National Commission on Law Observance and Enforcement, *Lawlessness in Law Enforcement*, p. 103.

89. Paul Jacobs, *Prelude to Riot* (New York: Vintage Books, 1968), pp. 13–60.

90. William A. Geller and Michael S. Scott, *Deadly Force: What We Know* (Washington, D.C.: Police Executive Research Forum, 1992).

91. Ibid.

92. Lawrence W. Sherman, *Policing Domestic Violence* (New York: Free Press, 1992).

93. Geoffrey P. Alpert and Roger G. Dunham, *Police Pursuit Driving* (Westport, Conn.: Greenwood Press, 1990).

94. American Bar Association, Standards for Criminal Justice, *The Legal Status of Prisoners* (Boston: Little, Brown, 1983), pp. 23-3–23-4.

95. Ibid., p. 23-57.

96. Standard 23-3.1, in ibid., p. 23-32.

97. Standard 23-7.1, in ibid., p. 23-132.

98. National Council on Crime and Delinquency, *A Model Act for the Protection of Rights of Prisoners* (Hackensack, N.J.: NCCD, January 1972).

99. American Correctional Association, *Standards for Adult Correctional Institutions*, 2d ed (College Park, Md.: ACA, 1981).

100. Michael Walzer, *Spheres of Justice: A Defense of Pluralism and Equality* (New York: Basic Books, 1983), p. 31.

Chapter Six: The Limits of Communitarianism

1. Preamble to "The Responsive Communitarian Platform: Rights and Responsibilities," *The Responsive Community* 2 (Winter 1991/92): 4. The Platform is also reprinted in Amitai Etzioni, *The Spirit of Community* (New York: Crown Books, 1993), pp. 251–267.

2. Etzioni, *The Spirit of Community*, chap. 4, "Back to We."

3. An earlier critique is found in Samuel Walker, "The Communitarian Cop-Out," *National Civic Review* 82 (Summer 1993): 246–254.

4. John Rawls, *A Theory of Justice* (Cambridge, Mass.: Harvard University Press, 1971).

5. Michael J. Sandel, *Liberalism and the Limits of Justice* (New York: Cambridge University Press, 1982). See also his more recent book, *Democracy's Discontent* (Cambridge, Mass.: Harvard University Press, 1996).

6. This phrase is repeated throughout the communitarian literature. See, for example, the Communitarian Network Platform in Etzioni, *The Spirit of Community*, pp. 251–267.

7. Cass R. Sunstein, *Democracy and the Problem of Free Speech* (New York: Free Press, 1993).

8. Etzioni's two recent communitarian manifestos are *The Spirit of Com-*

munity and *The New Golden Rule: Community and Morality in a Democratic Society* (New York: Basic Books, 1996).

9. Etzioni, *The Spirit of Community*, pp. 251–267.

10. William A. Galston, *Liberal Purposes: Goods, Virtues, and Diversity in the Liberal State* (New York: Cambridge University Press, 1991).

11. In retrospect it appears that President Clinton's favorable comments about communitarianism were simply another example of his habit of trying to please whomever he happened to be talking to at the moment. On welfare reform, see Peter Edelman, "The Worst Thing Bill Clinton Has Done," *Atlantic Monthly,* March 1997, 43ff.

12. Shlomo Avineri and Avner de-Shalit, eds., *Communitarianism and Individualism* (New York: Oxford University Press, 1992); Stephen Mulhall and Adam Swift, eds., *Liberals and Communitarians*, 2d ed. (Cambridge: Blackwell, 1996).

13. Etzioni, *The Spirit of Community*, pp. 124–125. See Katha Pollitt's comments on this "toothless" aspect of communitarianism in "Subject to Debate," *The Nation,* July 25/August 1, 1994, 118.

14. Mary Ann Glendon, *Rights Talk* (New York: Free Press, 1991).

15. Galston, *Liberal Purposes;* Sandel, *Liberalism and the Limits of Justice.*

16. Etzioni, *The Spirit of Community*, pp. 251–267.

17. Because the Platform is relatively short, I will not clutter the text with footnote references to specific quotes. The Platform is readily available in the source in note 16.

18. Ronald D. Elving, *Conflict and Compromise: How Congress Makes the Law* (New York: Simon and Schuster, 1995).

19. Ian Brownlie, ed., *Basic Documents on Human Rights*, 3d ed. (Oxford: Clarendon Press, 1992), pp. 21–27.

20. "Convention on the Rights of the Child" (1989), in Brownlie, *Basic Documents on Human Rights*, pp. 182–202.

21. Glendon, *Rights Talk,* chap. 6, "Rights Insularity."

22. Samuel Walker, *In Defense of American Liberties: A History of the ACLU* (New York: Oxford University Press, 1990), pp. 313–314, 376–377. Materials on the debate—position papers, board of directors minutes, and Biennial Conference papers—are available in the ACLU archives in the Mudd Library at Princeton University. See also the ACLU handbook: Sylvia Law, *The Rights of the Poor* (New York: Avon Books, 1974).

23. Walker, "The Communitarian Cop-Out."

24. On the legislative battle over the 1993 Family and Medical Leave Law, see Elving, *Conflict and Compromise.*

25. U.S. Bureau of the Census, *Statistical Abstract of the United States, 1995* (Washington, D.C.: Government Printing Office, 1995), p. 480.

26. Lenore J. Weitzman, *The Divorce Revolution* (New York: Free Press, 1985). Weitzman's book has had an enormous influence on public thinking. However, there is much controversy over her interpretation, including allegations of serious and possibly even fatal errors with her data. See Richard R. Peterson, "A Reevaluation of the Economic Consequences of Divorce," *Amer-*

ican Sociological Review 61 (June 1996): 528–536, and the responses that followed.

27. U.S. Bureau of the Census, *Statistical Abstract of the United States, 1995,* p. 391.

28. Andrea H. Beller and John W. Graham, *Small Change: The Economics of Child Support* (New Haven, Conn.: Yale University Press, 1993), p. 4.

29. Ibid., pp. 162–169.

30. The literature on this subject is vast. For an introduction, see Patricia Smith, ed., *Feminist Jurisprudence* (New York: Oxford University Press, 1993).

31. See, for example, how the discussion veered in the direction of the rights of children in the symposium "Who Owes What to Whom?" *Harper's,* February 1991, 43ff.

32. Etzioni, *The Spirit of Community,* pp. 13, 40–43.

33. The battle over the textbooks in Oakland, California, described by Todd Gitlin and referred to here in Chapter 1, is only one example of a struggle that has played out across the country. See Todd Gitlin, *The Twilight of Common Dreams: Why America Is Wracked by Culture Wars* (New York: Henry Holt, 1995).

34. Allan Bloom, *The Closing of the American Mind* (New York: Simon and Schuster, 1987): Dinesh D'Souza, *Illiberal Education* (New York: Free Press, 1991).

35. Gitlin, *The Twilight of Common Dreams.*

36. Arthur M. Schlesinger, Jr., *The Disuniting of America: Reflections on a Multicultural Society* (New York: Norton, 1992).

37. Leslea Newman, *Heather Has Two Mommies* (Boston: Alyson Wonderland, 1989).

38. Toni Marie Massaro, *Constitutional Literacy: A Core Curriculum for a Multicultural Nation* (Durham, N.C.: Duke University Press, 1993).

39. Gerald Graff, *Beyond the Culture Wars: How Teaching the Conflicts Can Revitalize American Education* (New York: Norton, 1992).

40. Sandel, *Democracy's Discontent;* Sunstein, *Democracy and the Problem of Free Speech.*

41. National Council on Research on Women, *Directory of National Women's Organizations* (New York: NCRWO, 1992); Gale Research, *Encyclopedia of Associations,* 32d ed. (Detroit: Gale Research, 1997).

42. Gale Research, *Encyclopedia of Associations.*

43. On the latent authoritarianism in communitarian-style theories, see Burt Neuborne, "Ghosts in the Attic: Idealized Pluralism, Community and Hate Speech," *Harvard Civil Rights–Civil Liberties Law Review* 27 (Summer 1992): 379–380.

44. Robert Puttnam, "Bowling Alone: America's Declining Social Capital," *Journal of Democracy* 6 (January 1995): 65; Robert Puttnam, "The Strange Disappearance of Civic America," *The American Prospect,* 34 (Winter 1996): 34.

45. Andrew Greeley, "The Other Civic America: Religion and Social Capital," *The American Prospect,* no. 32 (May–June 1997): 68–73.

46. Eldon Eisenach, *The Lost Promise of Progressivism* (Lawrence: Universi-

ty Press of Kansas, 1994), for example, finds three disparate perspectives within Progressivism: populism, managerial efficiency, and constitutional liberalism.

47. Robert H. Wiebe, *Businessmen and Reform: A Study of the Progressive Movement* (Cambridge, Mass.: Harvard University Press, 1962).

48. Jack Temple Kirby, *Darkness at the Dawning: Race and Reform in the Progressive South* (Philadelphia: Lippincott, 1972).

49. James H. Timberlake, *Prohibition and the Progressive Movement, 1900–1920* (Cambridge, Mass.: Harvard University Press, 1963).

50. Etzioni, *The Spirit of Community*, p. 15; Glendon, *Rights Talk*, pp. ix–x.

51. Herbert E. Alexander, *Financing Politics: Money, Elections, and Political Reform*, 4th ed. (Washington, D.C.: CQ Press, 1992).

52. On the free speech issues, see Rodney Smolla, *Free Speech in an Open Society* (New York: Knopf, 1992); Sunstein, *Democracy and the Problem of Free Speech*.

53. Cass Sunstein, writing from a civic republican perspective, recommends free television time for political candidates. Yet he quickly passes over the subject without addressing the question of equal time for all of the fringe candidates. See Sunstein, *Democracy and the Problem of Free Speech*, p. 85.

54. Etzioni, *The Spirit of Community*, p. 200.

55. American Civil Liberties Union, *Policy Guide* (New York: ACLU, nd.), Policy No. 72a, "Free Speech and Bias in College Campus."

56. A good account of the political reaction to Warren Court decisions on the police is found in Fred P. Graham, *The Self-Inflicted Wound* (New York: Macmillan, 1970).

57. The most substantive communitarian proposal is found in David Schuman, "Taking Law Seriously: Communitarian Search and Seizure," *American Criminal Law Review* 27 (1990): 583–617. A shorter version appears as "Communitarian Search and Seizure," *The Responsive Community* 3 (Spring 1993): 32–42. Schuman proposes that the ground rules for searches and seizures be defined legislatively. Presumably, this is a more "democratic" approach to defining the balance between rights and responsibilities. Yet he does not take into account what every police officer knows: that no two situations are alike, and that it is impossible to define them in advance. His proposal offers no practical alternative to broad, judicially defined principles of reasonableness.

58. For a discussion of this issue, see Samuel Walker, *Sense and Nonsense About Crime and Drugs*, 4th ed. (Belmont, Calif.: Wadsworth, 1998), pp. 86–90.

59. *Michigan Department of State Police v. Sitz*, 496 U.S. 444 (1990).

60. Etzioni, *The Spirit of Community*, pp. 181–183.

61. Walker, *Sense and Nonsense About Crime*, pp. 90–92.

62. Samuel Walker, "Historical Roots of the Legal Control of Police Behavior," in *Police Innovation and Control of the Police*, ed. David Weisburd and Craig Uchida (New York: Springer Verlag, 1993), pp. 32–55.

63. The most comprehensive review of the data on gun ownership, gun crimes, and gun control policies is Gary Kleck, *Point Blank: Guns and Violence in America* (New York: Aldine de Gruyter, 1991).

64. Ibid.

65. Glendon, *Rights Talk*.

66. Ibid., chap. 6, "Rights Insularity."

67. Mary Ann Glendon, *Abortion and Divorce in Western Law: American Failures, European Challenges* (Cambridge, Mass.: Harvard University Press, 1987). Glendon's argument, which posits a sharp dichotomy between American and Western European law on these subjects, will have great difficulty withstanding close empirical investigation. Even she acknowledges common "overall trends" (p. 2). For a short but devastating critique of Glendon's analysis of abortion law, see Lawrence H. Tribe, *Abortion: The Class of Absolutes* (New York: Norton, 1990), pp. 73–76.

68. Glendon, *Rights Talk*, p. 65.

69. Brownlie, *Basic Documents on Human Rights*, pp. 21–27.

70. Ibid., pp. 125–143.

71. Walker, *In Defense of American Liberties*.

72. *Abrams v. United States*, 250 U.S. 616 (1919). The classic account is Zechariah Chafee, *Free Speech in the United States* (Cambridge, Mass.: Harvard University Press, 1941).

73. Catharine MacKinnon, *Only Words* (Cambridge, Mass.: Harvard University Press, 1993). And see the reply by the ACLU's president, Nadine Strossen, *Defending Pornography* (New York: Scribner's, 1995).

74. Glendon, *Rights Talk*, p. 153.

75. Ibid., pp. 146–158.

76. Ibid., p. 153. *Bowers v. Hardwick*, 478 U.S. 186 (1986).

77. Etzioni, *The Spirit of Community*, p. 127. See also Glendon, *Rights Talk*, pp. 29–30.

78. Barry Bluestone and Bennett Harrison, *The Deindustrialization of America* (New York: Basic Books, 1982), pp. 49–81.

79. Glendon, *Rights Talk*, p. 30; *Poletown Neighborhood Council V. City of Detroit*, 410 Mich. 616, 304 N.W. 2d 455 (1981); Jeannie Wylie, *Poletown* (Urbana: University of Illinois Press, 1989).

80. Bluestone and Harrison, *The Deindustrialization of America*.

81. Glendon, *Rights Talk*, pp. 29–30.

82. Etzioni, *The Spirit of Community*, p. 127.

83. Bluestone and Harrison, *The Deindustrialization of America*, pp. 3–21.

84. G. A. Hillery, Jr., "Definitions of Community: Areas of Agreement," *Rural Sociology*, 20 (1955): 111–123. Colin Bell and Howard Newby, *Community Studies: An Introduction to the Sociology of the Local Community* (New York: Praeger, 1973), p. 15.

85. Etzioni, *The New Golden Rule*, p. 127.

86. Preamble, *The Responsive Community* 2 (Winter 1991/92), 4.

87. The Communitarian Network, Position Paper, *The Rights and Responsibilities of Potential Organ Donors: A Communitarian Approach* (Washington, D.C.: 1993). The proposal is explained and defended in James Lindemann Nelson, "Routine Organ Donation: A Communitarian Organ Procurement Policy," *The Responsive Community* 4 (Summer 1994): 63–68.

88. Communitarian Network, *The Rights and Responsibilities of Organ Donors*, p. 19.

89. Ibid., p. 20.

90. Ibid.

91. Ibid., p. 9.

92. Howard Mulvey, "Patients' Rights: Organ Transplantation and Brain Death in Japan," in *Case Studies on Human Rights in Japan*, ed. Roger Goodman and Ian Neary (Surrey, England: Japan Library, 1996), pp. 184–221.

93. Donald Irish, Kathleen F. Lundquist, and Vivian Jenkins Nelsen, eds., *Ethnic Variations in Dying, Death, and Grief* (Washington, D.C.: Taylor and Francis, 1993); Robert B. Hill and Robert E. Anderson, *The Autopsy: Medical Practice and Public Policy* (Boston: Butterworth, 1988).

94. Bell and Newby, *Community Studies*, p. 15; cited in Etzioni, *The New Golden Rule*, p. 127. The original estimate of ninety-four is found in Hillery, Jr., "Definitions of Community: Areas of Agreement": 111–123.

95. Charles Humana, comp., *World Human Rights Guide*, 3d ed. (New York: Oxford University Press, 1992), p. 8.

96. These issues are discussed in Michael Freeman, ed., *Children's Rights: A Comparative Perspective* (Brookfield, Vt.: Dartmouth Press, 1996); and Rebecca J. Cook, ed., *Human Rights of Women: National and International Perspectives* (Philadelphia: University of Pennsylvania Press, 1994).

97. Roger Goodman, "On Introducing the UN Convention on the Rights of the Child into Japan," Goodman and Neary, *Case Studies on Human Rights in Japan*, pp. 109–140.

98. Benjamin Barber, *Jihad v. McWorld* (New York: Times Books, 1995). A more serious scholarly approach to the same subject is Samuel P. Huntington, *The Clash of Civilizations and the Remaking of World Order* (New York: Simon and Schuster, 1996).

99. Arati Rao, "The Politics of Gender and Culture in International Human Rights Discourse," in *Women's Rights, Human Rights: International Feminist Perspectives*, ed. Julie Peters and Andrea Wolper (New York: Routledge, 1995), p. 167.

100. Steven L. Pevar, *The Rights of Indians and Tribes*, 2d ed. (Carbondale: Southern Illinois University Press, 1992), p. 129.

101. Ibid., chap. 14, "The Indian Civil Rights Act."

102. Quoted in Bell and Newby, *Community Studies*, p. 15.

103. Neuborne, "Ghosts in the Attic," p. 380.

INDEX